BYZANTINE CHRISTIANITY

FURTHER PRAISE FOR THIS SERIES:

"The concept of this 'people's history' represents a virtual revolution in the writing of Christian history, a change that means something dynamic, something that should draw the attention of many who do not think of themselves as likers of history. . . . These stories may come up from the basement of church history, but news about their existence deserves to be shouted from the housetops."

MARTIN E. MARTY, *University of Chicago Divinity School*

"Hidden for centuries by their anonymity and illiteracy, the people of God—the body of Christ, the church!—are finally having their story told, and by some of today's finest historians of the church. The saints, bishops, and theologians of traditional histories can now be placed against the panoramic and fascinating backdrop of the lived religion of ordinary men and women of faith. Highly recommended."

MARK U. EDWARDS, JR., *Harvard Divinity School*

A PEOPLE'S HISTORY OF CHRISTIANITY

Denis R. Janz
General Editor

Volume 1
CHRISTIAN ORIGINS
Richard Horsley, editor

Volume 2
LATE ANCIENT CHRISTIANITY
Virginia Burrus, editor

Volume 3
BYZANTINE CHRISTIANITY
Derek Krueger, editor

Volume 4
MEDIEVAL CHRISTIANITY
Daniel E. Bornstein, editor

Volume 5
REFORMATION CHRISTIANITY
Peter Matheson, editor

Volume 6
MODERN CHRISTIANITY TO 1900
Amanda Porterfield, editor

Volume 7
TWENTIETH-CENTURY GLOBAL CHRISTIANITY
Mary Farrell Bednarowski, editor

A PEOPLE'S HISTORY OF CHRISTIANITY

Volume 3

BYZANTINE CHRISTIANITY

DEREK KRUEGER

Editor

FORTRESS PRESS

Minneapolis

BYZANTINE CHRISTIANITY
A People's History of Christianity, Volume 3

Publishing team: Scott Tunseth (Publisher), J. Michael West (Acquisitions Editor), James Korsmo (Production Editor, interior design), Laurie Ingram (cover design), Lynette Johnson (permissions), Beth Wright (copyeditor), Zan Ceeley (typesetter), David Thorstad (proofreader)
Cover art: St. Mamas, Church of Sts. Peter and Paul, Kalyvia, Attica, Greece. Photo by Sharon E. J. Gerstel.

Scripture quotations are from the New Revised Standard Version Bible, copyright © 1989 by the Division of Christian Education of the National Council of Churches of Christ in the USA and used by permission.

Further materials on this volume and the entire series can be found online at www.peopleshistoryofchristianity.com.

Library of Congress Cataloging-in-Publication Data

Byzantine Christianity / Derek Krueger, editor.
    p.   cm. — (A people's history of Christianity ; v. 3)
  Includes bibliographical references and index.
  ISBN 0-8006-3413-6 (alk. paper)
  1. Byzantine Empire—Church history. 2. Byzantine Empire—Religious life and customs. 3. Christian life—History—Early church, ca. 30–600. 4. Christian life—History—Middle Ages, 600–1500. I. Krueger, Derek. II. Series.
  BX300.B99 2006
  274.95'02—dc22

2006001842

Manufactured in Canada
10   09   08   07   06   1   2   3   4   5   6   7   8   9   10

CONTENTS

Part 3. Devotional Life and Artifacts

CONTRIBUTORS

Charles Barber is Associate Professor of Art History at the University of Notre Dame. His research has focused on the aesthetics of the icon. His publications include *The Theodore Psalter: An Electronic Facsimile* (Urbana: University of Illinois Press, 2000) and *Figure and Likeness: On the Limits of Representation in Byzantine Iconoclasm* (Princeton: Princeton University Press, 2002).

Nicholas Constas is an independent scholar who was formerly Associate Professor of Theology at Harvard Divinity School. His interests range from christological controversies and the patristic interpretation of scripture to the theological study of icons and iconography. He is the author of *Proclus of Constantinople and the Cult of the Virgin in Late Antiquity* (Leiden: Brill, 2003).

Georgia Frank is Associate Professor of Religion at Colgate University. The author of *The Memory of the Eyes: Pilgrims to Living Saints in Christian Late Antiquity* (Berkeley: University of California Press, 2000), she has written articles on ancient Christian pilgrimage, liturgy, visual piety, and monasticism.

Sharon E. J. Gerstel is Associate Professor of Byzantine Art at the University of California, Los Angeles. A specialist in Byzantine art and archaeology with interests in the history of religion, Gerstel is author of *Beholding the Sacred Mysteries: Programs of the Byzantine Sanctuary* (Seattle: College Art Association and University of Washington Press,

1999). She has edited *A Lost Art Rediscovered: Architectural Ceramics of Byzantium* (University Park: Pennsylvania State University Press, 2001) and *Thresholds of the Sacred: Architectural, Art Historical, Liturgical, and Theological Perspectives on Religious Screens, East and West* (Washington, D.C.: Dumbarton Oaks, 2006).

Peter Hatlie is Academic Director and Visiting Associate Professor of the University of Dallas Rome Program. Specializing in early Byzantine social and religious history, he has published articles about letter writing, friendship, women, and various issues relating to monastic life. His forthcoming monograph on early Byzantine monasticism, *The Monks and Monasteries of Constantinople*, will be published by Cambridge University Press.

Derek Krueger is Professor of Religious Studies at the University of North Carolina at Greensboro. A student of early Byzantine hagiography and monasticism, his publications include *Symeon the Holy Fool: Leontius's* Life *and the Late Antique City* (Berkeley: University of California Press, 1996) and *Writing and Holiness: The Practice of Authorship in the Early Christian East* (Philadelphia: University of Pennsylvania Press, 2004).

Vasiliki Limberis is Associate Professor of Ancient Christianity at Temple University, Philadelphia. She is the author of *Divine Heiress: The Virgin Mary and the Creation of Christian Constantinople* (London: Routledge, 1994) and articles on the social and cultural history of the Christianity of the Cappadocian Fathers.

Jaclyn Maxwell is Assistant Professor in the Department of History and the Department of Classics and World Religions at Ohio University. Her research focuses on the interaction between different social classes in Late Antiquity. She is the author of *Christianization and Communication: John Chrysostom and Lay Christians in Antioch* (Cambridge: Cambridge University Press, 2006).

Brigitte Pitarakis is a researcher at the Centre d'Histoire et de Civilisation de Byzance, Collège de France—CNRS in Paris. Her main field is the study of Byzantine metalwork and its use in private and public contexts, both secular and ecclesiastical. Recent publications include *Les croix-reliquaires pectorales byzantines en bronze* (Paris: Picard, 2006) and *A Treasured Memory: Ecclesiastical Silver from Late Ottoman Istanbul in the Sevgi Gönül Collection* (Istanbul: Vehbi Koç Foundation, 2006).

James C. Skedros is Associate Professor of Early Christianity and Byzantine History at Holy Cross Greek Orthodox School of Theology in Brookline, Massachusetts. He is the author of *St. Demetrios of Thessaloniki: Civic Patron and Divine Protector (4th–7th c. CE)* (Harrisburg, Pa.: Trinity, 1999). He has written about popular religious practices in Late Antiquity, early Christian and Byzantine hagiography, pilgrimage, early Christian and Byzantine archaeology, and the Byzantine church.

Alice-Mary Talbot, Director of Byzantine Studies at Dumbarton Oaks, focuses her research on hagiography, monasticism, and the life of Byzantine women. She has served as Executive Editor of the *Oxford Dictionary of Byzantium* and as director of two hagiography projects at Dumbarton Oaks. Among her publications are two collections of saints' lives in translation, *Holy Women of Byzantium* (Washington, D.C.: Dumbarton Oaks, 1996) and *Byzantine Defenders of Images* (Washington, D.C.: Dumbarton Oaks, 1998), as well as *Women and Religious Life in Byzantium* (Aldershot: Ashgate, 2001).

ILLUSTRATIONS

Color Plates (following page 108)

FOREWORD

This seven-volume series breaks new ground by looking at Christianity's past from the vantage point of a people's history. It is church history, yes, but church history with a difference: "church," we insist, is not to be understood first and foremost as the hierarchical-institutional-bureaucratic corporation; rather, above all, it is the laity, the ordinary faithful, the people. Their religious lives, their pious practices, their self-understandings as Christians, and the way all of this grew and changed over the last two millennia—*this* is the unexplored territory in which we are here setting foot.

To be sure, the undertaking known as people's history, as it is applied to secular themes, is hardly a new one among academic historians. Referred to sometimes as history from below, or grassroots history, or popular history, it was born about a century ago, in conscious opposition to the elitism of conventional (some call it Rankean) historical investigation, fixated as this was on the "great" deeds of "great" men, and little else. What had always been left out of the story, of course, was the vast majority of human beings: almost all women, obviously, but then too all those who could be counted among the socially inferior, the economically distressed, the politically marginalized, the educationally deprived, or the culturally unrefined. Had not various elites always despised "the people?" Cicero, in first-century BCE. Rome, referred to them as "urban filth and dung"; Edmund Burke, in eighteenth-century London, called them "the swinish multitude"; and in between, this loathing of "the meaner sort" was almost universal among the privileged. When the discipline called "history" was professionalized in the nineteenth century, traditional gentlemen historians perpetuated this contempt if not by outright vilification, then at least by keeping the masses invisible. Thus when people's history came on the scene, it was not only a means for uncovering an unknown dimension of the past but also in some sense an instrument for righting an injustice. Today its cumulative contribution is enormous, and its home in the academic world is assured.

Only quite recently has the discipline formerly called "church history" and now more often "the history of Christianity" begun to open itself up to this approach. Its agenda over the last two centuries has been dominated by other facets of this religion's past such as theology, dogma, institutions, and ecclesio-political relations. Each of these has in fact long since evolved into its own subdiscipline. Thus the history of theology has concentrated on the self-understandings of Christian intellectuals. Historians of dogma have examined the way in which church leaders came to formulate teachings that they then pronounced normative for all Christians. Experts on institutional history have researched the formation, growth, and functioning of leadership offices, bureaucratic structures, official decision-making processes, and so forth. And specialists in the history of church-state relations have worked to fathom the complexities of the institution's interface with its socio-political context, above all by studying leaders on both sides.

Collectively, these conventional kinds of church history have yielded enough specialized literature to fill a very large library, and those who read in this library will readily testify to its amazing treasures. Erudite as it is, however, the Achilles' heel of this scholarship, taken as a whole, is that it has told the history of Christianity as the story of one small segment of those who have claimed the name "Christian." What has been studied almost exclusively until now is the religion of various elites, whether spiritual elites, or intellectual elites, or power elites. Without a doubt, mystics and theologians, pastors, priests, bishops and popes are worth studying. But at best they all together constitute perhaps 5 percent of all Christians over two millennia. What about the rest? Does not a balanced history of Christianity, not to mention our sense of historical justice, require that attention be paid to them?

Around the mid twentieth century a handful of scholars began, hesitantly and yet insistently, to press this question on the international guild of church historians. Since that time, the study of the other 95 percent has gained momentum: ever more ambitious research projects have been launched; innovative scholarly methods have been developed, critiqued, and refined; and a growing public interest has greeted the results. Academics and nonacademics alike want to know about this aspect of Christianity's past. Who were these people—the voiceless, the ordinary faithful who wrote no theological treatises, whose statues adorn no basilica, who negotiated no concordats, whose very names themselves are largely lost to historical memory? What can we know about their religious consciousness, their devotional practice, their understanding of the faith, their values, beliefs, feelings, habits, attitudes, their deepest fears, hopes, loves, hatreds, and so forth? And what about the trouble makers, the excluded, the heretics, those defined by conventional history as the losers? Can a face be put on any of them?

Today, even after half a century of study, answers are still in short supply. It must be conceded that the field is in its infancy, both methodologically and in terms of what remains to be investigated. Very often historians now find themselves no longer interrogating literary texts but rather artifacts, the remains of material culture, court records, wills, popular art, graffiti, and so forth. What is already clear is that many traditional assumptions, time-worn clichés, and well-loved nuggets of conventional wisdom about Christianity's past will have to be abandoned. When the Christian masses are made the leading protagonists of the story, we begin to glimpse a plot with dramatically new contours. In fact, a rewriting of this history is now getting under way, and this may well be the discipline's larger task for the twenty-first century.

A People's History of Christianity is our contribution to this enterprise. In it we gather up the early harvest of this new approach, showcase the current state of the discipline, and plot a trajectory into the future. Essentially what we offer here is a preliminary attempt at a new and more adequate version of the Christian story—one that features the people. Is it comprehensive? Impossible. Definitive? Hardly. A responsible, suggestive, interesting base to build on? We are confident that it is.

Close to a hundred historians of Christianity have generously applied their various types of expertise to this project, whether as advisors or editors or contributors. They have in common no universally agreed-on methodology, nor do they even concur on how precisely to define problematic terms such as "popular religion." What they do share is a conviction that rescuing the Christian people from their historic anonymity is important, that reworking the story's plot with lay piety as the central narrative will be a contribution of lasting value, and that reversing the condescension, not to say contempt, that all too often has marred elite views of the people is long overdue. If progress is made on these fronts, we believe, the groundwork for a new history of Christianity will have been prepared.

The volume before us features a major though frequently neglected chapter in this history. Westerners have all too often allowed Catholicism and Protestantism to eclipse their view of the Orthodox East. *Byzantine Christianity*, this fabulously rich sibling to Western Christianity, flourished in the Byzantine Empire for over a millennium, from the founding of Constantinople in 324 to its fall in 1453. Still today, well over 200 million Christians claim it as their heritage. Here our focus is drawn to the "performance" of a distinctive piety—by clergy in the liturgy to be sure, but even more so by the laity, ordinary women, children, and men, whether at night vigils, for example, or at shrines, or in the home. This entire panoply of religious practice has been unfolded for us by the contributors to this volume under the leadership of volume editor Derek Krueger. I am deeply grateful to him for accepting the task and seeing it through to completion. His extraordinary grasp of the big picture, his attention to detail, and his flair for making the seemingly arcane lucid have left a major imprint on the work as a whole.

Denis R. Janz, General Editor

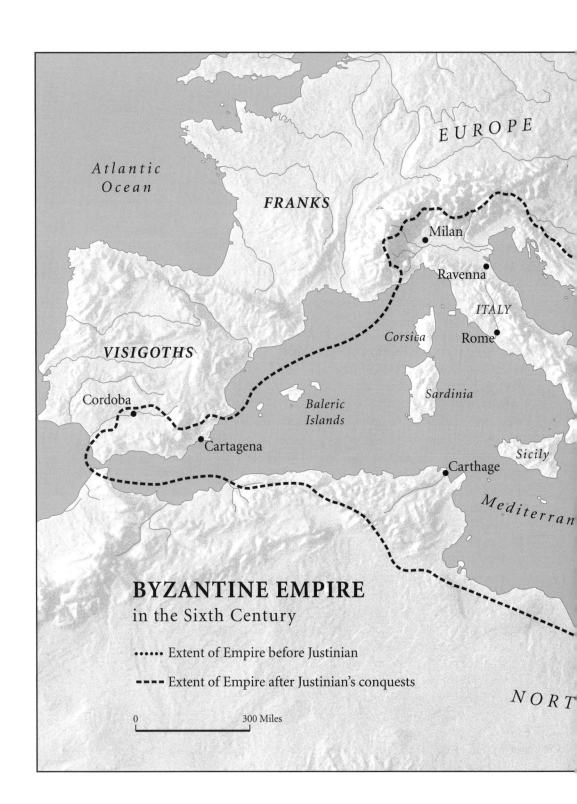

EUROPE

Atlantic
Ocean

FRANKS

Milan

Ravenna

ITALY

VISIGOTHS

Corsica

Rome

Cordoba

*Baleric
Islands*

Sardinia

Cartagena

Sicily

Carthage

Mediterran

BYZANTINE EMPIRE
in the Sixth Century

•••••• Extent of Empire before Justinian

----- Extent of Empire after Justinian's conquests

0   300 Miles

NORT

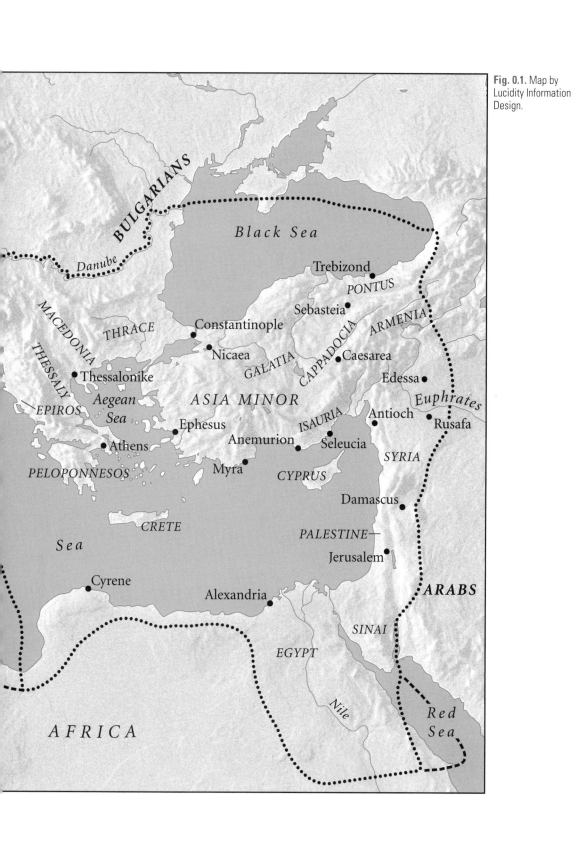

Fig. 0.1. Map by Lucidity Information Design.

BULGARIANS

Black Sea

Danube

Trebizond

PONTUS

Sebasteia

MACEDONIA

THRACE

Constantinople

ARMENIA

Nicaea

CAPPADOCIA

Caesarea

THESSALY

Thessalonike

GALATIA

Edessa

Aegean
Sea

ASIA MINOR

Euphrates

EPIROS

ISAURIA

Antioch

Rusafa

Ephesus

Anemurion

Seleucia

SYRIA

Athens

Myra

CYPRUS

PELOPONNESOS

Damascus

CRETE

PALESTINE

Sea

Jerusalem

ARABS

Cyrene

Alexandria

SINAI

EGYPT

Red
Sea

Nile

AFRICA

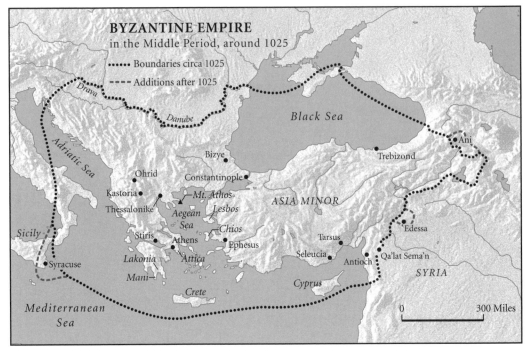

BYZANTINE EMPIRE
in the Middle Period, around 1025

••••• Boundaries circa 1025
----- Additions after 1025

Drava

Danube

Black Sea

Adriatic Sea

Bizye

Trebizond

Ani

Ohrid

Constantinople

Kastoria

Mt. Athos

ASIA MINOR

Thessalonike

Aegean Sea

Lesbos

Edessa

Sicily

Stiris

Chios

Athens

Ephesus

Tarsus

Lakonia

Attica

Seleucia

Qa'lat Sema'n

Mani

Antioch

SYRIA

Crete

Cyprus

Mediterranean Sea

Syracuse

0   300 Miles

Fig. 0.2. Map by Lucidity Information Design.

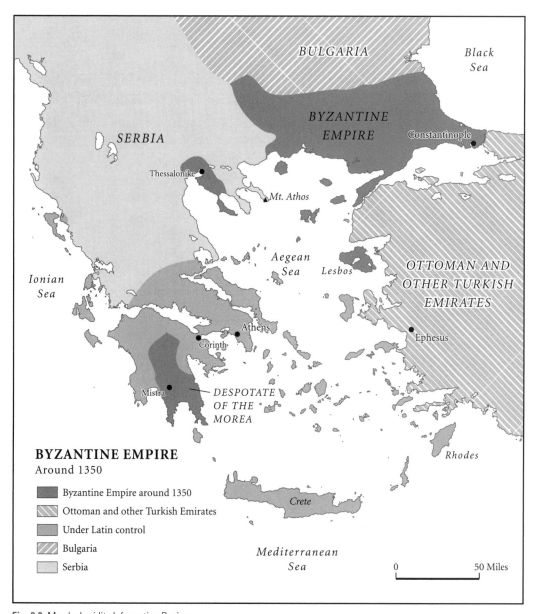

BLACK
Sea

BULGARIA

SERBIA

BYZANTINE
EMPIRE

Constantinople

Thessalonike

▲ Mt. Athos

Ionian
Sea

Aegean
Sea

Lesbos

OTTOMAN AND
OTHER TURKISH
EMIRATES

Athens

Corinth

Ephesus

Mistra

DESPOTATE
OF THE
MOREA

Rhodes

BYZANTINE EMPIRE
Around 1350

Byzantine Empire around 1350

Ottoman and other Turkish Emirates

Under Latin control

Bulgaria

Serbia

Mediterranean
Sea

Crete

0   50 Miles

Fig. 0.3. Map by Lucidity Information Design.

Fig. 0.4. Wooden panel icon of the Virgin Mary and child, two saints, and two angels painted in the sixth or seventh century, now at St. Catherine's Monastery at Mount Sinai, Egypt. During the early Byzantine period, Mary came to be venerated as *Theotokos* or "God-bearer." Photo: Erich Lessing/Art Resource, NY.

THE PRACTICE OF CHRISTIANITY IN BYZANTIUM

DEREK KRUEGER

In sixth-century Palestine a circle of women gathered to weave curtains for two monasteries in the Judean desert. In the seventh century a merchant from the island of Chios spent three months living and sleeping at the shrine of St. Artemios in Constantinople waiting for the saint to heal his hernia. In eighth-century Constantinople young mothers routinely adorned their babies with amulets to protect them from demons.[1] In the twelfth century, in a small church in the Peloponnesos, villagers attended liturgical services surrounded by life-size images of the saints; in another church, in the mountains of Cyprus, colorful scenes of major events in the lives of Christ and the Virgin, painted throughout the church, enveloped congregants in the world of the Bible. In fifteenth-century Thessalonike mourners marked the third, ninth, and fortieth day after a family member's death by bringing offerings of boiled wheat with nuts and raisins to the parish church.[2] Such acts shaped lay Christianity in Byzantium.

This volume of A People's History of Christianity, dedicated to Byzantine Christianity, explores the practices of lay Christians during the eleven centuries between the foundation of the city of Constantinople in 324 and its fall to the Ottoman Turks in 1453. Lasting from Late Antiquity to the threshold of the early modern period, the Byzantine Empire began as the eastern half of the Roman Empire and ended as a small medieval state. In the intervening centuries, Byzantine Christianity developed as a distinct system of religious practice and devotion, different from the medieval Roman Catholicism emerging simultaneously farther west. While some doctrinal issues divided the Orthodox East and the Catholic West, most differences stemmed from cultural practices. Different ways of performing Christianity produced separate identities for these two groups of medieval Christians. Even as their empire shrank, Byzantine emperors and churchmen exported their Eastern Orthodoxy to neighboring peoples. The direct heirs of Byzantine Christianity remain numerous among Greeks, Slavs, Arabs, and others to this day. Today there are more than 200 million Orthodox Christians worldwide.

This volume introduces the religion of the Byzantine Christian laity by asking the question "What did Byzantine Christians do?" To answer, we must consider how people prayed and how often they attended services; how they celebrated, married, and mourned; how they interacted with priests, monks, nuns, and holy people; where they went on pilgrimage and why they visited shrines; how they transmitted religious values to their children; and how they performed acts of charity. Indeed, questions about what ordinary Christians did in church or in their homes or workshops, about their veneration of saints or their use of icons, about their visual and material culture, and about the place of religion in the course of their lives illuminate a people's Christianity.

Fig. 0.5. The Church of the Holy Apostles, Athens, Greece. Built in the eleventh century, the building's modest scale, central plan, elaborate brickwork, and domed cupola are typical of Byzantine church architecture after the ninth century. Photo: Vanni/ Art Resource, NY.

Many Western readers tend, not surprisingly, to know less about Orthodoxy than about Catholic and Protestant forms of Christianity. And while Byzantine sources offer fairly detailed and accessible documentation for the religious lives of Byzantine aristocrats, clergy, and monastics, the piety of ordinary Christians and the patterns of their religious lives remain less familiar even to scholars. Researching the lives of ordinary Byzantines can be difficult. Most written sources derive from powerful church leaders who used their texts to shape proper practice rather than leave behind an unbiased and unfiltered description of what people did. Yet careful interpretation of sermons, saints' lives, hymns, canon law, and histories, together with architecture, icons, church decoration, and devotional objects, enables a rich description of lay religion among nonelites. Drawing on the techniques of social and cultural history, the essays in this volume contribute to a historical anthropology of Byzantine Christianity.

The focus on religious practice complements and sometimes challenges other ways of telling the history of Christianity in Byzantium. Neither the history of Christian doctrine nor the institutional history of the Byzantine church is sufficient in itself to tell the story of Byzantine religious life. Townsfolk and tradesmen, women and children, village peasants, the poor and the powerless rarely feature as agents in these narratives. The history of popular religious practice affords perspectives on religion in their everyday lives. Moreover, the interest in practice rather than doctrine draws on recent insights within the modern academic study of religion. Scholars increasingly understand religions not simply as the assent to a series of intellectual propositions but rather as richly embodied cultural systems. To understand people's religious lives, we must explore their customs and habits. Only in this way can we begin to understand the logic that grounded Byzantine piety, the basic assumptions that made such widespread practices as visiting the saints or worshipping before icons a matter of common sense.

While Orthodox theology investigated ways to understand God and creation, humanity's participation in Christ's work of redemption, and how the divine might be present in images, much Byzantine religious activity sought solutions to practical problems. Christianity offered therapies for physical ailments, protection from illness and demons, and the salvation of the soul after death. Observing pious activity uncovers patterns of Christian devotion both public and private. Festivals and vigils provided opportunities for collective expressions of devotion to Christ and the saints, often standardized through hymns and liturgies. Christians performed their piety, engaging in behavior to be witnessed by other worshippers, by the saints, or perhaps only by God and the self. Modern scholars have little access to the interior religious life of individual persons, but we can begin to reconstruct collective practice. Depending on the era, forms of private devotion—such as wearing small cross-shaped reliquaries, collecting and saving holy oil, or kissing icons—were often consistent across the broader population. Even intimate acts displayed common modes of self-presentation and comportment before the holy. To provide a people's history of Byzantine Christianity, this volume investigates a wide variety of religious expressions as they developed and changed over time.

CHRISTIANITY IN BYZANTINE HISTORY

Modern scholars divide Byzantine history into four periods, marking distinct phases in the territorial expansion and contraction of the empire, together with distinct forms of political and military organization, social and economic structure, and cultural and religious life.

The period from 324 to 641, early Byzantium, overlapped with the later Roman Empire and maintained many continuities with antiquity. At its height, under Emperor Justinian, who reigned from 527 to 565, the empire stretched from the eastern Mediterranean to include North Africa, the Italian Peninsula, and southern Spain. This multicultural, multiethnic, and multireligious empire boasted the great cities of Constantinople and Alexandria, with as many as half a million inhabitants each; other large cities such as Antioch and Ephesus, with roughly 120,000 inhabitants; and numerous smaller cities, especially in Asia Minor and Syria, with 10,000 to 25,000 inhabitants. Despite the vitality of urban life, the vast majority of Byzantines lived on farms and in villages in rural districts. This period also saw the formation of an imperial Christianity, distinctive of Byzantium, in which the emperor had effective control over the church, convening councils and appointing patriarchs and prominent bishops. Church leaders articulated Christian teachings on the incarnation and the Trinity under imperial guidance, although the supposedly definitive articulations of the faith at Nicaea (325), Chalcedon (451), and Constantinople (553) tended to perpetuate division as well as unity. Moreover, not all the empire's inhabitants were Christians. Jews remained an integral part of Byzantine society throughout its history, and traditional polytheists (or "pagans") survived in locally significant populations into the sixth century, despite imperial edicts expropriating temples and restricting public practice.

Byzantine society and economy suffered decline in the century after the 540s, as recurrent plague, disastrous earthquakes, wars with Persia, and the rise of Islam took their toll. The loss of the Levant and the southern Mediterranean to the Arabs in the 630s and 640s marked the beginning of the Byzantine "Dark Ages," 641 to 843. The population in the remaining lands in Asia Minor, Greece, and the Balkans was primarily Greek-speaking and Orthodox, although there were significant numbers of Slavs, Armenians, and Jews. With coastal cities in decline and a collapse in trade and coinage, Byzantine high culture nearly disappeared. Many people retreated to walled fortresses, or *kastra*, built on hills and promontories for safety. While earlier Byzantine Christians had decorated churches and religious paraphernalia with images of Christ and the saints, the characteristic Orthodox veneration of icons appears to have emerged for the first time in this period, together with a violent reaction to icon piety known as iconoclasm. From 717 to 787 and again from 815 to 843, imperial policy condemned worship before images even as the practice spread among monastics and laity alike.[3]

The middle Byzantine period, lasting from 843 to 1204, saw the revival of the Byzantine state and successive centuries of flourishing culture. Although cities never regained the central status that they had achieved in late antiquity, they regularly expanded beyond their walled fortifications. New forms of church architecture and decoration spread quickly throughout the empire together with new forms of liturgy. The cultural embrace of icons meant that the interiors of even the simplest churches were covered with images of the saints and scenes from the life of Christ. During the reign of Basil II (976–1025), church authorities in Constantinople standardized the calendar of the saints and rewrote their *vitae*, or biographies, into versions short enough to read during morning prayer. The liturgy of the Great Church of Hagia Sophia disseminated from Constantinople

Fig. 0.6. A late Byzantine icon depicting Christ crucified with the Virgin Mary and John the Evangelist grieving at the foot of the cross. Thirteenth century. Icon Gallery, Ohrid, Macedonia. Photo: Photo: Erich Lessing/Art Resource, NY.

to provincial churches. In the 860s began the first of many missions to convert the Slavs to Byzantine Orthodoxy, a development with momentous consequences for the peoples of Eastern Europe, especially the Bulgarians, Serbs, and Russians. By the end of the period, the empire's population included some Muslims.

Beginning already in the ninth century, the Byzantine church found itself in conflict with Rome over such issues as the text of the Nicene Creed and papal supremacy. The Orthodox objected to the Latin addition of the *filioque* to the creed, the assertion that the Holy Spirit proceeded not only from the Father but from both the Father "and the Son." And while the Patriarch of Constantinople recognized his counterpart in Rome as a "first among equals," Byzantines rejected the claim that the pope was the sovereign of the entire church. Perhaps more important for the self-understanding of ordinary Christians, Byzantines began to distinguish their practices from what they regarded as Latin aberrations, which included priestly celibacy, crossing oneself backwards, and using unleavened bread at the Eucharist. Despite the mutual anathemas that Western and Eastern church leaders pronounced against each other in 1054, the schism between Byzantine Orthodox and Roman Catholic Christians did not have a feel of finality until the thirteenth century; even so, Byzantines and Latins were still attempting to heal the rift in the 1430s. The middle Byzantine period also saw the rise of Western Christian crusades to wrest the eastern Mediterranean and the Holy Land from Islamic control; but during the Fourth Crusade, in 1204, Latins sacked the city of Constantinople, bringing a glorious period in Byzantine history to a decisive end.

The final phase of Byzantine history, from the restoration of Byzantine rule in 1261 to the fall of Constantinople in 1453, witnessed a dramatic revival under the dynasty of the Palaiologos family. This development is perhaps odd, since the empire was little more than a rump state encompassing the regions of Constantinople, Thessalonike, and parts of the Peloponnesos. Palaiologan elites commissioned beautiful churches, rich in mosaic and fresco, while on the peninsula of Mount Athos and elsewhere, Byzantine monasticism experienced a golden age. At the same time, lay practice coalesced in forms that would survive the centuries of Turkish rule to come.

DEFINING BYZANTINE CHRISTIANITY

"Byzantine Christianity" is not quite the same thing as "Christianity in Byzantium." First, there is the problem of self-designation. The Byzantines understood themselves to be Romans (*Rhomaioi*); they did not refer to themselves as Greeks (*Hellenes*) before the thirteenth century. Their empire was the Roman Empire, and Constantinople was the New Rome, founded on the site of the earlier town of Byzantion. Only after Constantinople's fall did sixteenth-century Western humanists begin to refer to the Eastern Roman state as "the Byzantine Empire." In some sense Byzantine Christianity here could be understood as the medieval phases of Roman Orthodoxy, and indeed Arabic speakers still refer to those in communion with the Patriarch of Constantinople as "Rum Orthodox."

Then there are the problems of geographical and temporal scope. Byzantine Christianity is not a phenomenon coterminous with the shifting boundaries and temporal limits of a medieval state. This volume focuses on piety and devotional practice among Christians in the eastern Mediterranean, and particularly the northeastern Mediterranean, in the regions that are now Turkey, Greece, the Balkans, and Syria, Israel, and Palestine. Not all of the Christians in this region, however, were (or are) in communion with Constantinople. The communities that would emerge as the Syrian Orthodox, Coptic (or Egyptian) Orthodox, and Armenian churches were distinct in doctrine and organization. These groups, which split decisively with Byzantine Orthodoxy and the Patriarch of Constantinople in the course of the sixth century, in part because of the controversies following the Council of Chalcedon (451), lie beyond the scope of this volume.[4] Even so, and despite different conceptions of the relationship between the human and the divine in the person of Christ and allegiances to separate—and often competing—hierarchies, these Christians often shared the everyday practices typical in Byzantium, even when these communities found themselves beyond the bounds of Byzantine political control.

After the rise of Islam in the eastern Mediterranean, many Greek Orthodox Christians in Syria and Palestine, under the patriarchates of Antioch and Jerusalem, respectively, continued their allegiance to the Byzantine church, even as they began increasingly to speak Arabic. Moreover, through diplomacy and missionary work, the Byzantines exported their imperial orthodoxy northward, beyond the bounds of their empire, among various Slavic peoples, including Bulgarians, Serbs, Ukrainians, and Russians. For the most part, and regrettably, these Arabic- and Slavic-speaking Christians fall beyond the scope of these essays.

Byzantine Christianity also outlasted Byzantium. As parts of eastern Anatolia fell to Seljuk Turks beginning in the eleventh century and the rest of Anatolia and the Balkans to the Ottoman Turks in the fourteenth and fifteenth centuries, more and more Byzantine Christians found themselves practicing Christianity beyond the bounds of the imperial territories. Even after the fall of Constantinople in 1453, Christians in former Byzantine lands continued to practice Christianity in many of the same ways, engaging in similar practices at home, in church, and throughout the course of their lives. Greek Orthodoxy today is both an heir of Byzantine Christianity and the product of a long encounter with modernity that began in the seventeenth century and endures into the present. This volume's focus on Christianity in Byzantium tells only part of Byzantine Christianity's story.

THE PEOPLE'S RELIGION

The quest for the people's Christianity in Byzantium implies, at least in part, that the religion of the common people differed from that of political and ecclesiastical authorities and religious specialists. And yet the religious lives of the elites and of the masses were not truly distinct. Rather, all Byzantine Christians participated in a shared system of religious practice, even as they experienced and took on different roles.

Many forms of piety spread throughout the social ranks. For example, one important locus of Byzantine piety was the healing shrine. The tombs of saints and repositories of their relics dotted major cities such as Constantinople and Thessalonike and were scattered throughout the eastern Mediterranean basin. Supplicants came to these shrines in search of relief from a wide variety of ailments, applying salves of holy oil and wax to their afflicted parts or ingesting infusions of water and holy dust. Some of the sick would sleep at the shrine, hoping that the saints would appear to them in a vision. The same saints would also appear to supplicants sleeping in their own beds. While modern scholars have often regarded such behavior as "popular religion," and earlier scholars might have thought of this as "folk religion," such labels are misleading. Byzantines at all social levels engaged in such practices, from peasants to members of the imperial family. According to the sixth-century historian Procopius of Caesarea, Sts. Cosmas and Damian appeared to the emperor Justinian in a vision when he was gravely ill (*On the Buildings* 1.6.5–8). The difference between the emperor and the average layperson, of course, was that, after the cure, Justinian had the means to entirely remodel the Church of Cosmas and Damian just up the Golden Horn from the capital (at modern Eyüp) as a token of his gratitude. Nevertheless, humbler Christians shared the impulse to adorn the shrines of the saints with votive offerings.

Fig. 0.7. Pilgrims continue to visit the shrine containing a miracle-working icon of the Virgin Mary at the Greek Orthodox Convent of Our Lady of Seidnaya, Syria. Since before the Crusades, the faithful have made supplications, collected holy oil, and presented votive plaques to commemorate their healing. Photo: Derek Krueger.

The religious lives and outlooks of the lower ranks of the clergy, in particular, may not have differed so greatly from those of their lay parishioners. Even as they presided over the liturgy, administered sacraments, and offered spiritual guidance, ordinary priests, together with deacons and subdeacons, were usually long-standing residents of the communities they served. Unlike their Western counterparts, Byzantine priests could marry and raise families. In rural districts, the priest often farmed his plots alongside his fellow villagers. Some priests were dependent peasants on large estates.

And while the rhythms of monastic life shaped monks and nuns differently from laypeople, it would be a mistake to overemphasize the differences between monks and the laity. Byzantine monasticism tended to be less institutional and hierarchical than its Western counterparts; in the absence of a standardized Rule, such as the *Rule of St. Benedict*, or of centralized systems of interrelated monasteries, as in the Cistercian movement, monasteries remained in a dynamic relationship with the lay world from which their members were drawn. In many cases, wealthy lay patrons founded monastic communities, and often members of the family would join these monasteries and govern them. Although, beginning in the late tenth century, monks might retire to the remoter wilderness of Mount Athos in increasing numbers, many monasteries were situated within the walls of cities and towns or on their edges. Here the laity might go for counsel or healing; here they might easily join. Indeed, the twelfth-century poet and historian John Tzetzes sneered that "every disgusting and thrice-accursed wretch has only to put on a monastic habit . . . dress himself up to look self-effacing in an ostentatious and highly theatrical way . . . [and] immediately the city of Constantinople showers him with honors."[5] Such comments reveal an uneasy tension with monasticism, but also its abiding presence.

The influence of monastic life on ordinary Christians was enormous. Church authorities sought to shape lay observance in the image of monasticism. Already in the fourth century, in Easter letters to communities of Christians up and down the Nile, Athanasius of Alexandria called on lay Christians to spend Lent "imitating the behavior of the saints," cultivating self-control through prayers and vigils, the renunciation of sex, and fasting.[6] An elaborate system, completely in place by the eleventh century, prescribed fasts for forty days before Christmas and seven weeks before Easter, for a variable period after Pentecost, for the first two weeks of August, during vigils preceding communion, in advance of various minor feasts, and on Wednesdays and Fridays. Some fasts forbade only meat, others meat and cheese, and some, such as the Easter vigil, demanded total abstinence from all food and drink. The rules demanded that, while fasting, lay Christians also avoid sexual relations. Thus all Christians were called to periods of rigorous, semimonastic observance: monks and nuns provided the model for a form of lay life that was particularly ascetic in character.

Even the distinction that obtained in the early Byzantine period between the cathedral and parish liturgies on the one hand and monastic liturgies on the other disappeared after the ninth century, as monastic leaders imposed their offices on lay parishes. And yet, while the laity came to observe the monastic rites, the boundaries between parishioners and their clergy during services increased. In the early Byzantine period, the urban laity participated in stational liturgies that processed through city neighborhoods between major churches and shrines and rendered the entire city a ritual space. By the eighth century the outdoor processional liturgies had come to an end, and most religious activity moved indoors. Processions still took place within the church building, but with less active lay participation. In the Little Entrance, during the first half of the liturgy, the laity sang psalms and hymns while the deacons and priests processed with the Gospel book. In the offertory, or Great Entrance, the laity watched as deacons and priests brought eucharistic gifts from the nave to the altar. Especially in the sixth and seventh centuries, lay Christians participated in elaborate vigils on the eves of feasts, listening to readings and sermons and singing hymns. Over time, church architecture changed to mark a stronger boundary between laity and clergy. Toward the end of the middle Byzantine period and increasingly in the late Byzantine period, the low barrier, or *templon*, separating the laity in the nave from the clergy in the sanctuary around the altar, grew in height to become a wall covered with images of Christ and the saints, an "iconostasis." Services became less participatory. Lay Christians could no longer see the priest during much of the service. Churches became smaller; the number of private chapels increased. What had once been a public service was increasingly private and screened from view.

Even the later Byzantine tendency to separate clergy from laity in liturgical settings, however, does not change the fact that laypeople shared—and shared in—many practices with clergy and monks. Moreover, the laity included most members of the upper classes. Therefore, an interest in lay Christianity does not and cannot exclude insights into elite modes of worship and observance. Indeed, lay piety is a useful lens through which to understand the common religion of most Byzantines, regardless of their class or status. Supplementing and broadening other ways of doing church history, this project explores a common history from another vantage point.

THE RITUAL MARKERS OF BYZANTINE CHRISTIANITY

The essays in this volume look for Byzantine Christianity by observing its outward signs. One place to watch for this Christianity is in and around the parish church. Although in late antiquity most Christians received baptism in adulthood, by the late sixth century nearly all Byzantine Christians were baptized in infancy. And although the baptized received communion at least weekly in the earlier church and at every eucharist that they attended, by the late fourth century the frequency of communion began to decline, in correlation with a high theology of the sacraments. By the middle Byzantine period most lay Christians received communion only a few times a year, on the Great Feasts appointed by the liturgical calendar and especially at Easter.[7] The sacramental liturgies thus provide too narrow a picture of lay religious life.

Preaching offers a different sort of evidence. In literary sources, church elites tended to present images of the laity as profoundly pious. Indeed, they sought to influence the collective imagination so that Byzantines would conceive of themselves as a pious people. But as Jaclyn Maxwell and Vasiliki Limberis show, a preacher's conception of appropriate religious activities often conflicted with his congregant's ideas about how to behave in church, at shrines, and in the home. Maxwell listens carefully to sermons that John Chrysostom preached in fourth-century Antioch to hear the preacher's attempts to change ingrained modes of lay Christian behavior while making concessions about habits so widespread that no condemnation, however eloquent, could alter. Limberis attends to the roughly contemporary orations that the Cappadocian Fathers delivered at festivals of the martyrs to hear the creation of new and local forms of piety. Not only does she discover a negotiation between enthusiastic throngs and the bishops who sought to restrain them, she charts how aristocratic families presented themselves to their dependents as models for emulation.

Much of the excitement in collective religious activity took place beyond the bounds of the Divine Liturgy, the eucharistic service of the church. Georgia Frank visits the night vigil in sixth-century Constantinople, during which a crowd gathered to hear a dazzling poet and cantor named Romanos bring the Bible to life on the eve of major festivals. Over the course of a year those in attendance entered the story of Judas's betrayal and Peter's fecklessness; they stood with the apostles at Christ's ascension. Like Limberis, James Skedros investigates the shrines and festivals of the saints to discover a mix of public celebration and private devotion. With a view spanning much of Byzantine history, he follows pilgrims to the shrines of St. Demetrius in Thessalonike and St. Menas outside of Alexandria, to the pillar of St. Lazarus of Mount Galesion, and to the Holy Land, watching devotees collect portable "blessings" in simple material substances: oil, water, and dust.

Closer to home, the local church still set the stage for the ritual action at the core of Byzantine observance. Sharon Gerstel visits churches in small country parishes from middle and late Byzantium, surveying architecture and decoration for clues about how villagers used their sacred spaces: how they entered and exited, where they stood, and what they saw. A simple structure, filled with icons, chanting, and incense, became the image of heaven on earth. Here, too, Byzantine Christians marked key moments in their lives: baptism, marriage, and death. Nicholas Constas considers this last rite in detail, providing a broad history of dying, death, and mourning in Byzantium. Along the way he articulates Byzantine notions of the afterlife, of rewards and punishments, and of the world to come.

The veneration of icons sets Orthodoxy apart from all other forms of Christianity. While Byzantine theologians contributed treatises to explain and defend the practice, the question of what ordinary Byzantines expected might happen when they addressed prayers to a saint through his image is harder to answer. Charles Barber turns to monastic evidence for clues about what Byzantines thought icons did in response to prayer and uncovers basic assumptions undergirding this practice. In another approach to Byzantine visual culture, Brigitte Pitarakis examines the small crosses and pendants that people wore around their necks. By reading the shapes and iconography of devotional objects, she traces their owners' private pieties as they expected protection, salvation, and divine assistance.

Religious practice was not uniform for all members of the laity. Indeed, the religious lives of children and women differed from those of adult men. Peter Hatlie takes up the question of the formation of the young from the fourth to the ninth century, as boys and girls received religious instruction and filled their parents with anxiety and hope. Alice-Mary Talbot considers the religious lives of laywomen from the ninth to the fifteenth century: their worship at home and in the church; their interaction with priests, monks, and nuns; and their works of charity and largesse.

Histories of Christianity, usually centered on the West, often omit Byzantium or mention it only in passing. Many surveys of Christian doctrine abandon the Christianities of the East after the fifth-century Council of Chalcedon. Icons and iconoclasm feature as little more than a footnote, and the Great Schism justifies ignoring centuries in the development of Orthodoxy. Students of Byzantium know a different story, a rich cultural heritage bridging antiquity and the early modern. While the essays collected here cannot offer a comprehensive history of Byzantine Christian life and practice, they help to correct this imbalance, to reinscribe Byzantine Christians in a people's history of Christianity.

FOR FURTHER READING

The Blackwell Dictionary of Eastern Christianity. Ed. Ken Parry et al. Oxford: Blackwell, 1999.

Cunningham, Mary. *Faith in the Byzantine World.* Downers Grove, Ill.: InterVarsity, 2002.

Meyendorff, John. *Byzantine Theology: Historical Trends and Doctrinal Themes.* 2nd ed. New York: Fordham University Press, 1979.

The Oxford Dictionary of Byzantium. Ed. Alexander P. Kazdan and Alice-Mary Talbot. 3 vols. New York: Oxford University Press, 1991.

The Oxford History of Byzantium. Ed. Cyril Mango. Oxford: Oxford University Press, 2002.

Safran, Linda, ed. *Heaven on Earth: Art and Church in Byzantium.* University Park: Pennsylvania State University Press, 1998.

CONGREGATIONS
AND PREACHERS

Part 1

Byzantine Christianity

Fig. 1.1. An elegant miniature mosaic of St. John Chrysostom from Constantinople, made in the early fourteenth century. Photo: Dumbarton Oaks, Byzantine Photograph and Fieldwork Archives, Washington, D.C.

LAY PIETY IN THE SERMONS OF JOHN CHRYSOSTOM

JACLYN MAXWELL

By the late fourth century, Christian communities in Antioch were well established and could trace their lineage back to apostolic times. John Chrysostom's sermons, however, give the impression that most Christians did not live up to his expectations. Like many other church authorities of his time, Chrysostom envisioned a more intensely Christianized world, where the laity would be just as religious at home, at work, and in the streets as they were in the church. The laity did not always fit this mold and sometimes actively disagreed with their preacher. This, of course, is not in itself unusual: preachers have always criticized their congregations. But while Chrysostom was promoting new elements of religious life and condemning practices that had been, until then, perfectly acceptable among Christians, he and his congregants were participating in the formation of orthodoxy as a system of practice.

Antioch was one of the most important cities in Late Antiquity: an occasional imperial residence, a city of merchants, administrators, and scholars, and the place where Christians were first called "Christians." Vibrant Jewish and pagan communities continued to flourish in this period, as did several Christian sects—orthodox Christianity was far from being without rivals. We have access to a great deal of information about Antioch during this transitional period because of an orthodox priest named John who preached frequently to lay Christians between 386 and 398 CE. Hundreds of his sermons were recorded, preserved, and circulated because of his eloquence (which later earned him his title "Chrysostom"—Greek for "Golden Mouth") and also because his subsequent career as patriarch of Constantinople catapulted him into the history books.

Although it is difficult to tell to what extent a congregation accepted or rejected advice from sermons, a preacher's instructions can provide important insights into the Christianization of the Roman world because they reveal aspects of the religious views of both the church leader and his more ordinary listeners. These texts should not always be taken at face value because of their rhetorical and prescriptive nature: much of the behavior that Chrysostom condemned or promoted were stock subjects tracing back even to pagan moral treatises. Moreover, sermons reflect first and foremost the preacher's point of view; Chrysostom's view may or may not have corresponded with contemporary standards of lay piety. Nevertheless, the sermons' purpose was to provide spiritual guidance for laypeople who lived in a world with many alternatives to orthodox Christianity, requiring the preacher to speak with the needs of his audience in mind.[1] Indeed, the points of contention between the preacher and his audience reveal many elements of lay piety, allowing us to examine the doctrines and behaviors that people refused to accept, the condemned traditions that many Christians continued to observe, and the elements of Christian piety that people cherished.

This chapter will examine how Chrysostom attempted to convince his listeners to integrate Christianity into the entirety of their lives and how they responded. At the center of the issue of Christianization on the part of both the preacher and laypeople were old customs, the force of habit, and differing conceptions of common sense. What lay Christians viewed as acceptable behavior was determined to some degree by their lessons in church but also by their observance of the authority of traditional practice and common sense. The laity's reluctance to adopt some of Chrysostom's teachings together with their embrace of other Christian practices reveals that the famous preacher addressed people who were neither passive nor particularly impious.

CHRISTIANIZATION OF HABITS

Chrysostom expected Christians to incorporate their religious outlook into all aspects of their lives. He spoke of this transformation in terms of habit: if people could develop Christian habits, then a virtuous life would come naturally, without much effort or thought. Pagan thinkers had developed similar ideas about habits forming the backbone of morality, a point they emphasized in their treatises on raising children, teaching students, and influencing rulers. The ambition of Christian leaders to spread these standards to all levels of society, however, was new. In the fourth and fifth centuries, a number of church leaders made a concerted effort to reform Christian mores and behaviors, modeling them after their own ideals. Much of their labor was spent making over the habits of ordinary people—their choice of entertainment, manner of doing business, the way they dressed or ate their food, their celebrations. The scale of this interference in daily life and the preacher's motivation for doing so brought about many of the small social and cultural changes that created the process of Christianization.

In Chrysostom's sermons we are given a glimpse of some of his contemporaries' customs involving, for example, getting married, raising children, and burying the dead, as well as the preacher's plan for a broad transformation of everyday life. Chrysostom, like other church authorities of this period, called for people to think consciously about things that they normally would not question—their patterns of thought, their food, their clothes, their speech, their laughter. Everyone would have a Christian response to any situation, he believed, if their religious disposition structured all of their thoughts and actions.[2] In a few generations, for people raised with these tendencies from childhood, the Christian life would be effortless: their dispositions would develop in a Christian environment of mutually reinforcing beliefs and practice. Chrysostom's goal was not social change (or control) as an end in itself, but to encourage a lifestyle conducive to collective salvation, which would include his own. With the knowledge of sins and virtues automatic, embedded in their habits, people would reflexively withdraw from sin and temptation. In other words, the Christian ethos had to become common sense if it was going to work for ordinary people. In the end, as we shall see, it is clear that he and other Christian authorities of this time had limited success in reorienting the tastes and attitudes of the mass of Christians.

CHURCH ATTENDANCE

The preacher's ability to transform the laity depended on their attendance in church. Christians in Antioch took their religion seriously and attended church fairly regularly. They flooded the church during festivals and times of crisis. But when special events attracted Christians to the theater or hippodrome, the change in the size of the congregation was noticeable. The reason for the decline was not difficult for the preacher to guess: "Again there are chariot races and satanic spectacles in the hippodrome, and our congregation is shrinking" (*Catech. Hom.* 6.1). Presumably, many of the people at the races attended church on less eventful Sundays, or else they would not have been missed. As much as Chrysostom considered the attraction of the two venues to be antithetical, enthusiasm for races did not diminish enthusiasm for church: "Some of those who listen to this (for I do not condemn all of you, far from it) have forgotten everything and surrendered themselves again to the satanic spectacle of the races. . . . Following some habit, they applaud what we say, show us that they receive our words with pleasure, and afterwards run back to the race-course. They give greater applause to the charioteers and show an uncontrollable frenzy" (*On Laz.* 7, PG 48.1045). However critical he was of his congregants' behavior, Chrysostom was realistic enough to appreciate that they showed up at all. Even if they did not always listen to him or agree with what he said, their attendance at church demonstrated some level of commitment to the Christian life: "I do not blame you for forgetting where we left off. Rather, I should praise you for your

---

The Benefits of Going to Church

The Church of God, in fact, is a spiritual market and a surgery for souls, and like people going to market, we ought to acquire an abundance of good things from here and go home the better for it, and like patients at a surgery we ought to receive various remedies for the passions afflicting us and go off. I mean, our purpose in assembling each day is not simply to gossip inconsequentially with one another and then all part; rather, it is for each of us to learn something worthwhile, get healing for our troublesome ailments and take our leave in that condition. After all, how would it not be utterly absurd for us to send our children to school, expecting of them day after day some advantage from their lessons, and never to regret their going there idly and to no purpose if we do not see them making some improvement—whereas, on the other hand, we at our mature age attend this spiritual school without giving evidence of an eagerness equal to theirs, even though the lessons here redound to our good as far as the salvation of souls is concerned? So let each of us, I beseech you, examine his conscience daily as to the advantage derived from this day's sermon, and the next day's, and so on, lest we too seem to be attending here idly and to no purpose.

—John Chrysostom,
Homilies on Genesis 32, PG 53.293;
FOTC 82.254–55

earnestness, because you do not abandon me any Sunday" (*On Repent.* 3). Regular church attendance was a sign of piety among Christians, yet it was not completely necessary for salvation, since people who did not attend church were still considered part of the religious community. Some people received communion only a few times a year, while others did so more often. Hermits, as an extreme example, only participated in this communion once every few years. The frequency of communion did not matter, Chrysostom claimed, but only the way one lived one's life (*Hom. on Heb.* 17, PG 63.131–32).[3]

For Chrysostom, no single day at church held any more importance than another. Most people, though, disagreed. Not surprisingly, times of crisis attracted larger numbers of people to the church. The church overflowed with people "whenever we were in dire distress due to hunger, plague, hailstorm, drought, conflagrations, and enemy invasions" (*On Repent.* 4.9). He encouraged this reaction to natural disasters, pointing to them as demonstrations of God's anger at their sins. After an urban riot in 387, during which the statues of the imperial family were desecrated, crowds of people filled the churches, inspired by their fear of imperial wrath. Chrysostom welcomed this opportunity to have increased contact with the Christians of the city. The aftermath of the riots had led Christians to become more religious, and he encouraged them to cultivate their piety to outlast the crisis (*On Stat.* 17.2).

Unlike most Antiochenes, Chrysostom welcomed the emperor's response to the riot, which was to shut down the city's public baths and theaters. This action removed some of the options that distracted the laity from church attendance. Elsewhere, not wanting to criticize and scare off the people who had come because of the crisis, Chrysostom still attempted to explain that being pious without fear of sudden earthly danger would bring them more honor in the eyes of God (*On Repent.* 4.9). Nevertheless, even if his listeners had come to church inspired by the wrong reasons, the preacher was happy to have the opportunity to explain to them what they were doing wrong.

In addition to times of crisis, Christians attended church in greater numbers and more frequently during Lent.[4] The preacher naturally noticed the increased size of his Lenten congregation. Unimpressed by their observance of Lent, he explained that if their hearts were not in their religion, then they should not feel compelled to come to communion because of a particular festival. On the other hand, those who were pure of heart should not be discouraged from coming to church by the absence of a festival (*Hom. on 1 Cor.* 28, PG 61.232–33). In short, he did not want the liturgical calendar to have any effect upon anyone's habits of church attendance. What his complaints also make clear, however, is that the calendar *did* affect many ordinary Christians' interpretation of religious duties.

GOOD BEHAVIOR

Chrysostom attempted to convince his congregants that every part of their lives should be saturated with religion just as much as the time spent in church. He was practical in his approach to the Christianization of daily life: he advised people to adopt new Christian habits by associating them with established daily routines. For example, at mealtimes, his congregants could use the thanksgiving prayer of the monks in the nearby wilderness, which he dictated to them verse by verse. Singing psalms while working would infuse their workdays with their faith and serve as a replacement for the traditional songs of farmers, wet nurses, and women at their looms, which ranged from bawdy to merely inconsequential. Chrysostom also encouraged prayer while working, pointing out that repetitive motions did not prevent laborers from quietly worshipping (*Hom. on Matt.* 55, PG 58.544–47).[5]

Trying to direct more attention to almsgiving, Chrysostom suggested that the Antiochenes collect a small sum of money everyday. He gave them precise instructions on how to do this: they should put a small chest near the place in their houses where they prayed. When they went to pray, they would deposit alms into the box first. In addition to helping the poor, the presence of this box of money would protect the house from demons and the sleepers from bad dreams (*Hom. on 1 Cor.* 43, PG 61.372–73). The preacher's advice—which probably reminded people of a similar method of alms collection among Jews—took the fear of demons for granted, as well as prayer in homes, a practice well enough established to have space reserved for it.[6] Also, in this case, it is important to note that Chrysostom was attempting to add a Christian habit of almsgiving to the already existing habit of praying.

After attending church, the laity was advised not to hurry off to the market but to go home and contemplate the sermon they had just heard with their families, like children doing their homework (*Hom. on Matt.* 5, PG 57.55). After work, they should write down their sins of the day. If they wrote down their sins, acknowledging them and asking for forgiveness, then God would erase them. Otherwise, God would inscribe them and exact the penalty for them on Judgment Day (*Hom. on Matt.* 41, PG 57.450).[7] Later, between dinner and bedtime, instead of thinking about work, Christians should sit quietly alone and review the sins they had written down, like judges sitting undisturbed behind a curtain (*Hom. on Matt.* 42, PG 57.455). It is unclear, however, how many people would have been literate enough to follow this advice and, even if they were, whether they would have embraced these homework assignments. As we will see below, although Chrysostom attempted to persuade people to perceive the public sphere and the home as places for religious life, it is clear that many laypeople preferred to mark off the church as a holy place and the church service as fundamentally different from the rest of their daily lives.

How to Pray

The time after dinner is the time for thanksgiving, and he who gives thanks should not be drunk but sober and wide awake. After dinner let us not go to bed but to prayer, or we may become more irrational than the irrational beasts. I know that many will condemn what I say, thinking that I am introducing a strange new custom into our life; but I will condemn more strongly the wicked custom which now prevails over us. Christ has made it very clear that after taking nourishment at table we ought to receive not sleep in bed but prayer and reading of the divine Scriptures.

—John Chrysostom, *On Lazarus* 1, PG 48.974; On Wealth and Power, 27

I praise and admire the monks that have occupied the desert places. . . . For they, after having made their dinners—or rather after supper (for dinner they know not at any time, because they know that the present time is one of mourning and fasting)—after supper then, they sing certain hymns of thanksgiving to God. . . . So that you too may say them continually, I will rehearse to you the whole of that sacred song. The words of it then stand as follows: "Blessed God, who feeds me from my youth up, who gives food to all flesh; fill our hearts with joy and gladness, that always having all sufficiency we may abound unto every good work in Christ Jesus our Lord; with whom be unto You glory, honor and might, with the Holy Spirit, forever. Amen. Glory to You, O Lord, glory to You, O Holy One, glory to You, O King, that You have given us meat to make us glad. Fill us with the Holy Ghost, that we may be found well-pleasing before You, not being ashamed, when You render to every man according to his works."

—John Chrysostom, *Homilies on Matthew* 55, PG 58.545; NPNF 1.10.342)

Fig. 1.2. The widow's mite, a mosaic from the Church of S. Apollinare Nuovo in Ravenna, Italy. Preachers regularly encouraged Christians to donate charitably. Photo: Scala/Art Resource, NY.

Because of the proximity of monastic communities, laypeople could visit monks to observe their pious way of life and receive prayers and instruction. The monks, Chrysostom assured his audience, had moved to the mountains for the very purpose of instructing the townspeople in how to conduct their lives. Accounts of Syrian monks in Late Antiquity indicate that most of them were indeed amenable to visitors who sought blessings, cures, and advice or who visited out of curiosity. Chrysostom even offered to guide laypeople on this spiritual field trip to the place where he had once lived as a monk (*Hom. on Matt.* 72, PG 58.672).[8]

Even though their preacher offered many suggestions for how they could immerse themselves in Christian-oriented activities and thoughts, this was not because the congregants lacked their own initiative. The Antiochenes had their own Christian customs that had not necessarily been taught to them by church authorities. We know about these customs not from exhortations against them but from Chrysostom's passing references to them or his suggestions of ways in which these activities could be made more effective. In contrast to the preacher's complaints that his congregation was not sufficiently Christian in their behavior, these practices afford a different view of lay piety.

Some of the Antiochenes displayed their respect for scripture by using these writings as holy objects in their daily lives outside of the church. Chrysostom compared the phylacteries worn by Jews in the Bible to the miniature Gospels that many of the women in the congregation were wearing around their necks (*Hom. on Matt.* 72, PG 58.669). Material evidence also testifies to this practice. Miniature parchment and papyrus codices as well as papyrus amulets survive, ranging in size from ten by fifteen centimeters to five by six and a half centimeters. Such use of the scripture was popular but not universally approved: the Council of Laodicaea in 360 prohibited clergy from making these amulets. Some Christians hung scriptural verses above their beds in order to keep away evil spirits that brought bad dreams. In these cases believers observed Christian customs that were not specifically required or even encouraged (*Hom. on 1 Cor.* 43, PG 62.372–73).[9]

Another important Christian practice that had become well entrenched by this period was the Lenten fast.[10] Because of the frequency of sermons during Lent, many of Chrysostom's comments about Christian behavior and belief regarding this season survive, providing valuable evidence about lay piety. Ordinary Christians had made the fast part of their religious common sense: they did not need to be persuaded or reminded to take part in this observance. Chrysostom commented on their enthusiasm in this matter: if someone tempted them with food forbidden during the fast, none of them would give in. "We bear it all with fortitude, from the habit of our conscience" (*On Stat.* 6, PG 49.90).

During Lent, roles reversed, with lay Christians taking a stricter stance on proper Christian practice than their preacher. One year, when some members of the congregation stayed home from church after breaking the Lenten fast too soon, Chrysostom rejected their

Fig. 1.3. Round amulet from Syria or Palestine, fifth or sixth century, cast in bronze and engraved on both sides. The amulet was intended to protect the bearer from all evils. One side shows a rider on a galloping horse spearing a demon in the form of a lioness with a woman's head. To the right of the horse, an angel gestures with his staff toward the conquered demon. The inscription above the angel reads, "One God who conquers evils," while the inscription around the border quotes Psalm 91, "He who dwells in the shelter of the Most High will abide in the care of the God of heaven." The opposite side of the amulet depicts Christ enthroned, borne aloft by the four winged beasts of the book of Revelation with the inscription "Holy, holy, holy Lord God of Sabaoth." Below Christ are magical symbols and a lion, a snake, and a scorpion. At a later point, someone drilled a hole in the amulet so that it could be worn around the neck. Photo: Kelsey Museum of Archeology, Ann Arbor, MI. Used by permission.

excuse for staying home. He was not concerned about their premature ending of the fast; he countered that coming to church after a meal might improve one's approach to eating—perhaps they would not drink too much because they would not want to smell like wine in the presence of their fellow Christians. To Chrysostom, the believers' bodily purity was less important than their ability and willingness to pay attention to his sermons (*On Stat.* 9, PG 49.104). Indeed, his lessons appear to have changed some people's beliefs. He began his next sermon by announcing how happy he was that the fast breakers had come to church after all (*On Stat.* 10, PG 49.111).

Although it is possible that the absent congregants used their failed fast as an excuse to stay home from church, this attitude fits a broader pattern in lay thinking. In numerous instances, lay Christians placed a high value upon physical purity. Even though they were told that physical substances such as food and dirt did not pollute their bodies, they took care to wash their hands before prayer. Likewise, they believed that they should not pray after having sex with their spouses, even though this was permitted (*Hom. on Matt.* 51, PG 58.516). The *Apostolic Constitutions*, an important collection of church guidelines assembled during this period in northern Syria, also testifies to these beliefs about purity and condemns them. The compiler emphasized that legitimate sexual relations, nocturnal emissions, and menstruation did not pollute Christians or preclude them from holy activities. Likewise, Chrysostom attempted to convince his congregation that a misdeed such as insulting another person created more pollution than dirt or marital sex (*Hom. on Matt.* 51, PG 58.515–16).[11]

Chrysostom worried that his congregants' concern with purity stemmed from Jewish customs. After discussing Jesus' rejection of Jewish laws, he looked at his own congregation and noticed Christians

---

Sex within Marriage

"Well," says one, "and what do you require us to do? To occupy the mountains and become monks?" Why it is this that makes me sigh, that you think them alone to be properly concerned with decency and chastity; and yet assuredly Christ made His laws common to all. Thus, when He says, "if any one look on a woman to lust after her," He speaks not to the solitary, but to him also that has a wife; since in fact that mount was at that time filled with all kinds of persons of that description. . . . Do not condemn the severity of my speech. For I neither "forbid to marry," (1 Tim. 4.2) nor hinder your taking pleasure; but I would have this be done in chastity, not with shame and reproach, and imputations without end. I do not make it a law that you are to occupy the mountains and the deserts, but to be good and considerate and chaste, dwelling in the midst of the city.

—John Chrysostom, *Homilies on Matthew* 7, PG 57.81; NPNF 2.10.49

continuing suspiciously similar practices (*Hom. on Matt.* 51, PG 58.515–16).[12] The Antiochenes had adopted traditions or attitudes that connected physical cleanliness and holiness, which they had learned either from observing the Jews in their city, from their Jewish ancestors' traditions, or from their own spiritual logic that led them to believe that they must be clean when in church. Ritual bathing was difficult for Chrysostom to forbid, since, of course, people had to bathe and their desire to show respect to holy places was not objectionable. Despite his hostility to the adoption of seemingly Jewish practices by Christians, he did not forbid his listeners to wash themselves before religious activities but only asked that they consider washing themselves in virtues as well. All the preacher could do about this practice was to try to put it in perspective. He asked his listeners if they would dare to pray if they had dung on their hands. He assumed that they would not, and he asked them to think about the reasoning behind this. Why would anyone be reverential in ways that were inconsequential, such as bodily cleanliness, but negligent of sins (*Hom. on Matt.* 51, PG 58.516)? His listeners, however, presumably believed that concern for purity expressed their respect for religious places and rituals and was not a substitute for morality. These discussions reveal more than just a famous Church Father's loathing of Judaizing practices: clearly the laypeople's ways of thinking about and expressing holiness had inspired their preacher to dwell on this problem. Again, the preacher's complaints, when looked at carefully, reflect a different kind of piety among his listeners rather than a lack thereof.

BREAKING BAD HABITS

In addition to instilling good habits, Chrysostom strove to get his congregants to break bad habits. But many Christians were reluctant to believe that numerous socially accepted activities were actually sinful. It is not difficult to understand their doubt, since Chrysostom urged his listeners to avoid not only sinful activities but also the thoughts and deeds that "seem to be indifferent, yet by degrees lead us into these misdeeds" (*On Stat.* 15, PG 49.159). Such dangers, according to the preacher, lurked everywhere: in business transactions, birthday parties, the theater and other spectacles, dice playing, jewelry, cosmetics, moneylending, investments, conversations with friends, songs, hairstyles, clothing, and eating habits. Repeatedly, laypeople resisted labeling such commonplace activities as sins. In many cases the preacher's attempts to define new sins were met with indifference or hostility, revealing the limits of Christianization.

Chrysostom's frustration on certain points of moral instruction often indicates that the laypeople had good reason to disagree. In the case of oath swearing, putting an end to such a practical aspect of everyday life would be difficult without the creation of a suitable substitution. The Antiochenes swore oaths in a range of situations: to make guarantees in business contracts, to promise a personal favor, or to force others to change their behavior. Swearing was a sin that workmen and artisans were in particular danger of falling into: according to the preacher, they could spoil the value of their honest labor by using oaths in the course of business (*Hom. on Matt.* 61, PG 58.591). Not only did Christians swear oaths in business transactions, but some even used the communion table and the Gospels to make the bond stronger (*On Stat.* 15, PG 49.160). Even more disturbing for the preacher was the sight of a Christian man forcing a woman into a synagogue to swear an oath regarding business matters. When questioned, the man explained that oaths sworn in synagogues were considered to be stronger. The preacher rescued the woman and took the opportunity to lecture the man on the sinfulness of both oaths and Judaizing (*Against Jud.* 1, PG 48.847–48). Interestingly, Chrysostom told this anecdote in the context of trying to convince his listeners not to have such respect for Jewish holy places.

The problem of oath swearing illustrates the conflict between the preacher's moralizing and the audience's common sense. Chrysostom repeatedly spoke about this issue, assuming that most people would not suspect this was a sin unless it was explained (*On Anna* 1, PG 54.631–32).[13] Chrysostom's efforts had some success: after a number of consecutive sermons dealing with the issue, some congregants reported, "We have performed the precept, by making rules for each other, defining penalties for those who swear and enforcing punishment upon those who transgress this law" (*On Stat.* 9, PG 49.103). This triumph, however, was not complete. Later in the same series of sermons Chrysostom continued trying to convince his congregants that oath swearing was a serious sin, telling them to envision the disembodied head of John the Baptist and the blood dripping from it and to keep the image with them all day, imagining that the gory head was crying out "abhor my murderer, the oath!" (*On Stat.* 14, PG 49.144).

Apparently, there was a range of opinions among the laity. On one occasion the preacher worried that dwelling on this topic would bore the ones who understood the sinful nature of oath swearing (*Catech. Hom.* 10, SC 366.172–74). At a different time, however, Chrysostom complained that some congregants did not believe that swearing was wrong at all, while others conceded that it was a sin but a small one (*On Stat.* 6, PG 49.90). In a sermon on Matt. 5:33-34 he read out the verse, "Again, you have heard that it was said to those of ancient times, 'you shall not swear falsely, but carry out the vows you have made to the Lord.' But I say to you, do not swear at all.'" Despite such unambiguous instructions, a number of Christians agreed that perjury was a sin but not oaths in general (*Hom. on Matt.* 17, PG 57.261). The context of these passages makes clear that some Christians had heard the preacher's views—even Jesus' views, for that matter—but still held on to their own interpretation based on common sense: oaths simply did not seem inherently sinful.

In addition to swearing, Chrysostom called the morality of numerous other aspects of daily life into question. For example, women in the region of Antioch put marks of mud on their children's foreheads. If asked, the women would say that the mark kept away the evil eye, witchcraft, and envy. Chrysostom encouraged the women to stop this practice because, first of all, their mud did not possess special powers. If mud could protect someone from evil, he argued, then the practice would not be confined to children or to foreheads: everyone would cover their entire bodies in it. Instead, they should put the sign of the cross on their children's foreheads: "From earliest life encompass them with spiritual armor and instruct them to seal the forehead with the hand and before they are able to do this with their own hand, do you imprint upon them the Cross" (*Hom. on 1 Cor.* 12, PG 61.106). Chrysostom's instructions acknowledged that people were correct in their fears of evil spirits, that they should still attempt to keep them away, and that a sign or a mark would work. The sign, however, should be overtly Christian.

In the same sermon, the preacher also criticized the way some parents chose names for their children. Parents lit a number of lamps, named each of them, and then chose the name of the longest burning lamp for their child, as a sign of good luck for a long life. The preacher had no sympathy for the custom but offered a Christian alternative. The way to find a good name was to choose a saint (*Hom. on 1 Cor.* 12, PG 61.105).[14] Since most people did not perceive a conflict between traditional practices and Christian faith, Chrysostom had to argue that certain actions did seem insignificant but *would lead* to greater evils (*Hom. on 1 Cor.* 12, PG 61.106). It is unclear whether Chrysostom thought that the practices harmed the children, the parents, or both. At any rate, he most likely realized that if parents immersed their children in Christian customs from birth, thereby establishing a core Christian common sense, future preachers would be able to concentrate on theology and praising God. He looked forward to a time when he could take basic knowledge of Christian behavior for granted and spend his time on more advanced subjects (*On Stat.* 16, PG 49.164).

PROBLEMATIC CELEBRATIONS

Many lay Christians did not perceive the sharp dividing line between Christian and pagan behavior that was so clear to Chrysostom. In his sermon *On the Kalends* Chrysostom attempted to explain to his congregation why they should not participate in the New Year's celebrations. On the first of January the Antiochenes adorned the *agora* (the market), their workshops, and their own bodies, competing with each other for the best display. They lighted lamps in the *agora* and decorated the doors of their houses. At dawn both men and women filled their libation bowls and wine cups in order to drink unmixed wine. The traditional festivities also included night choruses, gift exchange, and the careful observation of omens to learn the luck of the New Year (PG 48.953–63).[15]

Chrysostom found the entire premise of the holiday problematic. Traditionally, the omens of this day would determine the luck for the entire year, but Chrysostom insisted that Christians should neither observe omens nor give such importance to any single day.

He suggested an alternative for the custom: "Let the entire year be a good omen to you, not if you get drunk on the first of the month, but if on the first of the month and on each day you do the things that seem good to God." A certain day did not bring good or bad luck because of its place in the calendar, but rather one's fortunes were determined by one's actions on that day. Simply put, chance played no role, since nothing led to evil but sin and only virtue led to goodness. Chrysostom told his potential augurers, "if you philosophize on these [Christian] things and are thus disposed, you will have an entire year with good omens, making prayers and giving alms each day. But if you neglect your own virtue, and you entrust the good cheer of your soul to the beginnings of months and the numbers of days, you will be deprived of all good things" (*On Kal.*, PG 48.955).

Chrysostom was well aware, however, that he could not prevent people from observing the Kalends of January. For one thing, church authorities could not change the fact that it was the day when newly elected political officials began their terms. Since many Christians were going to observe the Kalends regardless of its association with paganism, Chrysostom offered a compromise. Christians should celebrate the Kalends by giving thanks to God, by weighing their sins against their good works, and by meditating on the passage of time as it related to their Christian beliefs. Chrysostom expressed this advice quite eloquently: "When you see the year coming to completion, give thanks to the Lord that he brought you to this period of years. Put your heart to rest, count up the time of your life, say to yourself: The days move quickly and pass by, the years come to an end, we have already traversed much of the road—but what noble thing have we done? We will not go from here empty and lacking all righteousness. The judgment is at the doors. Life presses on and on toward our old age" (PG 48.956).

Ideally, Christians would contemplate their deeds in this manner without any special occasion to prompt them. Chrysostom was sensible enough, though, to realize that introspection once a year was better than nothing. From the traditions of a persistent pagan celebration he singled out the impulse to become preoccupied with the passing of time. Instead of looking for omens, Christians were to concentrate on their mortality and on Judgment Day. In this manner the different conceptions of time stemming from pagan and Christian beliefs could be reconciled to some degree, and old habits of mind could help support new ones.

In addition to New Year the Antiochenes refused to abandon their traditional celebrations of weddings and funerals. In a sermon on Paul's first letter to the Corinthians, Chrysostom tried to explain why many elements of marriage ceremonies should be put to an end: "marriage is accounted an honorable thing, both by us and by those without [non-Christians]: and it is honorable. But when marriages are solemnized, such ridiculous things take place." Chrysostom decided that his listeners needed a fresh look at these cherished traditions because most people, being "possessed and deceived by custom," needed to learn what was wrong with their traditions. Dancing, cymbal and flute music, traditional songs, drinking, and a bride made up with a painted face and colored eyebrows on the occasion of a wedding seemed perfectly acceptable to most believers. Chrysostom acknowledged this but carried on: "I know indeed that I shall appear ridiculous in finding fault with these things; and shall incur the charge of great folly with the generality, as disturbing the ancient laws: for, as I said before, great is the deceptive power of custom." Here he had reached the limits of his authority over people's lives and tried to appear humble in his hope for change in these matters. He claimed only to expect that a few would join him to be laughed at by the rest.

Chrysostom attacked the wedding ceremony for its inconsistency with all other rules of decorum: the benefit of a lifetime of feminine

Fig. 1.4. An early Byzantine marriage ring from Constantinople with portraits of Aristophanes and Vigilantia kissing beneath a cross. Late fourth or early fifth century. Photo: Dumbarton Oaks, Byzantine Photograph and Fieldwork Archives, Washington, D.C.

modesty and isolation was undone in one day's festivities. The logic of breaking everyday rules for a special occasion fell flat on Chrysostom's ears: "Tell me not of the custom: for if it be an evil thing, let it not be done even once: but if good, let it be done constantly" (*Hom. on 1 Cor.* 12, PG 61.103). Chrysostom described the ceremony from his perspective: to the sound of obscene songs, the garishly made-up bride paraded through the marketplace by torchlight, watched by many men. A customary law required people to insult the bride, and many made this into a competition. Chrysostom asked his congregants to stop and think rationally: Why should they enjoy being abused in public? If they could only remove themselves from their attachment to "custom" for its own sake, they would understand that these practices made no sense and that marriage required a solemn ceremony.[16]

Funerals were another occasion for conflict.[17] Here, as with the New Year's celebration, Chrysostom condemned both the traditional practices and the premise behind them. The funeral dinner was an acceptable practice because there was a "human law" that required it, and so he did not forbid his listeners to attend them if they were invited (*Hom. on 1 Cor.* 28, PG 61.235–36). This attitude is echoed in the discussion of funerary banquets in the *Apostolic Constitutions*, which considered the funeral dinner to be an acceptable custom so long as the participants did not overeat or become drunk (8.44.1–3). But any funerary observation beyond the dinner, according to Chrysostom, implied an un-Christian fear of death.

The attack on funeral customs focused on "excessive" mourning. The preacher viewed highly emotional displays of grief as a pagan tendency and an implicit denial of the truth of the Resurrection. After the coming of Christianity, true believers had no reason to be upset by death. Instead, Christians were to mourn living sinners, because although worms were not yet eating their bodies, their passions were shredding their souls to pieces (*Hom. on Matt.* 27, PG 57.347–50).[18] After the death of a loved one, men should not beat themselves and should not invite pagan women to sing dirges at funerals. On the other hand, inviting poor people to funerals and priests to pray in order to help the souls of the dead was, in Chrysostom's view, consistent with Christian teachings about death, so long as this was done with the proper acknowledgment that sin was the problem, not death (*Hom. on Matt.* 31, PG 57.374–75).

Chrysostom encouraged his listeners to impress their pagan neighbors by not mourning over death. The stark difference between the behavior of Christians and pagans would emphasize Christianity's superiority, if only the flock would behave in ways consistent with their faith. Unfortunately, Christians grieved as much as anyone else. Christian women claimed that they were blinded by passion and that their tears were unavoidable (*Hom. on 1 Cor.* 3, PG 61.28–29).[19] Men and women alike could not imagine any other possible reaction, because they believed that mourning the dead was natural (*Hom. on Matt.* 31, PG 57.374). To Chrysostom their mourning was not due to nature but to old customs and a failing in their Christian beliefs. Like celebrating the Kalends, insisting upon grieving for the dead reflected a non-Christian understanding of how the world worked, and so the preacher exhorted his congregants to leave behind these emotional habits. We can assume, however, that the laity in Antioch did not in the end accept this belief as a dominant part of their Christian worldview. Rituals of mourning remained a part of emerging Orthodox society.

The new ways of thinking and acting that Chrysostom tried to instill through his sermons would work together, he hoped, to manifest a truly Christian society. Chrysostom remarked that the adherents of different religions in Antioch were indistinguishable in the marketplace, on the streets, and in the theater. Christians, he claimed, were clearly separated from the rest only in church, once the uninitiated were taken away so that the baptized could participate in the mysteries (*Hom. on Matt.* 4, PG 57.48). From the preacher's point of view, this distinction *should* have been visible to everyone, always, in every aspect of the person. This vision of Christian life required many practices to be reflexive, natural parts of each day. The only problem preventing this new world from coming into existence—the replacement of old habits of thought and action with new ones—was easy to solve in theory but extremely difficult in practice. There was another difficulty, too, which Chrysostom did not acknowledge: many Christians disagreed with his views because they simply had different ways of defining proper and improper Christian behavior.

As we have seen in the cases of oath swearers and the ones who returned to church despite breaking their fast, some Christians did respond to their preacher's demands and changed their behavior. But the sermons also reveal instances when the laity rejected the preacher's program of Christianization. Most Christians apparently did not question the necessity of being baptized, receiving communion, or fasting during Lent, but they did argue back, require more explanation, or simply ignore proposed changes to some of their routine activities. In other words, the laypeople did not necessarily reject their preacher's demands because they were generally impious or unenthusiastic Christians; their values and customs indicate that they were actively engaged with their religion. They incorporated religion into their lives in ways that originated from their own experiences and logic, rather than solely following the instructions from church authorities. The congregation sometimes accepted and sometimes rejected the demands of the preacher, and this determined how they would live their lives, how their preacher could progress with his teachings, and ultimately how their society was Christianized.

FOR FURTHER READING

Allen, Pauline, and Mary B. Cunningham, eds. *Preacher and Audience: Studies in Early Christian and Byzantine Homiletics*. Boston: Brill, 1998.

Allen, Pauline, and Wendy Mayer. *John Chrysostom*. New York: Routledge, 2000.

Brown, Peter. "Christianization and Religious Conflict." In *Cambridge Ancient History*, 13:632–64. Cambridge: Cambridge University Press, 1997.

John Chrysostom. *Baptismal Instructions*. Trans. Paul W. Harkins. ACW 31. Westminster, Md.: Newman, 1963.

———. *On Wealth and Poverty*. Trans. Catharine Roth. Crestwood, N.Y.: St. Vladimir's Seminary Press, 1984.

Kelly, J. N. D. *Golden Mouth: The Story of John Chrysostom—Ascetic, Preacher, Bishop*. Ithaca: Cornell University Press, 1995.

Mills, Kenneth, and Anthony Grafton, eds. *Conversion in Late Antiquity and the Early Middle Ages: Seeing and Believing*. Rochester, N.Y.: University of Rochester Press, 2003.

Palladius. *Dialogue on the Life of St. John Chrysostom*. ACW 45. Trans. and ed. Robert Meyer. New York: Newman, 1985.

THE CULT OF THE MARTYRS AND THE CAPPADOCIAN FATHERS

VASILIKI LIMBERIS

CHAPTER TWO

Many Christian practices in Late Antiquity emerged locally and were already well established in various regions by the time of Constantine. During the course of the fourth century, with the encouragement of Christian emperors, church leaders moved to regularize aspects of the religion, including doctrines, church governance, and lay piety. While bishops sought to ensure that lay practices conformed to the Constantinian rhetoric of "one Emperor, one God, one Church," this did not mean that local customs were uniformly erased for a standard practice. Instead, bishops began to appropriate existing forms of local piety for themselves and for the broader church, in a process that legitimated regionally specific practices and reinforced episcopal control.

This process unfolds in the sermons, letters, and panegyrics of the Cappadocian Fathers: Gregory of Nazianzus, Basil of Caesarea, and Basil's brother Gregory of Nyssa. These powerful bishops of the second half of the fourth century tirelessly promoted the cults of the martyrs of Cappadocia and Pontus in Asia Minor. Their writings reveal that the majority of these cults were long-standing and that most of Cappadocian Christianity's rituals constellated around them. The Cappadocian Fathers delivered their panegyrics on the martyrs in order to impose a degree of control over local rituals and piety. They stressed a uniform calendar, promoted the building of shrines and churches, and attempted to shape the rites of the *panegyreis*, or the festivals of the martyrs. The Fathers also appropriated the rhetoric of the

Fig. 2.1. Gregory of Nazianzus and Basil the Great from the Church of the Holy Anargyroi (Sts. Cosmas and Damian), Kastoria, Greece, circa 1180. Photo: Sharon E. J. Gerstel.

cults in their funeral panegyrics, refashioning the lives of their relatives and friends as imitations of the Christian saints. These panegyrics promoted the Fathers' own conceptions of appropriate Christian piety and elevated members of the regional aristocracy as local saints and heroes. In this fashion the Cappadocians created a Christian social order that maintained the hierarchical status of their aristocratic families by merging the categories of sanctity and kinship, as well as inscribed ideas about appropriate gender roles and lay behavior. The Cappadocian Fathers thus sought to regularize and regulate Christian practice in Cappadocia.

CALENDARS, BUILDINGS, AND FESTIVALS OF THE SAINTS

By the time of the Cappadocians, devotion to the martyrs was already very popular, with at least 111 different saints being venerated in different parts of the empire, most in local or regionally specific cults.[1] The Cappadocians' writings reveal that at least twelve saints were venerated in that province alone. Their avid promotion of these cults secured their institutionalization, establishing certain modes of pious practice and creating an overriding ethos of imitation. Martyrs offered models for Christians to follow.

The feasts of the saints punctuated the year, shaping the rhythms of time for local clergy and laity alike, and were significant occasions for social, political, and economic activity. Basil himself often used festivals to conduct ecclesiastical business, and he scolded bishops who failed to attend them for "neglecting the martyrs" (*Letters* 282). For the laity, the martyr festivals provided opportunities for trading and family visits. These festivals encouraged civic and collective expressions of piety, bridged public and private devotion, and reinforced the proximity of holiness. Whether alive or dead and buried, people at the shrine were "with the martyrs," who themselves were with God.

The greatest display of piety for wealthy Cappadocians was to build a church or shrine. By such an extravagant gesture, they exercised considerable power. They publicly connected themselves to the martyrs or saints and guaranteed for their dead a safe place of repose in proximity to the saints that ensured their bodies would be among the first resurrected. In a homily on the Forty Martyrs of Sebasteia (2), Gregory of Nyssa relates that his mother, Emmelia, had constructed a shrine to these saints in the town of Ibora, close to their country estates in Annesi. The shrine was next to the family tomb. The inaugurations of the cult began with the translation of the saints' relics to the shrine. By having their relatives' remains in close physical proximity to the remains of the saints, wealthy Cappadocians connected the martyrs' lives and deaths with those of their families.

Church building was expensive, as Gregory of Nyssa reveals in a letter about his own construction of a church and martyrium, most likely dedicated to the Forty Martyrs.[2] Gregory expresses concerns about lazy workers, problems with contractors, inferior materials, and cost overruns (*Letters* 16). His description of the church shows that it required craftsmen of considerable skill. In his letter, Gregory's worldly role as controlling patron of his own church comes to the fore. While he understood his own act of patronage to be an act of devotion, it is unclear whether Gregory understood his laborers' efforts to be an aspect of their own piety.

Gregory's praise of church architecture typically elides the craftsmen responsible for the lovely details of these structures. Nevertheless, such beauty spoke loudly as a visual prayer. For example, Gregory expounds on the meaning of a previously built shrine as a location for ritual and worship. In his elaborate descriptive oration, or *ekphrasis*, on the shrine of St. Theodore of Euchaita, Gregory delights in the grand architecture and praises the structure's magnificent aesthetic qualities: "wood, in the shape of animals, beautiful flowers illustrating nature, the elaborate mosaic floor that is like a prayer in tiny stones to the martyr, polished stones that are as smooth as silver."[3] A large painting depicting Theodore's bravery in the face of his persecution brought the saint close to the faithful. Gregory

---

Martyrs Eulogized or Mentioned in the Works of the Cappadocian Fathers

Basil of Caesarea's Writings

St. Mamas	Sept. 2
St. Eupsychius	Sept. 7
St. Gordius	Jan. 3
Forty Martyrs of Sebasteia	Mar. 9
St. Julitta	July 3
St. Damas	Aug. 28

Gregory of Nazianzus's Writings

St. Cyprian*	Oct. 2 or 4
The Maccabean Martyrs	Aug. 1

*conflating Cyprian of Carthage with Cyprian of Antioch

Gregory of Nyssa's Writings

St. Gregory Thaumaturgus	Nov. 17
St. Stephen	Dec. 26
St. Theodore of Euchaita	Feb. 17
The Forty Martyrs of Sebasteia	Mar. 9

also describes an image of Christ as "presiding over the contest of the martyr." Though silent, "paintings speak on the wall and are of greatest benefit." Such architectural beauty inflamed the believer's desire to venerate the martyr.

These churches and shrines attracted and organized the laity, demonstrated the importance of the cult, and established the honor and power of the donors. The ceaseless stream of believers at St. Theodore's shrine expressed a reciprocal relationship between the martyr and the faithful. As Gregory describes it, Theodore had called to the faithful, who in turn flocked to him and begged him to preside over their celebrations. Together, the saint and his faithful generated the power to protect the shrines and churches, as well as the entire community of believers contained therein. "The prayers of many righteous people release the sins of many others. Remind Peter, wake up Paul and John the Theologian in order that they might care for the churches they established" (*Homily on St. Theodore*).

With the towns of Cappadocia ringed with martyrs' shrines, huge crowds would gather at the yearly *panegyris*, or martyr's festival. The Cappadocians' letters attest to the number of the festivals, as well as to their rites and theological importance. *Panegyris* rituals were both corporate and individual, as the faithful rendered certain acts of piety and respect to the saint in hopeful expectation that miraculous transactions would take place.[4] The community assembled to keep vigil on the night before the anniversary of the martyr's death. Keeping a strict fast, the faithful prayed by candlelight, chanted psalms, engaged in prayers of intercession, kept silence, and listened to homilies. The following day, festivities would culminate in the Divine Liturgy of the Eucharist, the delivery of a long panegyric to the martyr, and the procession of the martyr's relics on a decorated bier. Participation in the *panegyris* required physical stamina, devotion, and proper demeanor.

These festivals could last several days and were often boisterous communal occasions, despite the bishops' efforts to instill an aura of reverence. For example, one year the crowd's unruliness forced Gregory of Nyssa to deliver his first *Homily on the Forty Martyrs* (a–b) over two days. Although on the first day he was drowned out, Gregory makes no attempt to scold the huge audience, as this would have proven useless. His homily has one goal: to remember the martyrs as if they were alive. The martyrs call the people to the festival, and the people, by customs of hospitality, are expected to reciprocate. On the second day Gregory ends with an enticing theology of the martyrs: "And like the martyrs, may we enter into paradise, since we have passed through the contests confidently, because we are now empowered through their intercessions for a good confession of our Lord Jesus Christ." Rhetorically, Gregory tries to control the ambience of the festival, sobering the crowd's mood with his hint at Christ's judgment. Gregory's words suggest that the laity's behavior at the *panegyris* mixed socializing, piety, jocularity, and liturgical ritual in a manner that fell short of episcopal expectations.

Gregory of Nyssa and Basil both countered such behaviors by employing the legends of the saints to institutionalize their parishioners' ritual activities. Gregory writes that while Theodore's body had hung on a stake in tatters, the faithful had held a vigil around him, singing psalms and holding torches. Gregory's flock should thus imitate earlier Christians' actions. Basil notes that before St. Gordius died, he traced "the sign of the cross on himself," modeling proper piety, and "delivered himself into the hands of the angels, who immediately received him as a fresh corpse, and transferred him to the blessed life just like Lazarus." Moreover, Basil creates through Lazarus (Luke 16) a lineage of holiness from the poor beggar outside the rich man's house, through St. Gordius, to his lay audience. Thus Lazarus, who shared poverty, social abuse, and hunger with the laity, was also a martyr.

For the faithful, encountering the saint at the shrine meant the disruption of their daily lives. Devotees made physically taxing journeys to the shrine, and once there they endured fasting and prayer. Upon arrival, the first and most important ritual was to greet the body or relics of the martyr by touching them. This show of respect and devotion for the martyr would in turn sanctify the believer and perhaps even bestow a miracle. Gregory of Nyssa's elaboration on the ritual of greeting the relics brings the paradox of martyr piety to life, for not only was this greeting proper to convey respect, it also facilitated an exchange of spiritual and sometimes even physical gifts. The shrine of St. Theodore was so popular that, according to Gregory, people came "like ants all year long, since it was known especially as a healing shrine for all sorts of diseases, a storehouse for those in need, an inn for the weary, and an incessant festival for those celebrating."

Laypeople might experience anxiety, curiosity, or even terror in the presence of dead bodies or body parts. The Cappadocian Fathers coaxed the laity out of any queasiness in this regard by promising participation in the martyr's sanctity and miracles. For example, Gregory of Nyssa contrasts the revulsion most people experience at the sight of the dead with the delight of beholding the saint's remains: "Those who see the body see it as living and thriving, and they embrace it [with arms] and with eyes, by mouth [with kisses], with ears, with all the senses they come to it, pouring out tears either from reverence or emotions." "On account of this," he explains, "we believe in invisible things from perceptible evidence, and from the experience of the world we believe in the promise of the future." Once people know the "fruit of piety," they must emulate the saint in order to share the honors that Christ dispenses "according to the merits of the athletes" (*Homily on St. Theodore*). Gregory of Nazianzus reminds his listeners that the very bodies of the martyrs "possess equal power with their holy souls, whether touched or worshipped. . . . Even the drops of their blood and little relics of their passion produce equal effects with their bodies" (*Against Julian* 1). Basil explains that the reason for honoring the martyr "is to be found in the tie, as it were, of blood, which binds the life of exact discipline to those who have been made perfect by endurance" (*Homily on Psalm 115*). Greeting the relics expressed a bond of blood relation or kinship with the saint.

> ### Against Taking Pieces of Relics
>
> And above all else be careful: refrain from destroying the objects dedicated to the holy martyrs, so that you will not bring about a judgment that would negatively affect both you and your property, as you will end up ruining your property obtained by wicked means.
>
> —Gregory of Nazianzus, *Letter* 203: To Valentinianus

Most relics of the saints, however, were not whole bodies or even distinguishable body parts. Slivers, splinters, tiny rock-like bones, images, and even dust counted as relics, and these were greeted by touch with a kiss, a hug, or a delicate hand gesture. Physical contact was most important. As Basil stresses, "Those who touch the bones of the martyrs participate in their sanctity" (*Homily on Psalm 115*). Gregory of Nyssa's description of the shrine of St. Theodore evokes a complete process of sanctification involving the believer's ritual response to the shrine's overwhelming architectural beauty, creating a desire to venerate the holy tomb. Ritual touch initiated this process of sanctification since "the act of touch is a sanctification and blessing." In exchange, the pious might take away dust from the tomb as a gift and preserve it as a treasure.

The opportunity to offer intercessory prayer at the martyr's shrine motivated the laity to attend the festival. In the midst of collective rituals of chanting, formal prayers, and procession, the plea for intercession involved individual conversation between the believer and the saint. The festival and its rites concentrated holiness in place and time; there was a much greater chance that the request would be answered at the shrine than at home. As Gregory of Nyssa reminds the faithful, "The Forty Martyrs prevail against all enemies and are the most worthy beings to ask for intercession to the Lord and Master, and with their hope the Christian is strengthened. . . . Their power is sufficient for every need" (*Homily 2 on the Forty Martyrs*).

The laity also engaged in such rituals as incubation, or sleeping at the shrine, which they believed might result in a miracle. In a society in which an abscessed tooth could result in death, miracles were an important source of medical remedy. They were also the ultimate proof of the powers of the holy martyrs and the piety of their believers. While we do not know how many people were allowed to sleep in the martyr's shrine, who kept watch at night, or whether some were disqualified from incubation, we do know that sleeping at the shrine could induce fear. For example, Gregory of Nyssa himself was terrified by his incubation at the shrine of the Forty Martyrs. During the vigil of the *panegyris* in Ibora, he sneaked into a garden and fell asleep. There he dreamed that the Forty Martyrs came to him, scolded him for his laxity, and beat him with sticks. He awoke shaking and immediately returned to the shrine, begging the martyrs for forgiveness and mercy (*Homily 2 on the Forty Martyrs*). Soon afterwards he was baptized and ordained a reader!

Most incubations, however, were voluntary. For example, Gregory recounts how a lame soldier implored the martyrs to cure his foot when he went to the shrine at Ibora. During his incubation, the soldier dreamed that he discussed his disability with the martyrs. When he awoke, his foot was cured. Gregory himself had seen this miracle and heard the man's elation announcing his cure (*Homily 2 on the Forty Martyrs*).

FUNERALS AS MARTYRS' FESTIVALS

The patterns defining martyrs as Christian heroes also reshaped the rituals of death. The Cappadocian Fathers remade their relatives in the image of the martyrs, thus solidifying their families' status and power, and establishing their own reputation as elite Christians. To accomplish this, they recast their families' funerals as martyrs' festivals. Their preaching at the funerals of the elite had the effect of Christianizing death and its rites, offering to the laity patterns to replace or supplement the pagan rituals of lament, including funeral meals and the tradition of placing a coin in the deceased's mouth to pay Charon for passage across the river Styx. While nonelites participated enthusiastically in the funerals of the upper class, it remains unclear whether their own funerals figured as martyr festivals. Nevertheless, they could be understood to have joined the martyrs, especially if they were buried near martyrs' relics.

Describing his older sister's last days in the *Life of Macrina*, Gregory of Nyssa writes, "What I had seen before me was truly the remains of a holy martyr, one who had been dead to sin, but illumined by the indwelling grace of the Holy Spirit" (43). Never a victim of persecution, Macrina assimilated to the martyrs through a lifetime of rigorous ascetic discipline. When Gregory assisted in preparing Macrina's body for burial, he says that her body glowed like a martyr's, with rays of sanctity, despite being dressed in a black cloak. Macrina's vigil took on the character of a martyr's festival, with antiphonal chanting of psalms and responses, and a candlelight procession. Gregory reports, "We spent the whole night singing hymns around her body, just as they do in celebrating the death of martyrs." Many laypeople and important clergy flocked to the funeral and followed the procession

> ### Burial at Shrines
>
> I will share a part of the gift by placing my parents' bodies beside the remains of these soldiers [the Forty Martyrs], in order that they may rise at the time of the resurrection with those who are filled with greater confidence. I know they will prevail because I have witnessed their courage and faith before God.
>
> —Gregory of Nyssa, *Homily 2 on the Forty Martyrs*, PG 46.784B

to the family crypt. Gregory laid Macrina's body in the tomb next to her parents' remains, adjacent to the shrine of the Forty Martyrs.

In his funeral oration for Basil of Caesarea, Gregory of Nazianzus similarly links his friend's death to the death of a martyr and his funeral rites to a martyr's festival. When the funeral procession began, there was a crush of people. Everyone clamored to be in Basil's shadow or touch his holy remains, "for what could be more holy or pure than that body." Psalms gave way to unruly lamentations. Then violence erupted; people were killed, becoming "funeral victims." The laity's spontaneous response to the presence of Basil's body acclaimed him a saint. Basil had become "the martyr to the martyrs," as had those who died at his funeral celebrations.

GENDERING CHRISTIAN PIETY

The Cappadocian Fathers' funeral orations and hagiography also served to gender Christian piety. Their writings create the unequivocal impression that the women of their families were the architects of their piety, preserving the traditions of the martyrs, teaching their husbands and children the faith, performing good works in the community, and in two cases performing miracles. The Fathers constructed a strong family mythos through their representation of their female relatives as present-day martyrs.

Since the Cappadocians endorsed celibacy and virginity over married life, their funeral panegyrics reveal the tension embedded in their paradigm of the Christian family. This tension between asceticism and marriage was resolved through the lives of their grandmothers, mothers, and sisters, who (except for the younger Macrina) embodied both states, thus providing examples of the Christian life to the laity. For the nonelites, imagining the Cappadocian women as venerable martyrs only further exalted them. Nonetheless, these women served as examples of piety through their selfless service to their faith, families, and communities. Their acts were imitable, if not their status.

Each of the Cappadocians stressed that their religion came from their mothers and, in the case of Basil and Gregory of Nyssa, from their grandmother Macrina as well. This Macrina had lived through the persecution of Diocletian, had known disciples of the third-century saint Gregory the Wonderworker, and kept traditions of Gregory and the martyrs alive through stories she told her grandchildren. For Basil and Gregory, these stories were part of their family heritage. Although Basil acknowledged his grandmother's transformative influence on his life, it was his mother, Emmelia, who dedicated him and his brother to God. Similarly, Gregory of Nazianzus's mother, Nonna, herself the daughter of a fervent Christian matriarch, dedicated him. Nonna converted her own husband to Christianity and then served as the spiritual guide to her children, Gorgonia, Gregory, and Caesarius.

In their brothers' writings, the Cappadocians' sisters further demonstrated how aristocratic women might serve as teachers, miracle workers, and links to the laity. In his *Life of Macrina,* Gregory of Nyssa presents his sister as the Christian teacher par excellence, assuming the care of her youngest brother almost as soon as he was born and convincing her mother, Emmelia, to convert their entire household into a monastery. Unlike Macrina, the married Gorgonia had to balance the life of an upper-class matron with the rigors of her ascetic vocation. However, she not only passed the Christian life on to her three daughters but followed her mother's example in persuading her husband to be baptized.

According to their brothers, Macrina and Gorgonia were so infused with faith that they, unlike the men in their families, were able to perform miracles. After Gorgonia was injured in a carriage accident, she spurned medical care and stole into a church, where she approached the altar and "ventured on an act of pious and splendid effrontery" (*On His Sister Gorgonia*). Crying on the altar, Gorgonia refused to leave until she was cured. She then took consecrated bread and wine and applied them like a salve to her body. The next day she left the church cured, keeping the means of this miracle a secret. Similarly, Macrina once suffered from a tumor on her breast. Emmelia begged Macrina to see a doctor, but she refused out of modesty, choosing instead to perform a vigil in the family chapel. She took dirt moistened with her tears and applied the mixture as a salve to the growth, then asked her mother to make the sign of the cross over the tumor. "The sign of the cross worked and the affliction disappeared," leaving only a small scar. Macrina also cured a soldier's daughter of an eye infection. Gregory listed Macrina's deeds of exorcism, prophecy, miraculous feeding, and healing, all of which reinforced the laity's dependency on Christian aristocratic families for models of piety and veneration.

The Cappadocian matriarchs modeled acts of virtue, including a rigorous prayer life and unquestioning generosity for needy friends and relatives. Macrina and Emmelia opened their storehouses during a famine; Gorgonia was unstintingly generous to needy relatives who were a constant presence in her household; and Emmelia built the shrine of the Forty Martyrs at Ibora. These women were at the center of Christian life for their communities, preserving, nurturing, and propagating the rituals of everyday piety. As such, their brothers and sons memorialized them as exemplars of Christian piety for their congregations.

SACRAMENTS AND OTHER RITUALS

The Cappadocians spoke much more about the piety of the martyrs than they did about the sacraments or the liturgy. Nevertheless, their writings reveal how they shaped baptism and the eucharist into opportunities for lay piety. Their writings also offer glimpses of a lay piety that included such practices as using blessed bread in acts of healing, venturing on pilgrimage, and a variety of strategies for combating the evil eye.

Baptismal customs had not yet been standardized by the mid- to late fourth century. To receive baptism was to enter into a life of perfection, but fear of sinning after baptism deterred many from seeking the rite until life's end. Even such devoted Christians as Gregory the Elder, Gregory of Nyssa, Basil, Gregory of Nazianzus and his brother Caesarius, and Gorgonia and her husband Alypius delayed baptism. Despite their own trepidation, Basil and his brother delivered sermons appealing for early baptism. Basil urged the people to see themselves as slaves about to be freed in Christ, asking, "Why would a slave delay?" (*Homily on Holy Baptism*). In *Against Those Who Delay Baptism*, Gregory of Nyssa echoed Basil's concern. His congregation was filled with unbaptized elderly people fearful of sinning after the sacrament. Gregory stressed that forestalling baptism was a gamble; he lamented the confusion that ensued when a household attempted to assemble a deathbed baptism, with family members running around looking for the right pots, clean water, and even the priest. He concluded by contemplating what awaited the unbaptized soul in the afterlife: alienation, disorientation, wandering, and anxiety, since the angels would not recognize one without the seal of baptism.

Gregory of Nazianzus's sermon *On Baptism* integrates this sacrament into the lay life cycle, urging its addition among festivals of rejoicing "for our salvation," including weddings, birthdays, name days, housewarmings, and anniversaries. His frustration is apparent when he says, "The fear of sinning again, as a delay against baptism, is a specious argument of the devil. It is an insane thought." Gregory urges the laity to baptize their children around the age of three. He believed that children, even so young, "would be able to listen and to answer something about the sacrament, even though they may not perfectly understand it." He presents baptism as a replacement for the civic celebration of "registering your children," which involved the use of apotropaic jewelry. Gregory decries these amulets and the incantations that accompanied them as diabolical, "stealing worship from God." Far better, he asserts, is to "give your child to the Trinity, that great and noble guard." Baptism, he says, is the "medicine of exorcism, for the Trinity is more powerful than demons, and the sacrament a greater phylactery than amulets."

The connections between sin and disease were a given in Late Antiquity. Christians from the time of Paul understood the eucharist not only to be the means of participation in the death and resurrection of Jesus, but also as a "medicine of immortality" (1 Cor. 11:28–30; Ignatius of Antioch, *Ephesians* 20). By partaking of the Holy Mysteries, individuals received "the healing of soul and body" (Liturgies of St. Basil, St. Serapion of Thmuis, and St. John Chrysostom). What is striking about these connections is that both the laity and the fathers had a profound stake in them, but for different reasons.

In the *Great Catechism*, Gregory of Nyssa capitalizes on the connections between disease and sin and between the eucharist and healing. By merging sin with disease and healing with salvation, he explains how the laity should approach the eucharist. For Gregory, eucharistic bread is crucial for salvation. Describing the problem of fallen humanity in terms of disease, he asserts that eucharistic bread is the antidote. Gregory's graphic description of metabolizing the eucharist appealed to the laity, and his use of medical terms was gripping. The eucharist is the "antidote to poison," "solvent of our nature." "Like leaven to dough, immortality reconstitutes and transposes the whole into itself, when it is in our body." Indeed, Gregory describes the process of receiving eternal life as a type of ingestion:

> In no other way can anything enter the body but by being transfused through the vitals by eating and drinking. . . . Since then, that God-containing flesh partook for its substance and support of this particular nourishment, then by this communion with Deity mankind might at the same time be deified. . . . He disseminates Himself in every believer through that flesh, whose substance comes from bread and wine, blending Himself with the body of the believers; by this union with the immortal, humanity may be a sharer in incorruption.

Gregory's sermon enticed people to participate actively in the sacramental life.

Gorgonia's experience of healing following her carriage accident also highlights the potency of the eucharist as medicine. What is startling about this story is that Gorgonia assumed the healing powers of the consecrated gifts but would not consume them because she was still unbaptized. The application of the consecrated eucharist to her body and her resulting cure show the extent to which the sacrament was considered therapeutic.

In Cappadocia, as in other regions of the Mediterranean, not all loaves consecrated during the liturgy were consumed on the spot. Already in the first and second centuries, this blessed bread was distributed to those unable to attend the liturgy, including the sick and those in prison. The fourth-century *Apostolic Constitutions* indicates that this process was common. Bishops also sent friends gifts of consecrated host. The Cappadocian fathers indicate that these blessed breads, called *eulogia*, were often hoarded by the faithful to ward off evil or to bring a cure.

While discussing his parents, Gregory of Nazianzus reveals the centrality of these *eulogia* to Christian life in Cappadocia. His mother, Nonna, had become gravely ill while nursing her husband back to health. She was unable to eat, drink, or rest. Gregory relates that God sustained her through a dream of *eulogia*: "She saw me, who was her favorite—for not even in her dreams did she prefer any other of us—coming to her suddenly at night, with a basket of pure white loaves, which I blessed and crossed, and then fed her, and she became stronger. The nocturnal vision was a real action" (*On the Death of His Father*). Nonna awoke fully cured.

Some common lay practices met with the Fathers' opprobrium. For example, Gregory of Nyssa disapproved of pilgrimage. After Constantine and his mother, Helena, had built churches at the holy sites of Jesus' life, pilgrimage to Palestine had become popular. Gregory himself seems to have mixed piety and business on his trips to and from Palestine and Arabia. But the behavior he saw displayed by the pilgrims visiting these sites provoked him to reject the practice (*On Pilgrimage*). According to Gregory, the laity took advantage of their anonymity and distance from home to commit indecent acts, including the mixing of sexes in public, immodesty, lewd behavior, adultery, theft, idolatry, poisoning, quarreling, and even murder. Gregory argued that visiting these holy places was not commanded in the Gospel: "The Lord does not include a pilgrimage to Jerusalem amongst [the apostles'] good deeds" (*Letters* 17). Needless to say, Gregory's censure had little effect on this popular practice.

Other practices that caused concern for the Fathers were those relating to the evil eye. Having just been ordained in 364, Basil wrote his homily *On Envy* in response to significant factionalism, gossip, envy, and accusations of curses and bewitchment among his congregation in Caesarea. The worst manifestation of this unrest was the pervasive accusation of the evil eye. Because of intense competition for honor in the community, individuals and families often vied for top status through public donations or other acts of beneficence. The victor's reward was universal acclaim, honor, and good fortune. According to the reigning theory, losing competitors would grow jealous, unable to control their passions. Soon envy would overcome them, and, intentionally or not, they would "cast the evil eye" on the victors. Envious people transmitted the evil eye through their stares and glances or by polluting the air.[5]

Due to the prevalence of such practices, the laity were wary of neighbors and acquaintances who were overly complimentary, fawning, or attentive. Above all, they made sure their babies and small children could not be looked at directly in the eyes. Many believed that apotropaic amulets hidden in their clothes or worn around their necks could divert the evil eye. The most common amulet was in the shape of an eye, with blue surrounding the black pupil. The second most effective amulet was stamped or etched with the "sign of Solomon," depicting Solomon riding a horse.[6] People knew they had been cursed when they, their families, or their livestock were suddenly stricken with headaches, sickness, misfortune, or death. Other signs of having been cursed were broken matrimonial arrangements or infertility.

Many of the laity believed that the harm they suffered had come "through the eyes alone."[7] While dismissing these accusations as "popular stories, spread by women's groups and old ladies," Basil nevertheless took the evil eye seriously. He did not deny that the evil eye could have deleterious effects on people's lives, but he instead denied that it was controlled by random demons. Rather, the devil himself perpetrated the evil eye, and only the church, not a sorcerer, could overcome this evil. Through Christian moral and ascetic training, the believer was to pursue virtue, thus rendering envy powerless. Basil's solution did not eradicate belief in the evil eye; instead, it provided a doctrinal explanation for its workings and a set of Christian practices to combat it.

MARTYR PIETY AND THE CONSTRUCTION OF AUTHORITY

Though the Cappadocian Fathers did not invent the cult of the martyrs, their endorsement of it allowed them to shape lay practice while establishing their episcopal authority. As members of elite families, the Fathers appropriated martyr piety as their own. Through their lineage and pious behavior, they could control the cult. In funeral panegyrics and saints' lives they presented their family members as models of piety to be emulated and themselves as authorities worthy to enunciate and arbitrate pious Christian practice.

For example, Basil and Gregory of Nyssa's class and wealth are not the only markers establishing their episcopal authority; they also devised for themselves a spiritual lineage that went back to earlier Christian times. By doing so, Basil and Gregory establish themselves as double "elites," both patrician and apostolic. For both, the heroic stories of Gregory the Wonderworker are part of their family heritage, which both claim through their grandmother Macrina. Basil adopts Macrina's spiritual association with the Wonderworker as proof of his apostolic lineage, thereby confirming the apostolicity of his beliefs. "What clearer evidence can there be of my faith, than I was brought up by my grandmother . . . the celebrated Macrina who taught me the words of the blessed Gregory [the Wonderworker], which as far as memory preserved down to her day, she cherished herself, while she fashioned and formed me, while yet a child, upon the doctrines of piety" (*Letters* 204). Basil places Gregory "among Apostles and Prophets, a man who walked in the same Spirit as they" (*On the Holy Spirit*). Gregory of Nyssa also invokes Macrina and her association with Gregory the Wonderworker. He records his namesake's countless miracles, which Macrina recounted to him as a child, making this preeminent saint of Pontus a true spiritual relative.

Gregory of Nyssa's biography of his older sister also demonstrates how the Fathers framed their eulogies as acts of piety and family glorification. Gregory's biography of his sister Macrina serves as a work of liturgical thanksgiving and an act of piety to overcome grief.[8] As a funeral panegyric, the work's overriding perspective is one of martyrdom. In the same way that his description of Macrina's funeral conforms to a martyr's panegyric, Gregory's biography transforms Macrina's life into the *vita* of a saint.[9] As a virgin ascetic, Macrina participated in the ranks of the martyrs.[10] Gregory charts her spiritual ascent through ascetic discipline as she matured in imitation of the martyrs. It is telling that the *Life of Macrina* opens with a vision of the holy martyrs. Not having seen his sister for eight years, Gregory recounts his decision to visit her. While traveling, Gregory has a dream in which he is blinded while holding brightly shining martyr's relics. Through this dream, Gregory identifies Macrina as a martyr. When he arrives at Annesi, Gregory learns that Macrina is indeed dying. Most effectively, while on her deathbed, Macrina refashions the entire family through the prism of martyrdom.

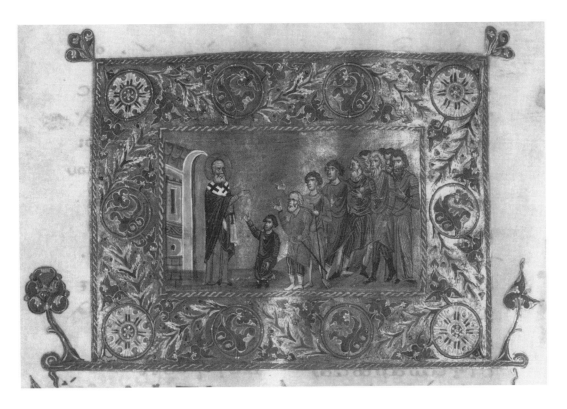

Fig. 2.2. Gregory of Nazianzus showing compassion for the poor, from a twelfth-century illustrated manuscript of his sermons (Sinai gr. 339). Photo: Reproduced through the courtesy of the Michigan-Princeton-Alexandria Expedition to Mount Sinai.

Gregory of Nazianzus also offers funeral orations for his two siblings, Caesarius and Gorgonia. Gregory's greatest challenge is writing about Caesarius, who was neither married nor a monk. However, by stressing Caesarius's roots in a saintly family and his courage in bearing witness before the pagan emperor Julian, Gregory locates him in the martyr tradition. "Such was the godliness of Caesarius," writes Gregory, comparing him to those who confessed Christ during the persecutions under Decius and Diocletian. On the other hand, Gorgonia's life is easier to conform to the pattern of martyrdom. Gorgonia's marriage was modeled on ascetic piety, the first step in the voluntary life of the martyr. Gorgonia was able to achieve a harmonious balance between the responsibilities of marriage and her personal goals of asceticism, for "she lived and died amid the word of piety." As Gregory presents them, the laity could easily relate to the lives of Caesarius and Gorgonia, the former an ambitious young man searching for a good career in court at Constantinople, the latter married with children. All Christians could imitate their piety and devotion, while still participating in lay life.

Through these eulogies the Cappadocian Fathers equate the extraordinary piety of their loved ones with the acts and powers of the martyrs. In this manner the Fathers not only prescribed normative models of Christian piety for the laity but mapped onto their own families' aristocratic pedigrees a genealogical embodiment of martyr piety, thus adding to their episcopal authority. As such, they made their relatives and themselves into local saints.

This survey of local piety in fourth-century Cappadocia has focused on efforts by an enterprising but small elite to appropriate the rituals of local martyr cults to establish themselves as model practitioners of the laity's martyr piety. The result is a rich hybrid of their own vision of Christian orthodoxy and the rituals of pre-Constantinian local martyr cults. In the centuries to come, the practices appropriated by the Cappadocian Fathers with their elite notions of Christian ritual and family piety would become the property of a much wider social circle, as the norm of Eastern Christianity as a whole.

Taken together, the panegyrics of the Cappadocian Fathers reveal that the power of the cult of the martyrs derived from the devotion of the laity. The laity presented the Fathers with a wealth of practices that they in turn appropriated and refashioned in a variety of ways. Indeed, it is only through the censorious comments of the Fathers that we know about the heterogeneous practices of the Cappadocian laity in the second half of the fourth century. In the Fathers' minds, some practices needed regularization, some needed prohibiting, while others needed encouragement. Above all, the Cappadocians as bishops were able to capitalize on an extraordinary devotion to the martyrs, promoting the cults and stabilizing their own authority on a host of ecclesiastical, political, and spiritual matters.

FOR FURTHER READING

Leemans, Johan, Wendy Mayer, Pauline Allen, and Boudewijn Dehandschutter. 'Let Us Die That We May Live': Greek Homilies on Christian Martyrs from Asia Minor, Palestine, and Syria (c. AD 350–AD 450). London: Routledge, 2003.

Limberis, Vasiliki. "The Eyes Infected by Evil." *Harvard Theological Review* 84 (1991): 163–84.

McGuckin, John A. *St. Gregory of Nazianzus: An Intellectual Biography.* Crestwood, N.Y.: St. Vladimir's Seminary Press, 2001.

Rousseau, Philip. *Basil of Caesarea.* Berkeley: University of California Press, 1994.

Van Dam, Raymond. *Families and Friends in Late Roman Cappadocia.* Philadelphia: University of Pennsylvania Press, 2003.

ROMANOS AND THE NIGHT VIGIL IN THE SIXTH CENTURY

GEORGIA FRANK

CHAPTER THREE

> The secret of the Great Stories is that they *have* no secrets. The Great Stories are the ones you have heard and want to hear again. The ones you can enter anywhere and inhabit comfortably. . . . They are as familiar as the house you live in. Or the smell of your lover's skin. You know how they end, yet you listen as though you don't.
>
> —Arundhati Roy[1]

What were the "Great Stories" for early Byzantine Christians? By the sixth century Christians boasted several kinds. They heard the events of Jesus' life, death, and resurrection retold throughout the liturgical year. They also knew stories about apostles, martyrs, desert ascetics, and other saints. To know the stories one simply had to listen. To "inhabit" them, however, required the entire body and its physical senses. The fourth-century pilgrim Egeria, for instance, marveled at how story and sense perception converged when she gazed at a holy place and listened to the appropriate reading from the Bible.[2] Tokens, amulets, and other "blessings" (*eulogiai*) from healing centers and shrines extended those sensory encounters to ever more distant locations. In various early Byzantine cities, newly baptized Christians were taught to enter the story of Christ's death as witnesses to a funeral cortège.[3] Preachers urged people to note the smells, sounds, and spaces that attended their Great Stories. All these rituals invited worshippers to enter and relive the story. They played the story by reenacting it.

And they played with the story by handling it, using the body's movements and sensations as entries into the episode's lost moments and its characters' hidden thoughts.[4]

One writer who invited worshippers to play with a variety of biblical stories was Romanos the Melodist (died circa 555). His chanted sermons, or *kontakia*, performed during vigils at churches around Constantinople, retold biblical stories with more characters,

Fig. 3.1. Elevation of the cross on the ambo from the *Menologium of Basil II*, circa 1000 (Vaticanus graecus 1613, 35). In larger churches preachers preached sermons and cantors chanted hymns from a raised platform in the nave called an ambo. According to a later Byzantine legend, one Christmas Eve after Romanos had arrived in Constantinople, he had a vision in which the Virgin handed him a scroll to eat. When he awoke, he mounted the ambo and sang his first *kontakion*, a celebration of the nativity of Christ. Photo: Biblioteca Apostolica Vaticana.

dialogues, and incidents to draw the audience into these dramas. Yet his expansions also provided many somatic cues for his audience. The attention to gestures, sights, smells, tastes, and sounds not only stretched stories but rendered them permeable, capable of absorbing the Byzantine worshipper. Romanos presented the biblical story as a site of numerous entrances, like the early Byzantine liturgy itself.

In addition to demonstrating Romanos's gifts as a raconteur, his *kontakia* reveal aspects of the experiences of early Byzantine worshippers at vigils. In many of his hymns, characters ask themselves what they heard in the distance or puzzle over a strange yet sweet smell. This chapter examines some of these deliberative moments, by which Romanos invited the congregation to enter the story. Although these hymns were not dramatizations, such as the passion plays of the medieval West, they did allow a variety of characters to interact and probe any given biblical story. In these exchanges Romanos unleashed sensory dramas that would breach what actors today might call the "fourth wall," the expectation that the audience is nonexistent to the performers on stage.

VIGILS IN EARLY BYZANTIUM

In many parts of the eastern empire, Christians gathered weekly at church for all-night vigils on the eve of Sunday mass or, in some parts of Egypt, on Thursday night in preparation for Friday eucharist.[5] Vigils were also held on the eve of major festivals in the liturgical calendar, such as Christmas, Epiphany, and Pentecost. The week leading up to Easter included several vigils. For instance, the pilgrim Egeria, who traveled to Jerusalem around 384, attended vigils on Great Tuesday, Maundy Thursday, Good Friday, and the eve of Easter.

The all-night vigil (*pannychis*) typically lasted from midnight until midday and involved various biblical and nonbiblical readings, the singing of psalms and hymns, prayer, prostrations, perpetual kneeling and rising, and preaching. As Basil of Caesarea described vigils, "the people rise early at night to go to the house of prayer, and in labor and affliction and continuous tears confessing to God, finally rise from their prayers and enter upon the singing of psalms." The singing might be antiphonal between two choirs or responsorial, with one leading the chant while the rest sang the response.[6]

Orations in praise of saints survive from these events, but with little direct description or explanation of any rites involved. Since vigils were festivals, however, a full engagement of senses and appetites was possible, providing occasions for large crowds to delight in drink, song, food, and dance. Even in remote Egyptian villages, payment receipts for wine, meats, breads, and sweets testify to available sensory delights.[7] Distressed by this highly exuberant enjoyment of the saints, some preachers sought to redirect sensory perceptions to the saint's tomb.[8] John Chrysostom, for instance, presented festival-goers with this advice: "Stay beside the tomb of the martyr; there pour out fountains of tears. Have a contrite mind; raise a blessing from the tomb. Take her as an advocate in your prayers and immerse yourself perpetually in the stories of his struggles. Embrace the coffin, nail yourself to the chest. Not just the martyrs' bones, but even their tombs and chests brim with a great deal of blessing. Take holy oil and anoint your whole body—your tongue, your lips, your neck, your eyes."[9] Here story and senses come together for the worshipper, as the immersion in the saint's story (*panegyris*) involves a full sensory immersion in the space. What remains unclear is specifically how the worshipper might relate to, or even participate in, the story itself. A fuller picture of how story and senses converge emerges in the retelling of Gospel events, performed as part of church vigils.

Late Antique Christians held various night offices in different settings, such as homes, tombs, monasteries, and churches. At these services Christians prepared for a feast with its eucharist or they would honor a martyr's memory on the anniversary of his or her death. Vigils were hardly silent. John Chrysostom, for instance, organized singing vigils in the streets of Constantinople to counteract Arian vigils that he claimed were disrupting his church services and depleting attendance. The popularity of night vigils continued well beyond the sixth century.[10] Repeated efforts by clergy to ban women's attendance at vigils suggest that such proscriptions had little lasting effect. The sixth-century *Life of Matrona of Perge* recounts how that heroine defied her husband's orders and spent the entire night singing psalms and praying at the Church of the Holy Apostles.[11] In urban churches and

---

A Hymn for Christmas

The prelude and first stanza of Romanos the Melodist's hymn "On the Nativity" are still used in Orthodox churches on Christmas.

Today the Virgin gives birth to him who is above all being,
and the earth offers a cave to him whom no one can approach.
Angels with shepherds give glory,
and magi journey with a star,
for to us there has been born
    a little Child, God before the ages.

Bethlehem has opened Eden, come, let us see:
we have found delight in secret, come, let us receive
the joys of Paradise within the cave.
There the unwatered root whose blossom is forgiveness has appeared.
There has been found the undug well
from which David once longed to drink.
There a virgin has borne a babe
and has quenched at once Adam's and David's thirst.
For this, let us hasten to this place where there has been born
    a little Child, God before the ages.

—*On the Life of Christ: Kontakia,*
trans. Ephrem Lash
(San Francisco: HarperCollins, 1995), 3.

suburban shrines, a long tradition of night vigils continued among Byzantine men and women. Romanos's *kontakia* form part of this nocturnal worship.

THE *KONTAKIA* OF ROMANOS THE MELODIST

Romanos composed hymns—more precisely, chanted sermons—for night vigils associated with feast days of the liturgical year.[12] He used his talents in the service of each Holy Week vigil, as well as for the feasts of the Epiphany, the Ascension, and Pentecost. These stanzaic poems were chanted by a soloist, who was joined by the congregation for a one-line refrain closing each stanza. For all the liberties Romanos took in making silent characters vocal and marginal characters central to some episodes, he remained true to the formal properties of these hymns. The *kontakia* normally consist of eighteen to twenty-four stanzas. The initial letters of each stanza form an acrostic to spell phrases such as "by the humble (*tapeinos/tapinos*) Romanos," "a *psalmos* by Romanos," or "praise (*ainos*) by Romanos." Even if that literary device escaped notice, his hearers would not have missed the common refrain distinctive to each poem and sung by all at the end of each hymn. In some hymns, the refrain comprised a single word, such as "alleluia" or *polyelee* (very merciful). Others were considerably longer, such as the "Judas" *kontakion*, whose refrain contained thirty syllables: "Be merciful, merciful, merciful to us, you who are patient with all, and wait for all" (33 [17]). A less skilled poet would have inserted refrains simply as musical punctuation, as in "and a partridge in a pear tree" in today's familiar Christmas carol. Romanos employed the refrain with far greater effect.

In any given hymn various characters would utter the same refrain. Thus hero and villain alike would eventually utter the same words. To cue his audiences for their entry, Romanos often introduced the refrain with a verb for speaking (*legein*) or some loud utterance, such as crying, yelling, even screaming (for example, *boan, krazein, kraugazein*). In other hymns, he directed the audience to "sing" (*psallein, adein*), to "supplicate" (*hiketeuin*), or to "pray" (*proseuchesthai*).

By this technique the stanza became the "green room" in which the audience waited offstage for their cue to take the stage and thereby rejoin the story.

This audience involvement is referred to directly in one *kontakion*:

> The people, faithful in their love of Christ,
>   have gathered to keep a night-long vigil with psalms and odes;
>   unceasingly they sing hymns to God.
> So, now that [the Psalms of] David ha[ve] been sung
>   and we rejoiced in the well-ordered reading of scripture,
> Now let us raise a hymn to Christ and pillory the enemy.[13]

This description suggests the cumulative effect of lessons, prostrations, and prayers, as well as the *kontakion* itself, on the audience's perceptions of the basic story. It is also likely that as the hour grew late, emotions ran high.

One also notices a participatory quality in the hymns' allusions to other rituals. Although the *kontakia* were performed in non-eucharistic settings, Romanos often inserted references to other rites. In "On the Resurrection I" (40 [29]) worshippers would have recognized various formulas from the Easter morning liturgy, including the "holy, holy, holy" (40.7), the "lift up your heart" (40.22), the beginning of the Lord's Prayer (40.24), and the "he has arisen, indeed," taken from the greeting for Easter morning (40.prol. 2; 40.21, 22; see also 7.8; 22.4; 24.8–9).[14] Equally resonant are the nonverbal dimensions of the ritual. In Romanos's reworking of Gospel accounts, Mary Magdalene enters the empty tomb not once but several times, suggesting the multiple entrances in the liturgy. He also evokes the processional quality of these rituals and possibly the choirs that attended them, as when the Magdalene invites women to light torches (40.12) and approach the tomb, to which a "choir of devout maidens" responds (40.15, 17;

A Hymn for Easter

The risen Jesus speaks to Mary Magdalene in Romanos's hymn "On the Resurrection I."

Hurry, Mary, and assemble my disciples.
I am using you as a loud-sounding trumpet.
Sound peace to the terrified ears of my friends in
    hiding.
Rouse them all as if from sleep,
that they may come to meet me and light torches.
Say, "The bridegroom has been raised from the tomb
and has left nothing within the tomb.
Apostles, banish deadness, for he has been raised,
who grants resurrection to the fallen."

—*On the Life of Christ*, 173.

see also 32.15). Outside the tomb, their good news to the male disciples is, first, to "form . . . choirs" and only then to say together, "The Lord has arisen" (40.22).

"On the Ascension" (48 [32]) illustrates well Romanos's ability to engage his audience. In recounting the events surrounding Christ's final instructions to the apostles before he rose to heaven, Romanos focuses more on the circumstances surrounding the Savior's imminent departure than on the ascension itself. Thus only three of the eighteen stanzas describe the ascension. Instead, Romanos emphasizes the apostles' distress prior to Christ's departure and their reaction in its aftermath. He calls on worshippers to "raise on high our eyes and minds . . . [to] make our sight together with our senses fly to heaven's gate" (48 [32].1). "Let us imagine we are standing on the Mount of Olives and that we bend our gaze on the Redeemer as he rides upon a cloud" (48.1). Christ's instructions to the apostles ("Now rise upright, stand firm and contemplate with blameless eye this taking up") echo the words deacons cried during the liturgy. The hymn also describes the path of Christ's ascent. When Christ is prepared, he signals the angels, who instruct the principalities to "lift up the gates and fling wide the heavenly and glorious doors. Bright air, prepare yourself for the One who journeys through you . . ." (48.10; cf. Ps. 24:7-9). Heaven's doors thus mirror the doors of the church itself: just as preparation for the eucharist included instructions to "close the doors" after the dismissal of the uninitiated, the Ascension calls for the opening of doors.[15] The call to open is made again, when "those in the heights immediately obeyed and open[ed] at once all the heights" (48.11). The scene returns to the beholders, as the apostles "were attentive . . . and all raised their faces to the heights as they watched his taking up" (48.12). Thus Romanos assimilates the audience to the apostles, blending Gospel event with familiar liturgical instruction.

For centuries, the *kontakion* remained a common expression of lay piety, enduring as community poetry.[16] The *Miracles of Artemios*, a seventh-century collection from Constantinople, mentions a young man who sang the verses of Romanos to laypeople at Artemios's tomb in the Church of John the Baptist in Oxeia. His shrine also served as an incubation center, where supplicants could participate in overnight vigils and, when sleep overtook them, encounter Artemios and his healing powers in their dreams. Thus, for more than a century after the Melodist's death, the *kontakia* continued to be performed in non-monastic settings.

PLAYING THE BIBLE

Romanos's *kontakia* bear a complex relation to the Bible. In the setting of the church the *kontakia* followed a series of lectionary readings, all taken from scripture and somehow related to the festival in question. As the description of the vigils quoted earlier suggests, several psalms and biblical readings preceded the chanted sermon. Thus the *kontakion* only perfunctorily rehearsed the story in order to proceed with the Melodist's concern, namely, the characters' inner thoughts and hidden actions. In his *kontakia* Romanos extended the story just heard to locate it in its larger moral universe. For every Bible passage read aloud, there were stories behind the story, as well as above it, below it, or even beyond it. In some *kontakia* Romanos weighed in on the current christological debates of his day, yet these polemics are rare among the sixty extant hymns. He did not hide polemics in his strong criticisms of Jews, heretics, and Greek culture. These enemies interested him less, however, than the potential in the portrayal of Christ's followers as their own worst enemies. He knew how to enter a story in its silences and recover the crippling emotions that consumed its characters. Their puzzlement, desires, and, above all, their most anguished deliberations were objects of intense scrutiny.

Romanos also knew how to repopulate familiar stories. In his cosmos, underworld figures spoke as witnesses to the crucifixion, and Roman soldiers aboveground overheard Christ's release of captives in hell. Like a jazz soloist improvising on a standard, Romanos preserved the steady cadences of a biblical story yet also "played tag" with the beat. Never quite landing squarely on this scriptural "beat," Romanos decentered the biblical drama, recovered lost voices, drew marginal characters to the center, and pushed central characters to darker recesses.

Dialogue is an important device for evoking and engaging sensory experience. In Romanos's hymns, underworld powers, such as Hades, Satan, and Death (all personified), are in constant conversation during the unfolding drama of Jesus' death. Even solitary characters carry on interior monologues with themselves and imagined interlocutors. In some cases Romanos uses invented characters, like a perfume seller who argues with the penitent prostitute (see Luke 7:36-50). Elsewhere, Romanos forges a conversation between characters from disparate episodes in the Bible, as in his second hymn "On the Nativity" (11 [2]), in which Mary interrupts her lullabies to the infant Jesus long enough to speak with Adam and Eve. Romanos takes full advantage of dialogue to probe characters' motives and emotions as well as to trace their sensory perceptions. He uses dialogue to connect internal dispositions, thoughts, and emotions with the bodily sensations that triggered them.

A Hymn for Good Friday

In this hymn "On the Lament of the Mother of God," written for Good Friday, Romanos has Jesus explain to Mary how he will heal Adam and Eve when he descends into hell.

Be patient a little longer, Mother, and you will see
how, like a physician, I undress and reach the place
     where they lie
and I treat their wounds,
cutting with the lance their calluses and their scabs.
And I take vinegar, I apply it as astringent to the
     wound,
when with the probe of the nails I have investigated
     the cut, I shall plug it with the cloak.
And, with my cross as a splint,
I shall make use of it, Mother, so that you may chant
     with understanding,
'By suffering he has abolished suffering,
     my Son and my God.'

—On the Life of Christ, 148.

JUDAS:
THE LITURGY OF SILENCE

The figure of Judas Iscariot evoked various emotions among Christians, who ruminated on his greed, deceit, and eventual despair. Already in the second century some Christians composed the *Gospel of Judas*, an effort to probe how Judas's actions actually benefited humankind by setting in motion the divine disclosure of salvific wisdom. Later generations of preachers recalled how Judas accepted thirty silver pieces, identified Jesus to his captors by a kiss, then hanged himself. On wall mosaics at S. Apollinare Nuovo in Ravenna (sixth century), for instance, not only does Judas press his cheek to Christ's, but he also gazes directly into Christ's eyes while placing his right hand over Jesus' heart. Set against Christ's rigid stance and frontal gaze, Judas's contorted torso, face, and limbs appear caught in a sensory tangle. Likewise, Romanos sought to express a similar tactile envelopment in song.

The story of Judas's betrayal was remembered liturgically on Holy Thursday, a time devoted to the commemoration of Judas's deeds as

Fig. 3.2. The Kiss of Judas from the Church of S. Apollinare Nuovo in Ravenna, sixth century. Christ is surrounded by the apostles as Roman soldiers arrive with Judas. Peter draws his sword to cut off one of the soldier's ears. Photo: Erich Lessing/Art Resource.

well as the Last Supper and the washing of the disciples' feet. Although Romanos mentions all three events, he focuses on the connection between Judas's betrayal and the foot washing. To do that, Romanos rearranges the Gospel's chronology of events. In Matthew Judas visits the high priests before the Last Supper (Matthew 26). But John, the only Gospel to recount the foot washing, ties Judas's betrayal directly to the Last Supper; only when he received the eucharistic bread did Satan enter him (John 13:26-28). To link foot washing and betrayal, then, Romanos places the foot washing before the meal and postpones Judas's visit to the high priests until after the Supper. Thus this composite tale has three movements: the preamble consists of a lengthy admonishment of Judas (33.1–5), followed by two foot washings (33.6–11)—first Judas's, including the angels' celestial reaction to the events below, then Peter's, including a dialogue with Christ. The second part (33.12–19) recounts Judas's visit with the high priests (who are portrayed as the devil), and the final part condemns Judas's kiss and his base motives by portraying his cruel demise.

Compared to artists' focus on Judas's kiss, Romanos calls attention instead to the feet. He mentions the kiss at the outset and near the end of the hymn (33.1, 21) to clear a space in which to concentrate on the foot washing. Instead, the prologue's opening line signals his intent: "when [Judas's] feet were being washed by the master's hands," he hatched his plot to betray Jesus. The rearrangement of Gospel events sharpens this focus. Judas lifts his heel into Christ's hand and then lifts his feet (that is, hastens) to the chief priests (33: 12, 14). The feet also symbolize his moral undoing: he descended to Hades having lost his footing. The final strophe exhorts the audience "to make firm our own feet./ So let us set our footsteps on the steps of the Creator's commandments" (33.23).

If the face was the site for betrayal through a kiss, Romanos finds the real story in the feet, the moment when Judas hatched the plot. Thus Romanos trades one tactile encounter for another and thereby decenters the story, while creating ideal conditions for dialogue, a hallmark of his hymns. Strangely, however, Judas himself is stripped of all dialogue. We are privy to no interior monologue or deliberation as Judas's feet are washed. In this hymn, dialogue belongs to others. Christ and Peter exchange tender words (33.9–11). Angels and audience take turns interrogating Judas: "What had happened to make you reject him? What had you seen to make you mindless like this? What had you suffered to make you hate like this? Had he not named you his friend?" (33.5). In all this Judas remains mute. This is not the Judas of *Jesus Christ Superstar*, an exasperated confidant who rebukes Christ. Romanos's Judas will utter only one phrase, taken directly from scripture: "What are you willing to give?" he asks the high priests (devil) (33.14; repeated at 33.15; see Matt. 26:14-15). Judas may be short on dialogue, but he is long on spectacle.

Bodily postures and multiple sight lines dominate Romanos's presentation of the foot washing. Jesus "bows [his] neck" over the basin and fills it with water to wash the disciples' feet. Freezing this pose, Romanos shifts vantage points from the earthbound to the celestial, as angels cry out at the shocking sight of the Creator girded like a slave and hunched over.[17] Trembling, the archangel Gabriel calls upon the angels to "look down" at the strange sight of a Creator "bending down and serving clay" (33.7). Below, Peter echoes the angels by confessing Christ's divinity yet refusing such subservience. How can he allow "the Potter of the world [to wash] the feet of a vessel of clay" (see Gen. 2:7)? One detects an echo of John the Baptist, when he deemed himself unworthy to untie the sandals of the one to come and tried to refuse to baptize Jesus (Matt. 3:11, 14). Peter, however, overcomes his compunction when Jesus explains that unless he agrees to have his feet washed, "I will not give you a part in me" (33.11). Ever obedient, then, Peter insists on having his entire body washed by Christ (33.11). Although Peter in the Gospel of John asks Christ to wash also his "hands and head" (13.9), Romanos transforms the request into the "whole body" (33.11), a reference to baptism that few in the audience would have missed. The whole body also emerges in those instances when Romanos links foot washing and Jesus' nourishment of the disciples with spiritual food (33.3, 4, 8).

This hymn thus gives the audience numerous points of entry into the biblical drama. They are the angels, reacting to events and singing the refrain. They know the intimacy of the act—the preparation of the basin, the crouched Christ, and the lifting of the heel into his hand—from the cosmic vantage point of angels. An important element for this identification will be the sensory memories Romanos interweaves, the references to eucharist (nourishment), to baptism, and to the sounds of the refrain, "Be merciful, merciful, merciful to us, you who are patient with all, and wait for all." Over the course of the hymn, the audience sings as disembodied angelic spectators and also with Peter as he offers his entire body to Christ. The same refrain also binds the audience to the poet-prosecutor, who rebukes the travesty of the kiss. Thus Romanos renders the intimate act of foot washing into a cosmic event.

ON PETER'S DENIAL:
THE LITURGY OF MEMORY AND FORGETTING

Peter's denial of Jesus was rarely a topic for sermons among early Byzantine preachers. Romanos, however, saw fit to highlight Peter's travails as part of Holy Week celebrations in his hymn "On Peter's Denial." It is difficult to pinpoint either the date of this hymn or its precise place in the liturgical calendar. According to some manuscripts, the hymn was performed on Holy Thursday, whereas others connect the hymn to Good Friday. Whatever the day, the hymn came close in liturgical time to Romanos's "On Judas." The proximity might explain their commonalities. Both "Judas" and "Peter" begin with the Last Supper. While the former deals with Judas's premeditated betrayal, the latter examines Peter's unwitting treachery. In both, Peter engages Christ in dialogue. Here, however, Romanos draws the audience into Peter's thought processes as he grapples with Jesus' prediction that soon he will be betrayed by one of his own. The greatest difference is in the use of speech: whereas Judas remains mute throughout much of his hymn,

Fig. 3.3. Peter's Denial, S. Apollinare Nuovo in Ravenna, sixth century. "Before the cock crows, you will deny me three times" (Matt. 26:34). Peter places his hand near his ear to hear the rooster on the column. Photo: Erich Lessing/Art Resource.

Peter remains in continuous dialogue with himself and others. Thus his shock, anger, and grief stay central to this rapid series of events that take the audience from the Last Supper to the Resurrection.

As is typical in his *kontakia*, Romanos takes great liberties with the biblical text. In the Gospel of Matthew, Peter is engaged in a double denial: resisting the prediction of his betrayal, then disowning Jesus. Despite explicit mention of a specific Gospel text, rare for Romanos, this episode (34.3) reworks several Gospel stories. Whereas Matthew's Jesus predicts that Peter will deny him three times (Matt. 26:34), Romanos's Jesus predicts that *all* his disciples will deny him (34.3). This shift from a prediction about an individual to one about a collective has dramatic consequences. In the Gospels, Peter must defend his honor by disproving a prediction about him. In Romanos's hymn, by contrast, Peter never felt that the prediction could refer to him. In other words, it is no longer a matter of Jesus singling out Peter, but a case of Peter singling himself out. To single out Peter, Romanos omits Jesus' anguish in Gethsemane (Matt. 26:37-41) and Judas's betrayal (Matt. 26:37-41, 47-56), moving directly to Christ's interrogation in the high priest Caiaphas's courtyard, with Peter looking on in silence (34.9–12). After a dialogue with a serving girl elicits the first of Peter's three denials (34.13–17), Romanos draws the hymn to a close with a series of Gospel vignettes: Peter's grieving and humiliated return to the disciples (34.19); the crucifixion, specifically Christ's pardon of the thief, interpreted as a pardon to Peter (34.20; see also Luke 23.43); and the women at the empty tomb (34.21; Mark 16:7), who are instructed by an angel to "tell Peter as well," further assurance of Peter's pardon, and thereby the audience's (34.22). Romanos combines a microscopic depiction of mental processes and emotions with a panoramic sweep of passion, pardon, and resurrection. Like the performer in Arundhati Roy's novel, "he can fly you across whole worlds in minutes, he can stop for hours to examine a wilting leaf." In this *kontakion*, however, the "wilting leaf" is memory itself.

Romanos's Peter is flooded by haunting memories. As Christ's words echo in his ears, Peter conjures a series of distant and fresh memories: "Would I deny you . . . and not remember your calling me?" he protests. "I still recall how you washed my feet and you say, 'You will deny me,' Redeemer?" (34.3). "I am still thinking," he declares, "how you approached my steps carrying the basin" (34.3). Piling memories like sandbags against rising floodwaters, Peter insists that they will serve as his bulwark against betrayal. Peter is riddled with memory, to the point of sputtering his protests: "I still (*akmēn*), Sinless One, I still (*akmēn*), Eternal One, have the taste of your supper in my mouth, and how can I deny your gift?" (34.5). He vows, now as one of the initiated (*mustēs*): "If I utterly forget (*lanthanō*) the mystery that I know (*oida*) and saw (*eidon*) and see again (*palin horō*)" (34.5), may he "run living towards hell." The list of memories does not end there: Christ replies with more memories: "Do you remember how a little time ago you would have been drowned had I not given you my hand?" (34.6). For Peter, his sole protection against betrayal is memory, specifically sensory memories: the sound of the call, the taste of the Supper, the touch of the foot washing or of the hand that pulled him out of the sea, the sight of Christ lifting the washbasin or showing the mysteries. So long as memory lives, reasons Peter, he cannot deny Christ. Thus Peter pits a past filled with sense perceptions against Christ's words about the future.

What the body remembers signals for the audience what the body will know. As Christ explains to Peter, the hand that pulled Peter from the sea must now pick up the pen and "write a pardon for all Adam's descendants" (34.7). Christ's flesh becomes paper, his blood ink. Playing on the dual sense of the word *kalamos* as both reed and writing implement, Jesus evokes at once the scarred body and the scarred page.

This string of sensory memories sets the stage for the spectacle of the blows Christ endures, an event Romanos shrouds in silence. Until Christ's arrest, Peter grieves aloud, cries, rebukes, beats his breast. Yet as witness to the brutality in Caiaphas's courtyard, Peter adopts a hushed tone, speaking "silently." "You are struck," he laments, "and do I still live and I look at you?" (34.11). Peter's perceptions soon shift to a set of cosmic witnesses. How can "earth see and hold firm," he asks, without seeking vengeance? Or how can heaven watch impassibly? How can the archangels Michael and Gabriel cap their rage? "Even if all the powers on high are silent," he proclaims, "I shudder and lament and cry to you" (34.11). These words usher in Peter's silence, as the curtain falls on this brutal scene.

For the audience, Peter's silence (34.12, 13) creates a space in which to engage his denial more directly. Up until this point the audience has entered *his* sensory past, by recalling the taste, touch, and sight of Christ's redemption. Led by Peter, they join in the angels' cosmic outcry as Christ suffers blows. With Peter's silence, however, they note the movements within the story. They picture the "serving girl" who approached Peter and "looked him all over and walked all round the disciple. Up and down she examined him closely" (34.13). This silent, circling dance prepares the audience for a "faltering voice" (*psellizousa*), which declares, "Clearly you too were once with the Galilean"(34.13; see also 34.14). After his vociferous denial Peter falls silent again, this time under the poet's prosecutorial barrage of questions: "You don't know the man, Peter, as you claim? You don't know the man? Don't you really want to say that you don't know a mere man, but God?" (34.16). Turning their back on Peter, the audience addresses Christ: "We hymn (*hymnoumen*) you, Master, for a chant (*psalmos*) is good" (34.17; see Ps. 147:1). During his silence Peter endures the audience's scrutiny, scolding, and denial. When he can bear no more, he shatters the silence, letting out "a howl" and weeping (34.18).

This howling and weeping suggests a transformation of Peter from an ardent protester into a mourner. His language and gestures are evocative of women's ritualized lament, as he "trembles" (34.2), "shudder[s]" (34.9), "lament[s] and cr[ies]" to Christ before falling silent (34.11). He returns to the disciples with his "hands [put] over his head," a gesture reminiscent of the grieving and humiliated Tamar after she was raped by her brother Amnon (2 Sam. 13:19). Peter beckons the disciples to "weep with me then, and as you lament say to me, 'Where are your love and zeal?'"(34.19). From his cross Christ is moved by "Peter's tears" (34.20).

In her study of ritualized lament in Greece, Margaret Alexiou observes a common pattern to women's laments: first the mourner addresses the dead, then remembers the past or imagines the future, and finally renews her opening address and lament. The laments are typically antiphonal, marked by a reiterated phrase as well as cries. The Greek lament is also marked by a barrage of questions. As Alexiou notes of another *kontakion*, "On the Lament of the Mother of God," Romanos "exploits all available forms, strophe-refrain, dialogue and three-part form."[18] One finds a similar three-part structure in "On Peter's Denial": Peter reproaches Christ's prediction (34.3), narrates their past (34.4–5), and ritualizes his lament before the disciples (34.19). Unlike male forms of mourning, such as the *elegos* or *epitaphios*, which commemorated and honored the dead, Peter's lamentation is marked by rage, rawness, and reproach. He cries, weeps, shudders, rends garments, and assumes the postures of female mourning. To cast this feminized mourner into sharper light, Romanos removes other women's speech. The story demands that the servant girls speak, but Romanos removes all grieving women from the crucifixion. There is no mention of the Virgin Mary's lament, the centerpiece of another *kontakion* (35 [19]). And Romanos preserves the women's shocked silence upon discovering the empty tomb (see Mark 16:8). In short, Peter's denial bears the signs of a women's ritual lament, or *thrēnos.*

Is this feminization of Peter a form of mockery? Probably not. The feminization of Peter can be misread as anti-Petrine polemic. This negative attitude toward Peter does not square with Romanos's positive portrayal of the disciples in other *kontakia,*[19] not least in "On Judas," where Peter as moral exemplar shows up the traitor. Peter's feminized grief serves another purpose. His lament invites both men and women in the audience to join him in mourning. The audience not only mourns with Mary, then, but also mourns with Peter, replicating his cries and sighs and sharing in his sensory memories and remorse. Ritualized lament intersects with sensory ritual to provide a vehicle for biblical memory during Holy Week.

Taken together, "On Judas" and "On Peter's Denial" form an odd couple. Romanos grants Peter a voice, while he condemns Judas to silence. He even allows Judas one line (33.14) and silences Peter for only one stanza (34.12) to underscore the contrast. Lacking speech, Judas's body—specifically, his feet—tells his tale. By contrast, Peter's wailing voice externalizes his grief into ritualized lament. Despite their differences, both characters equip the audience with a host of gestures, postures, and lingering sensations by which to enter the story. To ease that entry, Romanos presents each character in media res, still sensing past events while rushing headlong into the predicted future. To worshippers, recognizing the Gospel moment was not enough. Entering that moment required an embodied understanding of what came before and what was to come. Romanos furnished that understanding, so that the moment itself might open its doors.

RITUAL MEMORY AND ROMANOS

Romanos cued worshippers to sing with the angels, prosecute with the poet, wail with Satan, and weep with Peter. Song and sense came together, rendering biblical narrative into spiritual exercise. They were also deeply controlled exercises, as Romanos stirred emotions but always in connection with a specific sensory moment. Peter's grief was deep yet bounded by his sensory memories of the Last Supper and the foot washing. What the body might remember was central to Romanos's aims: to enter biblical events by means of sensory experience. It was also an affective piety that invited worshippers to connect sense impressions and discrete emotions with biblical narrative. Many pilgrims knew that type of bodily engagement with the biblical past in their visits to holy places, but the challenge, it seems, was to secure that engagement in the context of church worship over the course of the liturgical year. Romanos's *kontakia* provided that opportunity by his choice of characters and moments in close proximity to the core of a biblical episode.

Romanos's hymns also represent the emergence of biblical epic in the context of Christian worship. Centuries earlier, elite Christians had experimented with existing epic forms. The epic poems of Empress Eudocia (circa 400–460), known as *centos* (literally "stitchings"), retold biblical themes in verses quoted verbatim from Homer.[20] In worship, however, lay Christians did not require Troy's fallen heroes in biblical guise, so much as an embodied engagement with the biblical characters themselves. Romanos made that connection possible by putting marginal characters along with their emotions and sense perceptions in the spotlight. Over the course of the liturgical year these hymns revisited biblical stories from the margins. Romanos opened the margins of time, filling pregnant silences with intense interior speech on the meaning of lingering tastes, lost touches, and fading visions. He also pushed back the margins of space by inserting celestial and subterranean vistas into earthly events. Thus worshippers might join the angels in wonder and the underworld figures in dread. Most important, the margins provided entrances into the biblical stories, through which worshippers might engage their own bodies. In this epic they were instructed when to look up, look down, look away, stand up, or hold silence. All these moments were critical for a somatic engagement with the Bible.

Finally, the hymns mark an important transitional moment in Christian reflection on the power of ritual. Already in the fourth century, interpreters were divided on the meaning of liturgy. Some, following Origen, interpreted liturgy as a passage from earthly phenomena to the perception of celestial mysteries. This anagogical trajectory appears in the writings of Pseudo-Dionysius, whose *Ecclesiastical Hierarchy* charted the soul's progress through various rites of the liturgy. In the seventh century, Maximus Confessor (circa 630) extended that line of thought by interpreting the liturgy as a picture of the cosmos through which the soul might ascend. Other commentators, however, interpreted the liturgy as a memorial reenactment of events from the sacred past, such that worshippers revisited and reflected on mysteries of salvation history, regarding discrete elements of the liturgy as symbolic of historical objects, events, and personages. Although the historical always bore the promise of the anagogical, and the allegorical emerged from the historical, the two strands would not find a genuine synthesis until the eighth century, when Germanos of Constantinople (died circa 730) composed a commentary on the Divine Liturgy. In his *Church History*, or perhaps *Church Story*, Germanos treated each element of the liturgy and evoked its multiple layers of meaning. As Robert Taft has argued, Germanos held historical and allegorical meanings in complex tension, refusing to allow one to eclipse the other. He represents, according to Taft, "the victory of monastic popular devotion over a more spiritualist approach."[21]

Some 150 years before Germanos, Romanos's *kontakia* provided the groundwork for that synthesis in the context of the nightly

> ### A Communion Hymn
> During the reign of Justin II (565–578) Eutychius, Patriarch of Constantinople, added this *koinonikon*, or communion chant, to the liturgy for Holy Thursday, the annual commemoration of the Last Supper: "At Your mystical supper, Son of God, receive me today as a partaker, for I will not betray the sacraments to your enemies, nor give you a kiss like Judas, but like the thief I confess You: remember me, Lord, in Your Kingdom."

vigil. Before worshippers would scrutinize the design, decoration, and actions within church space, as Germanos's commentary does in exhaustive detail, Romanos helped worshippers find the layered meanings in sensory memories. His *kontakia* remind us that any synthesis of historical and allegorical would begin with the body—the sensory body of the biblical figures and its imitation in the worshipper's perceptions.

FOR FURTHER READING

Alexiou, Margaret. "The Lament of the Virgin in Byzantine Literature and Modern Greek Folk Song." *Byzantine and Modern Greek Studies* 1 (1975): 111–40.

Caseau, Béatrice. "Christian Bodies: The Senses and Early Byzantine Christianity." In Liz James, ed., *Desire and Denial in Byzantium: Papers from the 31st Spring Symposium of Byzantine Studies, University of Sussex, Brighton, March 1997*, 101–9. Aldershot: Variorum, 1999.

Dobrov, Gregory W. "A Dialogue with Death: Ritual Lament and the *Thrēnos Theotokou* of Romanos Melodos." *Greek, Roman, and Byzantine Studies* 35 (1994): 385–405.

Frank, Georgia. "Dialogue and Deliberation: The Sensory Self in the Hymns of Romanos the Melodist." In David Brakke et al. eds., *Religion and the Self in Antiquity*, 163–79. Bloomington: Indiana University Press, 2005.

———. "'Taste and See': The Eucharist and the Eyes of Faith in the Fourth Century." *Church History* 70 (2001): 619–43.

Krueger, Derek. "Christian Piety and Practice in the Sixth Century." In Michael Maas, ed., *The Cambridge Companion to the Age of Justinian*, 291–315. New York: Cambridge University Press, 2005.

———. *Writing and Holiness: The Practice of Authorship in the Early Christian East.* Philadelphia: University of Pennsylvania Press, 2004.

Mathews, Thomas F. *The Early Churches of Constantinople: Architecture and Liturgy.* University Park: Pennsylvania State University Press, 1971.

Romanos the Melodist. *On the Life of Christ: Kontakia.* Trans. Ephrem Lash. The Sacred Literature Series. San Francisco: HarperCollins, 1995.

Schork, R. J. *Sacred Song from the Byzantine Pulpit: Romanos the Melodist.* Gainesville: University of Florida Press, 1995.

[Ware], Kallistos, Bishop of Dioklea. "The Meaning of the Divine Liturgy for the Byzantine Worshipper." In Rosemary Morris, ed., *Church and People in Byzantium: Society for the Promotion of Byzantine Studies Twentieth Spring Symposium, 1986.* Birmingham, U.K.: Centre for Byzantine, Ottoman and Modern Greek Studies, University of Birmingham, n.d.

PLACES, SPACES, AND RITES

SHRINES, FESTIVALS, AND THE "UNDISTINGUISHED MOB"

JAMES C. SKEDROS

CHAPTER FOUR

The Byzantines loved a public celebration. Like their Greek and Roman forebears, they celebrated secular holidays, such as the birthday of the emperor, commemorations of the founding of cities, imperial triumphal processions, and installations of civic councils. Yet the vast majority of holidays that Byzantine Christians observed were religious. Participation in such holidays or feasts involved all levels of society: official government personnel (in Constantinople often including the emperor himself), members of the ecclesiastical hierarchy, and the lay faithful.

The richness of the Byzantine religious calendar can be seen in a law issued by emperor Manuel I Komnenos in 1166 that decreed which days the legal courts in Constantinople and throughout the empire were to remain closed. The law distinguished between full holidays, on which the courts shut down, and half-recess days, on which courts were closed "from dawn until the time of the holy liturgy, so that it may be possible for the judges to devote themselves to prayer and the praise of God."[1] Full holidays numbered seventy-three (not including Sundays, which had been considered a day of rest since the emperor Constantine proclaimed them such in 321) and half-recess days, twenty-eight. The courts were closed on feasts associated with the life of Christ—his birth and baptism (from December 20 to January 6) and his passion and resurrection (from the Saturday of Lazarus to the Sunday following Easter), as well as feasts of the Theotokos, the twelve apostles, and the great hierarchs of the church—John Chrysostom, Gregory of Nazianzus, Athanasius of

Alexandria, and Cyril of Alexandria. Half-recess days were appointed for feasts celebrating important relics in the city such as the bones of John Chrysostom and Gregory of Nazianzus, the girdle and belt of the Theotokos, and the chains of St. Peter. Half-recesses were also declared for some of the more popular saints and martyrs of the church, including Demetrius, George, Barbara, Nicholas, the two Theodores, and Prokopios. The great number of days that the court was in full or

Fig. 4.1. A procession in Constantinople to pray for rain during a drought. Mid-twelfth-century illustration from the *Chronicle* of John Skylitzes. Photo: Biblioteca Nacional, Madrid.

half recess because of religious holidays seems all the more astounding when one considers that the intent of Manuel's law was to limit the number of days the court would be in recess in order to facilitate the judicial process.

The observance of religious holidays in Constantinople took on its own distinctive expressions. Feast days associated with Christ, his apostles, and some of the great saints frequently included processions from the imperial palace to various churches or shrines, usually culminating at the church or shrine dedicated to the particular saint or event of the day. The abbot Symeon, writing from the Sakkoudion monastery inside the walls of Constantinople in the late tenth century, exhorted his monks not to pay attention to the "multitude of candles and lamps, or fragrances and perfumes, or the assembly of people, or the rich and elaborate table, or the boasting in the appearance of friends or the presence of men who are glorious upon the earth" that accompanied these feast days.[2] Indeed, feasts included all of these elements, and often more. Until the tenth century, chariot races in the hippodrome marked some celebrations. The feast of the Nativity demanded an elaborately staged procession from the imperial palace to the Church of Hagia Sophia and back again. The procession included eleven stops at which imperial chanters shouted acclamations with the crowd responding. In public gatherings, civic and ecclesiastical officials demonstrated their commitment to the urban and religious life of the city. Ordinary citizens participated, usually as spectators, often marching in processions, expressing their devotion, and enjoying the festivities, even if Symeon, the fifteenth-century archbishop of Thessalonike, regarded them merely as "the undistinguished mob."

SHRINES

In addition to the elaborate festivities, processions, and liturgical celebrations conducted in the presence of the emperor and patriarch in Constantinople, religious life also focused on the numerous shrines and churches that dotted the city and its suburbs. Literary and archaeological evidence from the seventh century attests some thirty-one shrines in the city associated with special healing or containing a saint's or martyr's relics.[3] The tomb of St. Artemios in the Church of John the Baptist in the Oxeia (now the hill where the Süleymaniye Mosque sits) was especially famous. Artemios had been martyred at Antioch during the reign of the emperor Julian (361–363). Shortly thereafter, when his remains were brought to Constantinople, his relics became a source of miraculous healing. The *Miracles of Artemios*, composed in the 660s, records many of these miracles.

The shrine of Artemios specialized in the healing of male genitalia and hernias. On Saturday evenings clergy, townsfolk, and suppliants gathered for an all-night vigil in the church. A crypt containing Artemios's coffin lay below the main altar. Suppliants descended into the crypt by one of two staircases. At the midnight hour, while venerating "the precious and life-giving cross," the afflicted men received a holy wax-salve known as *kērōtē*, a mixture of wax and oil, which they applied to their diseased body parts or ingested. This *kērōtē* was taken from the oil lamps and candles burning next to the saint's tomb. The individual seeking healing would then spend the remainder of the night inside the church and was often visited by the martyr in a dream. The following morning, a Sunday, the vigil ended with the celebration of the eucharist.

The fame of St. Artemios and his shrine spread far beyond the walls of Constantinople. One miracle involved an unnamed man from Africa who "had an only child, a male, who suffered terribly in his testicles." Doctors were unable to bring the young boy relief. Fortunately, the father heard of the miraculous shrine of St. Artemios in Constantinople and, leaving his sick son at home, he set sail for the imperial city. Arriving at the shrine, the man "made, in the name of his son, a votive lamp according to the prevailing custom with wine and oil. And this he did for as long as he stayed in the city. When he was on the point of sailing back, he put the burnt residue from the lamp into a glass vessel and brought it back to Africa . . . to anoint his son with the blessing" (*Miracles of Artemios* 4). However, when he returned, he found that his son had already been healed—in fact, at the precise moment when the father had made the first votive! This miracle documents one of the most common religious practices associated with Byzantine healing shrines, namely, burning votive oil lamps and then using the oil or burnt residue to transfer the power of the shrine and its saint to the afflicted. Stories of individuals receiving cures for their illnesses at holy shrines survive from all periods of Byzantine history.

In the first half of the seventh century, John, the archbishop of Thessalonike, penned a collection of miracles associated with that city's most famous shrine, the basilica of St. Demetrius.

St. Artemios Heals a Chatterbox

Another man, a Phrygian by birth named George, had swollen testicles and, suffering in the extreme, was waiting for a cure by the martyred saint. But this man chattered incessantly; for neither by night nor by day was his mouth at rest, nor would he allow anyone else to rest, and although everyone censured him, he would not be quiet. So the saint appeared to him in the small hours saying: "When day comes, withdraw from here. Since if you remain another moment, I will double your hernia. For I hate babblers." Rising early, he knew that he was cured and in accordance with what was said to him by the holy martyr, so he acted and did not remain but rejoicing went off blessing God.

—*The Miracles of Artemios* 8 in Virgil S. Crisafulli and John W. Nesbitt, trans., *The Miracles of St. Artemios: A Collection of Miracles Stories by an Anonymous Author of Seventh-Century Byzantium* (Leiden: Brill, 1997), 93.

John's collection contains various types of miracles, from the healing of individuals to the defense of the city from the attacks of the Slavs. The longest miracle in the collection relates the healing of Marianos, eparch (a civil official) of the Balkan diocese of Illyricum. Marianos suffered from total paralysis. Because of his high social and political status, he had access to the finest medical care available, but none of it worked. He refused magical amulets on account of his Christian beliefs. A dream encouraged him to visit the large basilica of St. Demetrius located in the heart of Thessalonike. He was brought to the church and placed on a bed on the basilica's floor, in an area of the church designated for the sick and injured. There he prepared to spend the night. That evening St. Demetrius visited the eparch, and when Marianos awoke the next morning, he discovered that he was miraculously cured. Marianos's experience of sleeping in a sacred place—a practice called "incubation"—was typical for supplicants at the basilica of St. Demetrius, the tomb of St. Artemios, and many other shrines. From the upper classes to pious townsfolk, healing shrines and sacred spaces attracted all types of people from all over the empire in search of cures.

The diversity of pilgrims visiting holy places for healing is perhaps reflected best in the histories of two famous shrines located outside of the city of Alexandria in Egypt: the shrine of Sts. Cyrus and John and the shrine of St. Menas. By the beginning of the seventh century the shrine of Sts. Cyrus and John at Menouthis (modern Abuqir) had become internationally renowned.[4] Our knowledge of the shrine depends almost exclusively on the writings of Sophronius, patriarch of Jerusalem (634–638), who wrote a collection of seventy miracle stories associated with the shrine after he himself had been healed of an eye ailment at the site. Here, too, incubation was by far the most common practice. Sophronius's *Miracles of Cyrus and John* suggests that pilgrims slept in various parts of the church, frequently overcrowding it with masses of supplicants. The pilgrim would sleep in the church, hoping for a visit from the saints in a dream. Often Cyrus and John would appear to the faithful to provide an immediate cure or prescribe a remedy that the pilgrim would obtain upon awakening. Although for some pilgrims cures did occur promptly, others waited one, two, or even eight years for healing. The prescribed remedies often included bathing in the bathhouse attached to the shrine complex.

Sophronius's account of late sixth- and early seventh-century visitors to the shrine of Sts. Cyrus and John provides a demographic catalog of Byzantine pilgrims. The patriarch arranged his miracle stories according to regional or national groups. The first thirty-five miracles tell of Alexandrians receiving cures. These are followed by fifteen miracles involving Egyptians and Libyans. The last twenty miracles involve foreigners from beyond the Nile and the North African coast. Sophronius records visitors from Asia Minor, Syria, Palestine, Cyprus, and Rhodes. Only one, John the Roman, came from the West. Sophronius himself noted the diverse nationalities of visitors to the shrine: "I speak of Romans, and Galatians, and Cilicians, people from Asia too, island-dwellers and Phoenicians, Byzantines and Bithynians and Ethiopians, Thracians and Medes and Arabs, Palestinians and Syrians and Elamites, in fact all the races that exist under heaven."[5] Although Sophronius emphasized the large number of non-Egyptian visitors, the majority of the miracles involved short journeys by inhabitants of Alexandria and its environs.

Some forty miles southwest of the shrine of Sts. Cyrus and John lay perhaps the most famous Late Antique pilgrimage site outside of Jerusalem, the shrine of St. Menas. Situated at the edge of Lake Mareotis (now Maryût), the shrine housed the relics of the early fourth-century martyr. Extensive archaeological remains at the site attest an enormous pilgrimage complex.[6] A series of structures formed the sacred core, and the sequence of their construction reveals the tremendous growth of the cult over time (fig. 4.2). A subterranean crypt housed the saint's bones. Above the tomb Christians initially erected a cenotaph; this was soon replaced by a three-aisled basilica, commonly called the Martyr Church. During the reign of Justinian (527–565) this basilica was replaced by a more elaborate tetrachonch church. In addition to the crypt and Martyr Church, a larger church, known as the Great Basilica, was built directly east of the apse of the Martyr Church to accommodate the ever-increasing number of pilgrims.

The Martyr Church and the Great Basilica shared a rectangular space, a type of a narthex, which connected the two structures. The nave of the Great Basilica measured more than fourteen meters wide, making it the largest church in Egypt in its time. A large baptistery with adjoining rooms attached to the Martyr Church facilitated multiple baptisms. From a cross-vaulted square antechamber pilgrims descended into the crypt, the shrine's focal point, and passed to a semidomed niche containing St. Menas's sarcophagus. There the pilgrim paused and offered prayers and private devotions before exiting by another staircase. The surrounding area developed to accommodate the masses of visitors and became known as the City of St. Menas,

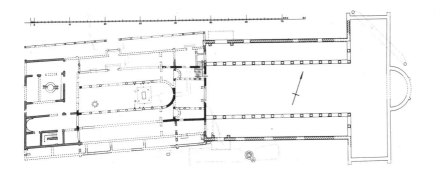

Fig. 4.2. Ground plan for the shrine of St. Menas, near Alexandria, Egypt. The pilgrim progressed from the baptistery, left, past the crypt below the Martyr Church, center left, to the Great Church, right. After Peter Grossman, *Abu Mina: A Guide to the Ancient Pilgrimage Center* (Cairo: Fotiadis, 1986).

with a large pilgrims' court, hostels, and a long colonnaded processional way leading from the lake to the shrine with shops, storerooms, and public buildings, including two bathhouses. Civil buildings and residential neighborhoods lay outside of the ecclesiastical precincts. To the south of the Martyr Church a semicircular two-story building accommodated the sick and infirm seeking a cure from the saint through incubation. In addition to these widely popular sites, other pilgrimage destinations and shrines of more local importance were scattered throughout the empire and usually centered on the tomb of a martyr or the spot of miraculous or divine intervention.

The holiest of all Byzantine shrines were those in Palestine, especially Jerusalem, associated with the life of Christ. Christian pilgrims began visiting the Holy Land as early as the end of the second century, yet it was not until the fourth century, with the assistance of imperial patronage, that Jerusalem began to attract Christians from throughout the Mediterranean and beyond. The Church of the Anastasis, or Resurrection, the well-known rotunda pictorially represented on later pilgrim ampullae, enclosed the tomb of Christ and was the focus of the entire Holy Sepulchre complex (fig. 4.3). The complex also included the rock of Golgotha, where Christ had been crucified and where, by the 380s, pilgrims flocked to see the true cross. A large basilica known as the Martyrium, in front of the Anastasis and Golgotha, hosted the

Fig. 4.3. Lead pilgrim's flask, circa 600, now flattened, depicting two key venues on an itinerary of the Holy Land. One side depicts the veneration of the cross at Golgotha, with a nimbed Christ between two crucified thieves. The other side depicts the two Marys approaching the tomb of Christ, as the angel speaks the inscription, "The Lord is Risen." The columns and the dome over the tomb show the shrine of the Resurrection, or Anastasis Rotunda, as it appeared to pilgrims from the fourth century on. Photo: Dumbarton Oaks, Byzantine Photograph and Fieldwork Archives, Washington, D.C.

more liturgically traditional gatherings, including the regular celebration of the Divine Liturgy or eucharist.[7]

An amalgamation of Holy Places in Jerusalem and its environs, with the Holy Sepulchre complex as a focal point, remained an important destination for Byzantine pilgrims. A Western pilgrim visiting Jerusalem around 570 offered a detailed description of the tomb of Christ:

> We entered the Holy City and venerated the Lord's Tomb. The Tomb is hewn out of living rock, or rather in the rock itself . . . and in the place where the Lord's body was laid, at the head, has been placed a bronze lamp. It burns there day and night, and we took a blessing from it, and then put it back. Earth is brought to the tomb and put inside, and those who go in take some as a blessing. . . . There are ornaments in vast numbers, which hang from iron rods: armlets, bracelets, necklaces, rings, tiaras, plaited girdles, belts, emperors' crowns of gold and precious stones, and the insignia of an empress.[8]

This description of the Anastasis Rotunda highlights typical accoutrements associated with religious shrines in Byzantium: endlessly burning oil lamps, a clutter of gifts offered by grateful devotees, and substitute relics, in this case dirt and oil brought daily to the site, capable of materially conveying the power and sanctity of the shrine (fig. 0.4).

The Arab conquest of the Levant in the seventh century reduced opportunities for imperial patronage of the Holy Land as well as access to Jerusalem and its environs. Yet pilgrimage continued: literary sources from the eighth through the fourteenth century attest the visits of thirty different Byzantine pilgrims (or groups of pilgrims) to the Holy Land.[9] Although this is a relatively small number, it does reflect that Byzantines continued to visit the shrines of the Holy Land. Several of these pilgrims produced accounts of their visits: Epiphanius Hagiopolites (the end of the eighth or ninth century), Lazarus of Mount Galesion (circa 991–1009), Constantine Manasses (1161/62), and John Phokas (1177 or 1195). The visits of these and other middle Byzantines differed from pre-Islamic pilgrimage to Holy Land shrines in two significant respects: first, all known Byzantine pilgrims from the middle and late Byzantine periods were men; second, these pilgrims were as interested in visiting the historic monastic communities of the Judean desert as they were the places associated with Christ's life and ministry. During his twelfth-century pilgrimage John Phokas visited the traditional shrines of the Church of the Anastasis in Jerusalem and the Church of the Nativity in Bethlehem. During his stay, Phokas also visited the famed centers of early Christian monasticism: the monasteries of St. Euthymius, St. Theodosius, and St. John the Baptist, as well as the celebrated monastery of St. Sabas. Phokas offered an account of the "desert" of these monasteries and of the spiritual athletes who continued the ascetic discipline of earlier Palestinian monasticism.[10] The focus of pilgrimage to the Holy Land had widened.

Arab ascendancy of the seventh century along with later Islamic expansion not only altered the geopolitical landscape of the Byzantine Empire but affected its sacred topography as well. Some shrines were completely abandoned in the wake of the seventh-century conquests, others met a slower demise in the absence of frequent travelers, while still others survived and even flourished. Jerusalem's shrines with their wide appeal remained; other shrines continued but drew their clientele almost exclusively from the local area. The shrine of St. Sergius at Rusafa in eastern Syria, which had received significant imperial patronage under Justinian in the sixth century, continued to flourish for some six centuries after the loss of that region to the Arabs in 638.[11] The great shrine of St. Menas in Egypt survived as well and even saw a renaissance during the ninth century under local, non-Chalcedonian patronage.

One city that remained a destination for Byzantine pilgrimage throughout most of the empire's history was Ephesus. A major port on the Aegean Sea linking the coast with the interior of Asia Minor, Ephesus was famous for its church and tomb of St. John. In addition to the magnificent church that Justinian built over the tomb of the apostle, Ephesus contained other sacred shrines, such as the tombs of Mary Magdalene and the apostle Timothy and the cave where the Seven Sleepers of Ephesus had been walled up during the persecutions of the third century, only to awake 190 years later in a Christian empire. Outside the city, on Mount Galesion, was the pillar upon which St. Lazarus stood in the eleventh century.

The church and tomb of St. John at Ephesus and the annual miracle associated with the shrine brought many visitors to the city. During the later Byzantine period the feast of St. John was celebrated on May 8. On the eve of the feast, before the customary all-night vigil, dust—or manna, as it was called—began to spew forth from the holes or grates in the slab covering the subterranean tomb. The yearly miracle of the manna reinforced the widely held belief that the apostle had not died but was asleep in his tomb. According to the legend, on the day commemorating his death or falling asleep (May 8) St. John would breathe and stir up the dust under the altar. This manna had amuletic powers: it could cure the sick, reverse infertility, and change the weather. A Catalonian described the phenomenon after a visit to the shrine in 1304:

> Every year, at the hour of vespers, there comes out of the tomb . . . manna like sand . . . a full palm high from the slab, as a jet of water rises up. And this manna issues out . . . and it lasts all night and then all Saint John's day until sunset. There is so much of this manna, by the time the sun has set and it has ceased to issue out, that, altogether, there are of it full three Barcelona quarts. And this manna is marvelously good for many things; for instance he who drinks it when he feels fever coming on will never have fever again. . . . And some of this manna is given to all pilgrims who come there; but it only appears once a year.[12]

The tomb of St. John at Ephesus attracted the faithful for almost one thousand years and was perhaps the most popular Byzantine shrine outside the capital.

From Constantinople to the city of St. Menas, from Thessalonike to the Byzantine-Persian frontier at Rusafa, the Byzantines participated in and helped maintain a vast network of holy shrines and places throughout the empire.[13] The shrines ranged from the biblically attested, holiest, and perhaps oldest Christian shrine, the Church of the Resurrection, to the person and pillar of St. Lazarus of Mount Galesion outside of Ephesus. In Asia Minor shrines of the Archangel Michael—one at Chonai, which contained a miraculous icon of the Mother of God, and another in Galatia, where a piece of the true cross procured miracles—attracted pilgrims. Elsewhere people flocked to shrines of early Christian martyrs or to those martyred later at the hands of the Iconoclasts. Members of all social, political, and economic groups visited shrines. The emperor Leo I (457–74) visited St. Daniel, who lived upon a pillar outside the imperial city; Juliana, a poor woman who did not have the financial means to secure a bed for incubation inside the tomb of Sts. Cyrus and John, was healed as she slept on the ground outside the shrine's gate. Men, women, and children visited the holy shrines of Byzantium. While literary and material evidence highlights how those seeking cures from all sorts of ailments filled these shrines, many others visited out of devotion or curiosity, perhaps because they happened to be in the vicinity or because they supplied materials and food to the shrine and to monastics who lived nearby and cared for the shrine. The religious shrine was a ubiquitous feature in the landscape of Byzantium.

"RECEPTACLES OF DIVINE ENERGY"

Like the shrine of the Holy Sepulchre with its oil and oil lamps that pilgrims could take home with them, many other Byzantine shrines produced tangible and portable means for the distribution of the shrine's sanctity. Moreover, the world of the faithful offered many opportunities for accessing the power of living saints, whom the eighth-century theologian John of Damascus called "receptacles of divine energy."[14] The numerous shrines commemorating a miraculous event, the resting place of a martyr, or the home of a once-famous living saint offered souvenirs, called *eulogiai* or "blessings." These *eulogiai*, available and often manufactured at the shrine itself, might take the form of small loaves of bread, lead or clay tokens, or flasks containing oil, water, or some other substance that pilgrims obtained at the shrine. The power of these souvenirs is poignantly illustrated by a story from the *Miracles of St. Symeon the Younger*, a stylite saint who stood upon a pillar at the Wondrous Mountain southwest of Antioch from 541 until his death in 592. A priest accompanied by his sick son visited the saint at his pillar. After receiving the blessing of the saint, the priest suggested that he and his son should remain at the base of the pillar, since "the presence at your side assures us of a more complete cure." In response Symeon stated, "The power of God . . . is efficacious everywhere. Therefore, take this *eulogia* of my dust and depart, and when you look at the imprint of our image, it is us that you will see." The priest did as he was told, and the same *eulogia* was used later to heal another child, who was assured that by means of the blessing "St. Symeon has the power to come and visit you here."[15] These *eulogiai* rendered the sanctity or holiness of a person or a place mobile, allowing the visitor to bring it home.

Fig. 4.4. Clay pilgrim's flask showing St. Menas at prayer, flanked by two camels (sixth or seventh century). Pilgrims purchased such tokens at shrines to collect and transport holy water or oil. Photo: Walters Art Museum, Baltimore.

The shrine of St. Menas in Egypt produced *eulogiai* in the form of small ceramic flasks, or ampullae. One side of the flask was stamped with an image of St. Menas praying with his arms outstretched in the traditional early Christian *orans* position and flanked on both sides by two sitting camels. The reverse side contained a cross or the small inscription "an *eulogia* of St. Menas" (fig. 4.4). The flasks were filled with oil from the lamps located above the saint's tomb or from an alabaster receptacle located in the ground directly in front of the altar of the Martyr Church, where oil was kept: the oil received its sanctity from its proximity to the tomb. The Menas oil flasks provided visitors with a sacred souvenir that brought the blessings of the site and the saint into the private lives of the individual believer.

Religious shrines in Byzantium and their powers to cure through contact with bones, sacred objects, or sacred space were not limited to the great centers that housed relics of Christianity's martyred heroes. One of the most popular sites associated with a living saint was Qal'at Sem'ān east of Antioch, the place where Symeon the Elder stood atop a pillar of some sixteen meters from 423 until his death in 459. After his death the column remained a place of pilgrimage; a large church was built to enclose the column. It was during the saint's lifetime, however, that he was most influential, acting as charismatic ombudsman in meting out justice to those who sought his counsel. Theodoret, bishop of Cyrrhus and Symeon's contemporary, described a typical day at the pillar: "He can be seen sitting in judgment and handing down proper and just sentences. These and similar activities are dealt with after three in the afternoon, for he spends the whole night and the day up till the ninth hour [three p.m.] in prayer. After the ninth hour he first delivers the divine teaching to those present and then, after receiving the request of each and effecting some healings, he resolves the quarrels of the disputants. Around sunset he then begins his conversation with God."[16] Symeon, the first stylite saint, became an international attraction, with visitors from all over the Mediterranean as well as from the Arabian Peninsula and the Persian hinterland. The remarkable sight of an ascetic living atop a pillar would be repeated many times in the following centuries. In the tenth century St. Luke the Stylite stood upon a pillar for some forty-two years in the city of Chalcedon, bringing healing to the lower classes of that city and nearby Constantinople.

Stylite saints attracted numerous pilgrims who, in part, were interested in viewing such a strange exhibition of piety and asceticism. Pilgrims returned home not only with the memory of what they saw but with a material token of their visit. The shrines of both Symeons produced and distributed pilgrim tokens or *eulogiae* made of lead or clay. These tokens bore an image of Symeon stamped on one side. The visitor would take the clay token with her or him as a souvenir, talisman, or blessing and could keep the token intact or, as many did, crumble it to be applied on the body either dry or in a paste. Symeon's pilgrim tokens were still being manufactured in the twelfth century, even though both sites had ceased to be significant centers of pilgrimage following the Islamic expansion of the 630s.

During the later Byzantine period the city of Thessalonike and its Church of St. Demetrius provided many Byzantines with *eulogiai*, conveying the power and strength of that city's patron. From the tenth century onwards the veneration of St. Demetrius in Thessalonike included the collection and distribution of *myron* or myrrh, a perfumed oil-like substance that exuded from the saint's bones. The holy *myron* flowed through a series of pipes into cisterns near the tomb. Visitors gathered the *myron* in small ceramic and lead ampullae or flasks that were decorated with images of St. Demetrius on one side and the Virgin, St. Nestor, or St. George and St. Theodora on the other. Such flasks have been found throughout the Balkans (fig. 4.5).[17] The thirteenth-century *chartophylax* (an important administrative functionary) of the Church of Thessalonike, John Staurakios, offered a vivid eyewitness account of how the faithful made use of the holy *myron*: "Men, women, and children extract the *myron* with their hands and straws and anoint their eyes, mouths and ears with it along with their chests and their entire bodies. . . . All ages and nations are endlessly being anointed with the *myron* of the martyr and, in particular, women ceaselessly anoint their eyes and chest, and their breasts and arms."[18] The production of *myron* was not limited to the cult of St. Demetrius; the practice arose after the end of Iconoclasm and also featured in the cults of St. Nicholas at Myra, St. Theodora at Thessalonike, and St. Nikon at Sparta, among others.

Shrines attracted Byzantine Christians for various reasons: physical and spiritual healing, justice, guidance, and intervention. Although the motives that drew individuals to shrines were diverse, the practices and activities that visitors participated in while at the shrine were relatively standardized. Private, individual prayer formed the core of religious activity at a shrine. Corporate prayer in the form of various liturgical services accompanied most shrines as well, though these depended in large measure on the popularity of the shrine and the availability of priests and monks to conduct and chant the services. Sleeping for one or more nights in the shrine or at a nearby hostel was commonplace. Incubation was an important tool in the treatment of maladies. Preferably, pilgrims would seek to touch the bones or secondary relics of a saint, and when they could not, a token or blessing from the shrine would serve the same function as a "receptacle of divine energy," a conduit of holiness for the believer.

Fig. 4.5. Small lead pilgrim's flask with an image of St. Demetrius. Thessalonike, thirteenth century. Photo: Archaeological Museum of Kavala.

FESTIVALS

Visitors to a Byzantine shrine usually found buildings for liturgical gatherings, housing relics, and accommodating visitors, as well as monasteries, cells, and workshops for producing pilgrims' *eulogiai*. Shrines were accessible year-round, yet visitation peaked during annual feast day celebrations. Most, if not all, shrines had one or more particular days or periods of time set aside as annual commemorations specifically associated with the history of the shrine or the saint.

The date of a saint's annual feast, or *panegyris*, was usually the anniversary of the saint's death or martyrdom. For some shrines this date could be fortuitous: the sixth-century bishop of Gaza noted the advantages of the feast of St. Sergius at Gaza on October 7: "[This is] the best time of the year, when the bodies are neither oppressed by cold nor enervated by heat, and when day and night have just made their truce with one another and agreed to have an equal share; when the weather is especially pleasant for everyone and gathers for us many people from everywhere, when there are no winter showers or the burning rage of the sun which ravage travelers."[19] The combination of religious, economic, and social activities in saints' festivals had a long history in the Mediterranean, stretching back to ancient Greece.[20] Like its predecessors, the Christian *panegyris* in Byzantium brought together men and women, old and young, rich and poor, native and foreigner in a celebration that often lasted several days. Many of the more important *panegyreis* were accompanied by a commercial fair that facilitated the trade of agricultural and manufactured products among local inhabitants and neighbors. Nevertheless, at the center of the festival were the liturgical rites conducted at the church or shrine, especially the all-night services on the eve of the feast and the celebration of the eucharist the following morning.

One of the earliest attested festivals was St. Thecla's, which was held at her shrine just outside of Seleucia in southeastern Asia Minor (modern Silifke). The shrine consisted of two large churches, one of which was built over the cave where, according to tradition, St. Thecla had descended into the earth to avoid her captors.[21] The commemoration of her feast day on September 24 was preceded by a weeklong festival that included a rhetorical contest and a commercial market. The festival concluded with the celebration of the eucharist on September 24: "On this day all rushed . . . to come together, to pray to God, to beseech the Virgin, and having partaken of the holy mysteries to go away blessed and as someone renewed in body and soul. Then they banqueted and set to discussing the wonders of the *panegyris*. One participant praised its brilliance, another the size of the crowd, yet another the culture of the teachers, and still another the harmony of the psalmody, another the duration of the vigil, and so they continued commenting on the liturgy and prayer."[22]

Not all Byzantines were as exuberant in their support of religious festivals as this description of the festival of St. Thecla suggests. Some church leaders complained about excesses associated with religious festivals. Basil of Caesarea described how a Christian ought to act at such festivals: "Scripture shows us that buying and selling conducted at martyrs' tombs is not fitting for us. For it is incumbent on Christians to be seen at the martyrs' tombs or in their neighborhood for no other reason than that of prayer."[23] Later ecclesiastical legislation attempted to reinforce appropriate behavior by restricting bartering and banqueting to spaces outside the shrine's precinct.

According to the *Life of St. Elisabeth the Wonderworker*, possibly composed in the sixth century, the annual festival of the martyr Glykeria was held in Herakleia, the capital city of the province of Thrace. The weeklong festivities drew visitors from the surrounding area who "participated in processions and all-night doxologies," feasting and celebrating "with the populace." A highlight of the festival was the procession carrying the martyr's head through the city. A visitor to the feast, Eunomianos, noticed the changing expression on Glykeria's face, "sometimes smiling slightly as though happy and sometimes with a sad and gloomy expression."[24] After "the throng" had made their final prayers, Eunomianos remained alone inside the martyr's

---

Canon Law Regulating the Sale of Food at Festivals

It is not right that those who are responsible for reverence to the churches should place within the sacred bounds an eating place, nor offer food there, nor make other sales. For God our Savior teaching us when he was dwelling in the flesh commanded us not to make his Father's house a house of commerce. He also poured out the small coins of the money-changers and drove out all those who made the sanctuary common. If, therefore, anyone shall be apprehended in the aforesaid crime, let him be excommunicated.

—*Canon 76* of the Council in Trullo [or Quinisext Council], 692 CE; NPNF 2.14.398–99 [modified]

church and beseeched the saint to end his wife's sixteen years of barrenness. Eunomianos prayed long into the night and finally lay down on the floor of the church and fell asleep. While sleeping, the martyr Glykeria, her head reattached to her body, appeared to him in a dream and promised that he and his wife would conceive a child whom they were to name Elisabeth, "for she will be shown forth like the mother of the Forerunner and Baptist John."

The festival of St. Demetrius in Thessalonike was one of the most popular, in part because of the saint's close association with that city and its citizens. The *panegyris* included a large commercial fair held outside the city walls that began six days before the feast and lasted for three days. A twelfth-century description of the fair highlights its international flavor, noting not only that it was the most important fair in Macedonia but also that it attracted pilgrims and merchants from throughout the Mediterranean: "the shores of the ocean send pilgrims and sightseers to the martyr, so famous is he in Europe."[25] Outside the city, merchants set up booths in two long rows facing each other, with smaller rows branching off of the central one. The length of the main two rows was impressive enough to have been noted by our twelfth-century observer, who compared the ground plan of the fair to a centipede with a long body and numerous extending feet. Expensive altar cloths were among the wares for sale, and the fair bustled with people, horses, cattle, sheep, pigs, and dogs.

The liturgical celebration of the festival of St. Demetrius began with three consecutive all-night vigils leading up to the martyr's feast day. "Many priests and monks, divided into two choirs, constantly chanted the hymn in honor of the saint."[26] The archbishop of Thessalonike presided over the entire festival. Torches burned throughout the nights, illuminating the vigils. The liturgical services filled the large five-aisle basilica of St. Demetrius, which was located inside the city walls and built over the place where it was said the saint had been martyred during the persecutions of Diocletian at the beginning of the fourth century. Symeon, archbishop of Thessalonike from 1419 to 1429, described the ritual procession on the eve of the feast, that is, on the evening of October 25. The procession began at the church of the Virgin Katafygeis, proceeded through the city, and ended up at the basilica of St. Demetrius, where an all-night vigil and liturgy followed. Representatives from the various churches of the city led the procession, each carrying their church's liturgical cross. After the crosses came readers, chanters, and priests. Behind them, four young readers carried a casket containing the holy *myron* of the saint, accompanied by six young men holding flaming torches and incense burners who censed the casket continuously. The archbishop followed, surrounded by several deacons; then came other bishops, abbots, priests, and officials. Behind them were monks who chanted the appointed hymns as the procession progressed. Finally, at the end of the procession were the laity—"the undistinguished mob" of men, women, and children—who, Symeon notes, were responsible for singing "Lord have mercy" at each stop along the way. Our anonymous twelfth-century source describes events on the morning of the last day of the festival, October 26, the actual feast day of the martyr:

> From those who had specially practiced the rituals of the festival . . . there was heard a most divine psalmody, most gracefully varied in its rhythm, order, and artistic alternations. For it was not only men who were singing; the holy nuns in the left wing of the church, divided into two antiphonal choirs, also offered up the Holy of Holies to the martyr. And when every part of the spectacle and service had been properly concluded, we too invoked the saint in the customary way, praying to the martyr for a safe return, after which we came out of the church.[27]

PUBLIC CELEBRATION AND PRIVATE DEVOTION

Responding to a friend from Cappadocia who had asked for advice on whether to go on pilgrimage to the Holy Land, the fourth-century bishop Gregory of Nyssa wrote, "What advantage is reaped by him who reaches those celebrated spots themselves? Does he imagine . . . that the Holy Spirit is in abundance at Jerusalem, but is unable to travel as far as us?"[28] Theologically speaking, Gregory was correct, yet his views did not curb the lure of the Holy Land and other shrines. Elsewhere, Gregory wrote about his own visit to Jerusalem in terms that seem to contradict the advice he gave his friend: "I was filled with joy so great that the description of its blessing is beyond the power of utterance." This latter observation is more representative of the Byzantines' experience of and response to the numerous shrines and holy places dotting their religious landscape. Periodically, clerics challenged the popularity of religious shrines and the activities associated with them. Iconoclasts—who rejected the use and veneration of images—at times also opposed to the veneration of relics. Yet, even with such reservations, the veneration of saints, relics, shrines, and other holy places endured throughout Byzantine history.

The religious shrine was a busy place, and some devotees sought more peaceful surroundings. The ninth-century St. Ioannikios, when visiting the tomb of St. John the Evangelist at Ephesus, "had no desire to enter [the shrine] along with the crowd streaming in there," but rather wanted to enter the church "privately at night."[29] Like other medieval societies, Byzantium was a mixture of public and private space, of communal liturgies and individual devotions. The shrine reflected both extremes. The large basilica of St. Demetrius in Thessalonike overflowed with people seeking the saint's assistance during a sixth-century plague. While at the shrine of St. Luke the Younger in Stiris, a civil servant once convinced the monks to remove an ill man so that he could remain "alone by the divine tomb, while the sick one was tormented with great despair, having been ordered to pass the night somewhere else."[30] Activity at a shrine peaked during annual festivals and feast days. In the late sixth or early seventh century, Theodore of Sykeon visited the bishop of Germia, in central Asia Minor, during the annual feast of the Theotokos; "all the citizens" of Germia and the neighboring town of Eudoxias turned out for the festival.[31] The city of Trebizond, in the fourteenth century, marked the feast of its most revered saint, the martyr Eugenios, with processions that included the emperor, the archbishop, the bishops, the abbots of monasteries, and "all the Christian people."[32]

From the empire's earliest days to its final demise, the shrines of saints, martyrs, miracle-working icons and relics, and places from the Bible formed an integral part of religious life. Some shrines had a long and continuous history of activity during the thousand-plus years of Byzantine civilization. Others had a shorter life span. However, the shrines' functions, religious activities, and festivals remained fairly consistent. There were organized processions, liturgical services, sermons, readings of the life and miracles of a saint, and banqueting. Commercial fairs accompanied many shrines and their feast days. Individual or private devotion at shrines consisted of prayer; contact with relics by touch, kiss, sight, or proximity; incubation; offerings; and the receipt of blessing, often mediated through oil, dirt, water, *myron*, or a clay token.[33]

In the literary sources, the most frequent reason given for visiting a shrine was healing. This is not surprising for a premodern society in which the practice of medicine left a lot to be desired. Byzantine hagiographic texts spill over with accounts of miraculous cures associated with a saint or shrine. Just as the Byzantines needed physical and spiritual healing, they also sought guidance. People visited shrines for other types of divine intervention as well: the resolution of infertility, assistance in childbirth, and the finding of lost items. Often people turned to the shrines of living saints, the holy man or woman, for counsel or justice.

Shrines and festivals were public spaces and events filled with private devotions. The qualitative difference between communal participation in a procession during the festival of St. Glykeria and individual devotion such as incubation at the shrine of St. Artemios is difficult to assess. A reassuring glance from the decapitated head of the martyr Glykeria may have been equally as powerful as a visitation from St. Artemios accompanied by the disappearance of pain from a hernia. Both experiences drew the Byzantines from their homes into very public spaces and brought them into contact with sacred space, sacred time, sacred objects, and sacred people. While believers could bring the blessing of these public spaces into their private homes, the primary encounter with the holy took place in the public arena of the shrines and their festivals.

FOR FURTHER READING

Davis, Stephen J. *The Cult of St. Thecla: A Tradition of Women's Piety in Late Antiquity.* Oxford: Oxford University Press, 2001.

Fowden, Elizabeth Key. *The Barbarian Plain: Saint Sergius between Rome and Iran.* Berkeley: University of California Press, 1999.

Grossman, Peter. "The Pilgrimage Center of Abû Mînâ." In David Frankfurter, ed., *Pilgrimage and Holy Space in Late Antique Egypt*, 281–302. Leiden: Brill, 1998.

Skedros, James Constantine. *Saint Demetrios of Thessaloniki: Civic Patron and Divine Protector, 4th–7th Centuries CE.* Harrisburg, Pa.: Trinity, 1999.

Talbot, Alice-Mary. *Faith Healing in Late Byzantium: The Posthumous Miracles of the Patriarch Athanasios I of Constantinople by Theoktistos the Stoudite.* Brookline, Mass.: Hellenic College Press, 1983.

Vryonis, Speros. "The *Panegyris* of the Byzantine Saint: A Study in the Nature of a Medieval Institutions, Its Origins and Fate." In Sergei Hackel, ed., *The Byzantine Saint*, 196–226. San Bernardino, Calif.: Borgo, 1983.

Fig. 5.1. Entrance to the Church of the Holy Anargyroi (Sts. Cosmas and Damian), Kastoria, Greece. The plain decoration of the exterior portal belies the intricate painted decoration of the church interior. Photo: Sharon E. J. Gerstel.

THE LAYPERSON
IN CHURCH

SHARON E. J. GERSTEL

In the Middle Ages, as today, portals and gates, whether of houses, public buildings, neighborhoods, or cities, marked important transitions between spaces of varied function and meaning. One of the most important portals for the Byzantine was the entrance to the church, which framed the passage between profane and sacred spaces (fig. 5.1). Within the church other portals were labeled with names such as the "beautiful gate" and the "royal gate," further emphasizing, through nomenclature, hierarchies of passage. Entrance into the church signified the elevation of the layperson into a sanctified ritual space where temporal and spatial perceptions were intentionally altered. In order to understand the relationship between the Byzantine layperson and the church building and rituals, the reader is encouraged to pass through the church portal, leaving worldly cares aside.

A picture of the religious lives of the Byzantine elite, whether the emperor or a high bureaucrat, is fairly easy to reconstruct. Written sources from the period following Iconoclasm describe the way in which the emperor experienced church rites and ceremonies and the manner in which members of the elite provided for ecclesiastical construction and enjoyed the reciprocal benefits of their patronage. Writers of the period also composed eulogies and epigrams that describe the funerals of their contemporaries and the elaborate furnishings of tombs, providing valuable information about church rites surrounding the deceased and the elaborate provisions to house and commemorate the dead.[1] Wills of high-placed individuals record donations to religious foundations and occasionally provide information about the kinds of books or icons that wealthier individuals may have commissioned and owned. An excellent example is the will of Eustathios Boilas, dated 1059, in which the official lists a number of liturgical objects—including service vessels, sacerdotal vestments, icons, and books—that were intended for the Church of the Virgin, which he had constructed.[2] These donations were the physical reminders of a spiritual exchange between supplicant and monk that guaranteed that the lay donor might find easier entrance to heaven through the commemorative prayers of the monastic community. Letters preserved from the period also reveal, for members of high society, the important relationship between laypeople and their spiritual mentors, who provided advice on a wide range of topics, both practical and religious. These valuable written sources are the literary products of a very small segment of Byzantine society—highly educated people who were associated with the court and civil service and who inhabited, for the most part, the Byzantine capital and the empire's larger cities. To these sources can be matched a large body of material evidence, including, but not limited to, standing churches, preserved tombstones, and small objects of personal use, from lead seals impressed with the names and holy portraits that were used to validate written documents to icons and manuscripts intended for private devotional use.

Little is known, however, about the religious lives of the humble laypeople who inhabited the small agrarian villages of the Byzantine countryside. Largely unlettered, Byzantine villagers left no written accounts of their religious experience, though it is generally assumed that they were deeply pious. Any written information about the religious life of the Byzantine villager is incidental. Saints' lives, for example, recount stories of laypeople who made pilgrimages to shrines or were affected by the works of holy men. The tenth-century *Life* of St. Nikon, for example, records the holy man's interactions with villagers in the Peloponnesos, who flocked to hear his fiery preaching and, after his death, approached his tomb to be healed of a variety of ailments.[3] The proliferation of this saint's portrait in small churches in the area of Lakonia, the center of his activity, demonstrates the significance of Nikon's cult to laypeople in the region. Church and civil court documents of the later centuries, particularly from provincial areas such as Epiros, provide information about the Byzantine laity far from the capital and offer another kind of information about the intervention of the church in the lives of lay petitioners. The study of tax documents and inventories of landholdings has shed light on naming practices, demonstrating that the vast majority of baptismal names derived from Orthodox saints.[4] In the absence of substantial written sources directly concerning the religious experience of laypeople from the lower strata of Byzantine society, however, the structures that housed Orthodox rites—the churches themselves—offer the fullest evidence for any analysis of lay piety in the countryside. These buildings, which are preserved in large numbers, contain inscriptions, portraits, and holy paintings, which provide important information about lay piety in Byzantium, particularly in the empire's distant provinces. Added to the evidence from standing structures are the remains of metal and ceramic objects that were worn and used by people in the Byzantine countryside. Small metal crosses or coins bearing a likeness of Christ and pierced for suspension may have served as the humble adornment of pious Christians, just as more well-to-do Byzantines favored objects carved or created from more precious materials.

It has been estimated that in modern-day Greece alone, painted churches dated between the seventh and the fifteenth century number around two thousand.[5] Of these, the majority are dated between the thirteenth and the fifteenth century and therefore constitute a valuable primary source for the study of late Byzantium. In southern Greece and the Greek islands, the thirteenth century witnessed the widespread construction and decoration of new churches serving local populations. Of approximately nine hundred medieval churches still standing on the island of Crete, for example, 5 percent date from the ninth to the twelfth century and 95 percent date from the thirteenth to the fifteenth century, the period when the island was under Venetian rule (1204–1669). The decoration of these unpretentious churches reveals valuable information about the practice of Orthodoxy under Latin rule. In the Mani, a rugged peninsula at the tip of the Peloponnesos, over 140 churches survive, most of them also dating from the thirteenth through the fifteenth century. Whether the high percentage of surviving churches from this period is accidental or reflects an upsurge in lay piety is unknowable. Their survival, however, is providential. Together with a close reading of *euchologia*, or service books, from the same period, one can gain great insight into the rites, services, and religious environments experienced by the Byzantine layperson.

THE SPACE OF THE CHURCH

Byzantine cities contained a multitude of churches. In the late period, large cities such as Thessalonike could host a number of parochial churches. The preserved texts of homilies delivered in these large churches by such ecclesiastical figures as the great theologian and archbishop Gregory Palamas (circa 1296–1359) provide a sense of the passionate sermons that would have inspired laypeople in Byzantium's civic centers.[6] The ecclesiastical infrastructure of the empire's large cities was also marked by churches that promoted the cults of specific saints or healing cults, as well as by monastic enclosures. Churches and church ceremonies were at the center of civic life. Religious processions between churches, vigils within churches, celebrations of church feasts, and regular services offered the layperson an annual cycle of events and religious obligations that ordered daily existence. Walking through a Byzantine city, the layperson could not have ignored the calls to hourly prayers or special services, summoned by the striking of a wooden beam (*semandron*) or, in the late Byzantine period, by the tolling of bells. Within many cities, commercial markets were associated with specific church celebrations, adding an economic dimension to the call to worship. It was to the church that Byzantines turned at moments of communal anxiety. The Byzantine church calendar recalls, for example, a number of devastating earthquakes. During moments of war and invasion, the army and cities were placed under the protection of holy figures, who were summoned, in spirit and through icons, to protect both citizens and ramparts.

For the villager also, the church stood at the center of religious and social life. In most cases, the church exterior was fairly simple. Constructed of brick or of local fieldstones, the small building was often undifferentiated from the surrounding houses—the only architectural distinction was the rounded apse that protruded from the east end, signaling the position of the altar within. More elaborate churches were outfitted with domes, enlarged in scale, and may have boasted external decoration such as immured sculpture, which was often taken from ancient or earlier medieval structures and invested with numinous or apotropaic powers. The decoration of village churches suggests that in outlying areas of Byzantium religion was closely linked to the agricultural cycle.

In stark contrast to the fairly plain exterior, holy images covered the interior of both city and village churches, from the base of the walls to the top of the vaults or central dome (color gallery, plate B). In some churches, particularly in Byzantine cities, wealthy patrons sponsored images fashioned from mosaic. More often churches were painted in fresco, the dominant medium for ecclesiastical decoration. Wooden icons of saints of heightened importance to the community or to individuals often supplemented the life-size images on the walls of the church. Icons of special importance were usually larger and encased in elaborate frames. Carrying poles affixed to the base of the panels facilitated their use in church processions. The proliferation of images of sacred figures lining the interior of religious space was a defining characteristic of Byzantine church decoration and shaped the religious experience of the layperson. Worshippers easily recognized the images of the saints by their physiognomy, costume, or attribute. Although in the period following Iconoclasm every saint was inscribed with his or her name, the average layperson would have been familiar with the facial characteristics of a wide range of saints whose images were repeated in public, ecclesiastical, and even domestic contexts. In the fifteenth century Sylvester Syropoulos recorded the reaction of a Byzantine church official to the interior decoration of an Italian church: "When I enter a Latin church, I do not revere any of the [images of] saints that are there because I do not recognize any of them."[7] It was to these *recognizable* saints that the Byzantine layperson addressed a variety of prayers and petitions, from the desire for spiritual healing to the wish for an abundant harvest. The worshipper expected the saint, represented with eyes forward and hand raised in a gesture of reception, to listen and respond.

But beyond the decoration of its walls, the Byzantine church held a special place in the Orthodox mind and soul, one that was not easily defined by words. Byzantines at every social level intuitively understood the interior of the church as trans-temporal and trans-spatial, a deliberate confusion of time and space. Upon entry, the church rendered impossible normal temporal cognition by purposefully inviting, within a single, enclosed space, the mystical intersection of the past and the present, the immediate and the eternal. The manipulation of natural lighting and the careful staging of artificial illumination encouraged this temporal confusion. For example, a strong beam of light entered the eastern window to touch the altar table during the morning service, a deliberate effort to unveil God's illumination for the faithful and to transfigure the church interior through the revelation of the Word and presence of God. The church's internal decoration, presenting saints long dead on the wall and, occasionally, woven or embroidered on ecclesiastical vestments, also played a role in confusing time and inviting the layperson, through faith, to enter another plane of existence. Moreover, the words and actions of the liturgy fostered the blurring of temporalities. That the dead were invoked in prayer together with the living further emphasized the suspension of normal divisions of time and hastened the mingling of those to be resurrected and those praying for resurrection. The vision of the bearded priest, who bore a superficial resemblance to the swarthy Christ represented overhead, suggested a further temporal fusion between he who had died and was risen and he who officiated over the sacrificial rite.

Spatially, the interior of the church, especially after Iconoclasm, offered a series of divided chambers that were metaphorically related to the earth and the uppermost reaches of the heavens (fig. 5.2). The sanctuary, or altar area, divided from the laity by a screen, was associated with heaven. This was the domain of the clergy and strictly prohibited to the laity, with the exception of the Byzantine emperor. The narthex, the church vestibule that often housed burials, corresponded to the earth. As architectural confirmation of this metaphorical notion, the narthex was lower in height and more dimly lit than the rest of the church. The central nave, which also evoked heaven, was the site where the laity stood for the service and the space through which liturgical processions passed, sanctifying the area through the movement of holy objects and the smoke of incense. This space was therefore a microcosm of the world, where the worshipper momentarily entered heaven through penitence and prayer. Often crowned

Plate A. Portable mosaic icon of the Forty Martyrs of Sebasteia. Constantinople, late thirteenth century. The popular cult of the Forty Martyrs celebrated men from eastern Asia Minor who were condemned by the Romans to stand naked and die on a frozen lake for refusing to renounce their Christian faith. Photo: Dumbarton Oaks, Byzantine Photograph and Fieldwork Archives, Washington, D.C.

Plate B. Church of the Virgin Phorbiotissa, Asinou, near the village of Nikitari in the Troodos Mountains of Cyprus, circa 1105/6, with additional painting in the fourteenth century. Looking east, from the nave toward the sanctuary. Near life-size images of John the Baptist, the Virgin Mary, and Christ frame the iconostasis. Images of saints and scenes from the lives of Christ and the Virgin cover the walls of the church. Above the apse, Gabriel *left* announces the incarnation to Mary *right.* Photo: Dumbarton Oaks, Byzantine Photograph and Fieldwork Archives, Washington, D.C.

Plate C. "Sinners Sleeping on Sunday." Church of St. John the Theologian, Selli, Crete. 1411. Photo: Sharon E. J. Gerstel.

Plate D. Blessing hand of God. Southwest chapel of Hosios Loukas near Stiris, Greece. Photo: Sharon E. J. Gerstel.

Plate E. Niches with tombs from the exonarthex of the Chora Monastery, Constantinople. On the *left* is the tomb of Irene Raoulaina Palaiologina, daughter-in-law of emperor Michael VIII Palaiologos, whose son John married the daughter of the monastery's founder, Theodore Metochites. Photo by Sharon E. J. Gerstel.

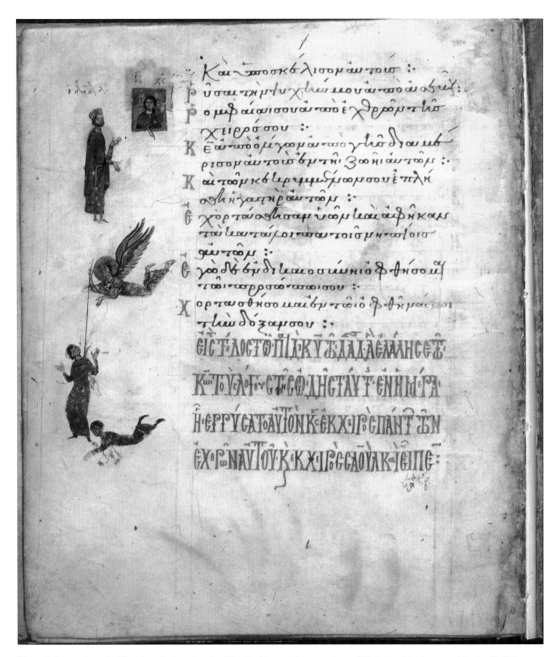

Plate F. A page from the Theodore Psalter showing King David speaking to an icon of Christ beside the text of Psalm 16. Below, an angel pierces one iconoclast, while another has already fallen. Folio 15v, British Library Add. 19.352. By permission of the British Library.

Plate G. Green jasper intaglio, tenth century, depicting the crucifixion and the woman with an issue of blood approaching Jesus (Matt. 9:2-22). Photo: Benaki Museum, Athens.

Plate H. (left and below) Enameled medallion, late twelfth to thireenth century, showing Christ enthroned surrounded by the symbols of the evangelists, and the Virgin and child surrounded by the inscription, "You who carry the Word purely, I carry on the breast for health of body." Vatopedi Monastery, Mount Athos, Greece. Photo used by permission.

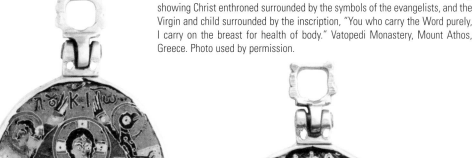

Plate I. Silver *enkolpion* with Daniel in the Lions' Den, late thirteenth to fourteenth century. See also figure 8.10. Photo: Istanbul Archaeological Museum, inv. no. H.K.95.278.

Plate J. Icon of Virgin Hodegetria, with silver revetment showing portraits of donors Constantine Akropolites, *lower left,* and his wife Maria Komnene Tornikina Akropolitissa, *lower right.* The icon dates from the fifteenth century, while the silver revetment dates from the late thirteenth to early fourteenth century. State Tret'iakov Gallery, Moscow.

by a dome decorated with a half-length image of Christ—as if the Lord peered into the church through an oculus—this space contained scenes from the Gospels, often arranged in the sequence of the church calendar but occasionally rearranged according to the demands of the congregation (fig. 5.3). These three spaces—sanctuary, nave, and narthex—were divided on a longitudinal axis by portals and screens, each decorated with suitable imagery of carved crosses, vines, or other vegetal ornament and even birds and animals. These dividers physically separated spaces but also served as liminal markers, signaling changes in levels of sanctity and ritual preparedness as one neared the holy altar. Within the church, therefore, discrete chambers recalled otherworldly spaces; the decoration and rite that unfolded in each confirmed these associations.

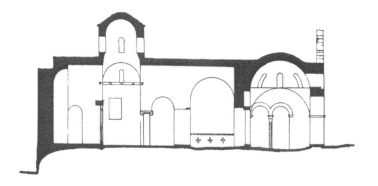

Fig. 5.2. St. Michael the Archangel, Upper Boularioi, Mani Peninsula, Greece. The ground plan and cross section of this village church reveal how the sanctuary, left, was separated from the nave by a barrier. At the center of the church is the nave, which is crowned by a tall dome. The narthex, which is smaller in size and darker, contains sarcophagi along the north and south walls. A domed porch was added to the west end of the church after its initial construction.

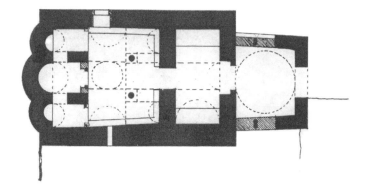

The interior of the nave was also subdivided on a vertical axis by intricately carved or colored cornices that separated full-length images of saints at the ground level, narrative scenes in the upper vaults, and dogmatic images in the dome and conch of the apse.[8] These divisions also indicated the direction of prayer, from the intercessory saints at the lowest level, to the supplicant Virgin in the conch of the apse, to the judging Christ represented at the apex of the dome. Thus the vertical division of the building mirrored the very practice of prayer, which sought access to Christ through a long series of intercessory figures and elevated the thoughts of the layperson toward heaven.

The decoration and furnishing of the church also attested its special position as a negotiated space between earth and heaven. Byzantine authors compared the church floor, paved with brightly colored marbles, to fields of flowers and flowing rivers. Beyond the portraits of saints the interior walls and vaults were covered with representations of vines and flowering plants so subtly placed that art historians have usually relegated them to the category of ornament. These motifs, found on carved barriers, portals, and icon frames, border figural decorations on the walls, but also form a kind of lattice that provides its own visual structure for the rest of the decoration. The frequent use of vine scroll decoration recalls the psalm referring to God looking down upon his vineyard (80:14-15; LXX 79:14-15) as well as other biblical references to vines and wine. In turn, such passages were inscribed within the church, encircling icons and reminding the congregation of the intersection of text, image, and rite, an intersection that seems noteworthy to modern scholars but was surely intuitive for medieval worshippers. The psalm text, for example, encircles the Pantokrator, the half-length image of Christ in the dome of the Church of the Virgin Peribleptos in Ohrid (1294/95) (fig. 5.3), effectively equating the protected vineyard with the Orthodox faithful standing below.

Fig. 5.3. Image of the Pantokrator, or Almighty, surrounded by Ps. 80:14-15 (LXX 79:14-15): "Look on us from heaven, and behold and visit this vine; and restore that which thy right hand hath planted: and look on the son of man whom thou didst strengthen for thyself" (KJV). Church of the Virgin Peribleptos, Ohrid, Macedonia. 1294/95. Photo: Foto Marburg/Art Resource, New York.

Throughout the service, prayer and images urged the lay congregant to enter an alternative world. The Cherubic Prayer, or *Cherubikon*, for example, invited the congregant to join the ranks of the escorting angels. An atmospheric change that was and is clearly perceptible upon entering the building assisted the mental leap from a profane to a sacred plane. Within the church, the temperature was cooler, the light dimmer, and the smell pungent. The empty church, deafening in its silence, contrasted greatly with the chants and rhythmic movements of the service. The physical response to the church interior was immediate and subconscious. Hands clasped before the body and head slightly bent, one waited, shifting one's feet on the hard floor. The legions of saints—painted on the walls or captured on wooden panels—also waited. Staring straight ahead, they anticipated the supplicant's entreaty, through which they would become animated. At that moment the martyrs of the past mingled with the faithful, blurring the line between the perceptible and that which is beyond human cognition.

By the last centuries of Byzantium, Orthodox churches, whether in the city or village, celebrated a fairly standard liturgy, one that had evolved over centuries and that, by the end of imperial rule, had synthesized texts stemming from both monastic and cathedral worship. The most common service in the period under discussion was the *Liturgy of St. John Chrysostom*, which could range in length from less than one hour to more than two, depending on the status of the church and number of celebrants. The *Liturgy of St. Basil* was used on Sundays during Lent and on important feast days. Laypeople were expected to attend church with some frequency and to obey church laws governing bodily and spiritual purity before taking communion or during periods of fasting, such as Lent. Sources suggest, however, that the laity did not strictly adhere to such regulations. In letters written to Andronikos II in 1306 and 1307, the patriarch Athanasios I implores the emperor to prohibit Orthodox Christians in the city from entering bathhouses and taverns during Lent.[9] The patriarch is equally troubled that many have ignored the prohibition

> **The Cherubic Hymn of the Divine Liturgy**
>
> We who mystically represent the Cherubim and sing
> the thrice-holy hymn to the life-giving Trinity, let
> us now lay aside all worldly care to receive the King
> of All escorted unseen by the angelic corps, alleluia!

against eating fish during the holy fast. Church decoration also bears out a certain lassitude in following church regulations. In a number of Orthodox churches in Crete, among sinners represented in the scene of the Last Judgment is a couple labeled "Sleeping on Sunday," referring to parishioners who did not abstain from sexual intercourse before attending church on Sunday or, perhaps, to those who did not attend services at all (color gallery, plate C). Once they were in church, we do not know how frequently Byzantine laypeople took communion. Most scholars assume that by the last centuries of Byzantium, laypeople received communion principally during Holy Week. Taking communion in the Orthodox church presupposed that the layperson had fasted and was spiritually cleansed. For laypeople who had not undergone such preparation, the church provided the *antidoron*, the "gift in place of the gift," a piece of the offering that had remained after the consecrated bread had been excised for use in the eucharistic rite. In this way, people who attended church could participate in the community of the faithful without taking communion while spiritually unprepared.

Written and visual sources suggest that men and women were separated within the church. In most churches men and women occupied opposite sides of the nave, standing along the north and south sides or, perhaps in some communities, the east and west ends.[10] Within the church interior, the laity was separated from the clergy, who, for a large part of the liturgy, remained within the sanctuary. By the last centuries of imperial rule the sanctuary was largely obscured from the laity by a tall screen covered with sacred images. These icons provided the laity with devotional images toward which to focus prayer during the services. Not surprisingly, since a large number of prayers within the liturgy were addressed to Christ and

From a Letter of Patriarch Athanasios I to Emperor Andronikos II, December 1307

I ask that the offerings of good deeds not be neglected, and especially at this time that all the baths and taverns in the capital be closed by an imperial command from Monday morning to Saturday morning, and that men, women and children should spend their time in the holy churches, and should stop eating fish [which is sold] by the old women at the seashore. For instead of these foods, boiled wheat and pulse and fruits and vegetables are sufficient for Orthodox Christians, so that by piously accepting the proclamation of fasting, we may be judged acceptable to God, and so that the Ruler on High will recompense your divine majesty with great rewards, thanks to your reverence for God.

—Alice-Mary Talbot, ed. and trans., *The Correspondence of Athanasius I, Patriarch of Constantinople: Letters to the Emperor Andronicus II, Members of the Imperial Family, and Officials*, Dumbarton Oaks Texts 3 (Washington, D.C.: Dumbarton Oaks Center for Byzantine Studies, 1975), 90–91.

the Virgin, the majority of the screens presented life-sized images of these holy figures, often with their hands extended in gestures of blessing or intercession. In many cases, inscriptions on the icons or portraits of laypeople painted adjacent to the holy figures record the supplications of petitioners and their families (fig. 5.6). In these cases, we can propose that the petitioners had a special devotional relationship to the saint, who may have shared a name or may have been adept at healing or military protection. Presumably, laypeople invoked these holy figures even outside the walls of the church.

Average Byzantines' connection with the church, where they attended services in life, continued after they were laid to rest to await judgment. Within Byzantium's great cities in the last centuries of imperial rule, families of the elite were buried within monasteries, where the monks or nuns were expected to commemorate lay patrons in perpetuity. Such commemorations were guaranteed by the act of institutional foundation or through the donation of large sums of money or precious gifts for the use of the monastic community. In the same period Byzantine villagers, echoing the pattern of city dwellers, banded together to construct and decorate churches through the communal donations of those who would use the church in life and would, they hoped, be buried around it in death. A well-known example is the church of Sts. Cosmas and Damian in the small village of Kepoula at

---

Dedicatory Inscription from the Church of Sts. Cosmas and Damian, Kepoula, Mani, 1265

The most sacred church of the holy physicians Cosmas and Damian, and of their mother Theodote, was constructed and painted thanks to the labor and expense of the priest Ioram and his son Elias, the church lector and notary, and his wife, Maria; the priest Eustratios with his brother Ioram and his wife, K[...]; Tromarchis and his wife, Thalo, and his son; Pantoleos and his wife, Maria, and his son. Of these, Father Stratis gave one nomisma, Tromarchis and Pantoleos one and a half nomismata, and the notary [=Elias] eight nomismata. The priest Michael and his wife; Leon and his wife, Kallarchos and his wife; Michael and his wife; Kyritzas, [...] Kalarchos and his wife, Kanakarea; and Kalarchos with his wife.

The most sacred church was constructed for fourteen and one half nomismata. The priest Michael [gave] one nomisma; his brother Leo one nomisma; Kalarchos one nomisma; Michael one-quarter nomisma; Kyritzas one-quarter nomisma, Kalarchos one-half [nomisma]. [The church] was completed by my hand, Nikoloas the painter from the town of Retzitza, with [the help of] my brother and student Theodoros. The third day of the month of June, the year 6773, the eighth indiction.

—Translation by the author. For the Greek text and commentary, see S. Kalopissi-Verti, *Dedicatory Inscriptions and Donor Portraits in Thirteenth-Century Churches of Greece* (Vienna: Österreichische Akademie der Wissenschaften, 1992), 67–69.

the southernmost tip of the Peloponnesos, which is surrounded by a medieval graveyard. The inscription on the south wall of this small church records the names of those who contributed extremely modest sums for its construction along with the amount of their donations. In addition to cash gifts villagers also contributed vineyards, olive trees, vegetable gardens, and even threshing floors for the upkeep of their local churches.

RITUAL LIFE

Built through the patronage of families, town residents, priests and their wives, and local donors, the decoration of non-monastic churches responded to the ritual needs of the congregations within their walls. For the layperson the church was, in essence, a second house, where the rites associated with the most critical events of the human life cycle, from birth to death and beyond, took place. Together with the guidance of the local priest, the paintings of this house led the faithful in correct church teachings and ritual that followed the life of Christ. The text of the liturgy also shaped the experience of the layperson—whether poor or powerful—within the church. It provides information about what a layperson heard and saw. Related sources describe the censing and lighting of the building, atmospheric conditions that also informed the worshipper's experience. Together these documents provide a potent image of the place of the layperson within the church during the liturgy. In addition to weekly services, the church facilitated equally important domestic rituals tied to the security and sustenance of the family and to the economic and physical health of the men and women of medieval Byzantium. These rites fell, for the most part, outside of the communion service but were arguably just as important in the lives of Byzantine laypeople. Limited space allows for the analysis of only a few such rites.

Betrothal and Marriage

Among the most important events in the lives of Byzantine families were betrothal and marriage, which the service books of the middle and late Byzantine periods include as separate rites. Girls were betrothed at a very young age in Byzantium, often before they turned twelve. Depending on family circumstances, the actual marriage could take place some years later. Since the rites of both betrothal and marriage took place within the church, the dissolution of these ecclesiastical contracts had to be overseen by church courts. Indeed, a number of cases brought before church courts by women concerned betrothal, marriage, adultery, and even divorce.

According to liturgical texts of the late Byzantine period, the betrothed couple stood in front of the sanctuary gates for the duration of the ceremony, the man to the right and the woman to the left. The service was short.[11] In the course of the rite, preserved in slightly varied forms, the priest asked the prospective groom if he would accept his betrothed, then posed the same question to the prospective bride. After swearing in the affirmative, the couple was blessed. Rings were given to the couple, a gold ring to the man and a silver ring to the woman. On occasion, the woman's ring was made of iron or copper. According to the theologian Symeon of Thessalonike (died 1429), the iron ring symbolized the firmness of character that the groom pledged to his bride; the gold ring represented the softness and purity of the woman.[12] The rings were exchanged three times, the more precious metal ultimately remaining with the man. The priest affirmed to each: "The servant of God [name] is engaged to the servant of God [name] in the name of the Father and of the Son and of the Holy Spirit." At the end of the ceremony the couple took communion, sealing the contract through the blessings of the church.

The subsequent marriage ceremony, or crowning, also took place inside the church. Texts from the period under discussion describe the blessing of the couple in front of the sanctuary portal, the reading of prayers, petitions regarding the propagation of children, the marking of the heads of the couple three times with marriage crowns, and the joining of the couple's hands before they took communion from a common cup.[13] As the priest held the marriage crowns over the heads of the bride and groom, he intoned a verse from Ps. 21:3 (LXX 20:3): "Thou hast set upon his head a crown of precious stone" (KJV). A nearly identical verse appears on a pair of tenth-century marriage crowns today in the Byzantine and Christian Museum in Athens (fig. 5.4). Each of the tin-plated copper crowns, nineteen centimeters in diameter, is incised with a cross and an inscription referring to the official Romanos, his wife, and their children. The use of the Psalm verse from the marriage ceremony as a supplemental inscription on the crowns suggests that these precious objects were used within the wedding rite.[14] The text of the rite is full of references to Old Testament marriages of renowned strength—Abraham and Sarah, Isaac and Rebecca, Jacob and Rachel—as well as to New Testament marriages, particularly the wedding at Cana. At the conclusion of the rite, according to several service books of the period, the couple was escorted from the church to their house.

Fig. 5.4. Marriage crowns naming the *spatharokandidatos* Romanos. Inscribed with a verse from Ps. 21:3-4 (LXX 20:3-4): "Thou hast set upon his head a crown of precious stone. He asked life of thee, and thou gavest him length of days for ever and ever" (KJV). The other inscription is an invocation: "Lord, help thy servant the *spatharokandidatos* Romanos, together with his wife and children." Photo: Byzantine and Christian Museum, Athens.

Health and Holy Water

The Byzantines often summoned the assistance of saints for help in healing a wide variety of ailments. The walls of churches were covered with images of healing saints carrying medical kits, surgical instruments, and vials of drugs. St. Anastasia the Pharmokolytria, for example, was easily identified by the vial she carried in her left hand, the antidote for poisons such as snakebites (fig. 10.1). Moreover, many churches constructed by laypeople, such as the aforementioned church of Sts. Cosmas and Damian at Kepoula, were dedicated to healing saints. Theodoros Lemniotes and his wife, Anna, a wealthy couple in the small city of Kastoria, redecorated a church dedicated to the same pair of medical saints around the year 1180. A verse inscription over the entrance to the nave demonstrates Theodoros's motive for the redecoration: "the recovery of my ailing flesh and the gift of bodily health." Orthodox Christians, as today, could also purchase inexpensive votive plaques to attach to sacred images. One eleventh-century plaque in the Dumbarton Oaks Collection in Washington, D.C., represents Hermolaos, the saint who was believed to have trained the popular healer Panteleimon (fig. 5.5). An inscription surrounds the central image of the saint: "For the health and salvation and forgiveness of the sins [of] . . ." The name of the donor is unfortunately lost, but this rare copper plaque provides precious evidence that Byzantines donated votive plaques to churches in order to seek the medical intervention of sacred healers.

Belief in the healing efficacy of holy water was widespread in Byzantium. Many monasteries contained sources of water considered therapeutic. Best documented is the Constantinopolitan Church of the Virgin, later called Zoodochos Pege (Life-Containing Source), whose miraculous

> **Dedicatory Inscription from the Church of the Holy Anargyroi, Kastoria, circa 1180**
>
> Time, the sower and in turn the destroyer of all things, has hastened to lay waste to your glorious house, holy dyad [Cosmas and Damian]. I, your faithful and humble servant Theodore, offspring of the Lemniotis [family], fighting against the ravages of time, have succeeded in bringing forth the decoration of the church from the very foundations up to the roof. But in vain I restore your columns through the desire of my tripartite soul. I raise the house of the holy dyad hoping to find there the ever-dewy grass and a place of the meek. And now, entreating to find the recovery of my ailing flesh and the gift of bodily health, and begging for this favor along with my wife and children.
>
> —Translation from Sharon E. J. Gerstel, *Beholding the Sacred Mysteries: Programs of the Byzantine Sanctuary* (Seattle: University of Washington Press, 1999), 89.

spring and association with the Mother of God effected numerous healings. The tenth-century *Life* of St. Luke of Stiris provides a different kind of information. The excellent preservation of his monastery offers the unusual opportunity to situate a written source within its physical setting. The monastery of Hosios Loukas (Holy Luke), where the saint's body was entombed, attracted local pilgrims, who sought healing through direct contact with the holy remains. At the southwest corner of the main church is a small chapel. The scene of the encounter of Christ and John the Baptist before Christ's baptism occupies the upper register of the east and north walls. The placement of the figures, as if in dialogue, on adjacent walls and the prominent inscribing of the very Gospel verses that were read during the service of the Great Blessing of the Waters on the eve of Theophany (January 6, corresponding to Western Epiphany) (Matt. 3:13-16) demonstrates that the chamber was employed for this rite. The discovery of a fragmented marble basin below the pavement confirms this function of the space. The apex of the chamber's vault, above the presumed site of the font, depicts the hand of God in a gesture of blessing against a background of stars (color gallery, plate D). The hand and sleeve constitute one arm of a cross. Thus the imagery in the chamber links the space with the rite that took place within. In likelihood, visiting pilgrims collected the blessed water.

The rite of the Great Blessing of the Waters followed vespers on the Feast of the Theophany. The ceremony could take place inside the church, as at Hosios Loukas, or over a *phiale*, a large basin, in the courtyard. From the ninth century, Byzantine service books attest both locations. At the conclusion of the liturgy the priest would approach the *phiale* preceded by candles and incense. According to one eleventh- or twelfth-century service book (Mount Sinai, Monastery of St. Catherine, ms. 973), "the priest, taking the holy cross, blesses the waters, saying: 'Christ is baptized, He who removes the sins of the world. John baptizes Christ, the remover of sins. Christ is baptized, He who removes the sins of the world.' And when everyone has been blessed by the sprinkling of water, the chanters begin the *troparion* 'In the Jordan' in the first tone. And this is sung three times at the *phiale*, and in the narthex, and in the nave."[15]

In communities that bordered the sea or were close to rivers or springs, the priest would consecrate the waters by throwing a cross into their depths. A member of the community would then retrieve the cross from the frigid waters. Although the casting of the cross into the sea is still practiced in modern Orthodox communities, surviving service books contain no reference to this practice. Most of these collected works, however, derive from monasteries that would have used a *phiale* for the celebration. Documentary evidence for the ritual retrieval of the cross, however, is found in a fifteenth-century Genoese statute from Kaffa that describes the Orthodox rituals that took place in this multicultural Crimean trading center. The text details the outlay of money for a number of feasts, including the Blessing of the Waters: "The expenses ought to take place yearly on the feast of the Epiphany as written below. First of all, the Greeks who come to the palace and sing the *kalimera* should be given two hundred asperi. Likewise to those boys who dive into the sea when the priest blesses the water, seventy-five asperi. To those priests who chant lauds in the palace courtyard, one hundred asperi. Likewise to the person who sounds the bell, six asperi."[16] Dated to January 4, 1440, this document confirms that at least as early as the mid-fifteenth century the cross was thrown into and retrieved from the sea during the feast.

Fig. 5.6. Portrait of St. Kyriake with adjacent inscription: "Supplication of the Servant of God, Kyriake, and of her husband, Nicholas Orphanos. Amen." Church of St. Panteleimon, Upper Boularioi, Mani, 991/92. Photo: Sharon E. J. Gerstel.

The importance of holy water in the life of the layperson also informed the decoration and furnishing of many late Byzantine churches. In smaller churches without narthexes the scene of the baptism appears at ground level rather than in the narrative sequence of images in the central vault. In churches with narthexes the scene of baptism often appears on the east wall of that space. Some churches preserve evidence of a small font or drain in this location. In all likelihood, the representation of the baptism together with a small basin signals that the rite of the *mikros agiasmos*, the Lesser Blessing of the Waters, took place at this site. This rite was celebrated on the first of every month except January and September.[17] Service books place this rite within the church. One service book of 1027 (Paris, Bibliothèque Nationale, Coislin 213) was written for a priest named Strategios, who served at the church of St. Sophia in Constantinople.[18] The text states that the service of the Lesser Blessing of the Waters takes place "in various churches on Sundays and holidays in the narthex or in other parts of the church, using a *phiale* or a basin.... [The ceremony] takes place after the beginning of the holy liturgy, the chanting of the antiphons, and following the end of the blessing of the waters, the entrance takes place and the rest of the holy liturgy follows."[19] The service, inserted into the liturgy before the First Entrance of the Gospels, includes prayers to both the Virgin and Christ, who heal the body and soul. A series of petitions also concerns spiritual and physical cleansing. The short service concludes with intercessory prayers to

Fig. 5.7. Basin for holy water and scene of the baptism of Christ. Narthex, Church of Sts. Peter and Paul, Kalyvia, Attica, Greece. Photo: Sharon E. J. Gerstel.

popular medical saints, including Cosmas, Damian, Panteleimon, and Hermolaos, Panteleimon's teacher. These prayers and the selection of specific intercessory saints attest the Byzantine belief in the curative powers of the blessed waters.

The relationship of the baptismal imagery and the Lesser Blessing of the Waters is clearly seen in the early thirteenth-century church of Sts. Peter and Paul at Kalyvia, near Athens. In this village church, a font is embedded in the north wall of the narthex. On the east wall, immediately adjacent, is a niche containing a scene of Christ's baptism (fig. 5.7). An attendant angel represented on the adjacent wall offers a cloth to Christ. Depicted above the baptism are the prophets David and Isaiah, who extend their right hands in gestures of benediction. Isaiah holds in his left hand an open scroll inscribed, "Wash yourselves and be clean. Put away the evil of your deeds" (Isa. 1:16). The exhortation to spiritual cleansing offered warning and guidance to the parishioners and is related to the monthly rite that took place in this part of the church. The laity and clergy alike preserved the blessed water for times of sickness, for sanctification, and for ritual celebration.

Work and Prayer

The stories of the lives of saints, prayers within service books, and the decorated church all reveal a concern with the agricultural activities of Byzantine villages. Byzantine Christians attributed to a number of their saints the power to save crops and heal livestock. In the tenth-century *Life* of Elias Speleotes, for example, villagers call upon the saint to heal a horse. The saint sends a monk to bring him a cup filled with water. The saint, "making the sign of the cross says, 'Go, my brother, and opening the mouth of the horse, pour into it this blessed water and the Lord God will perform his charity quickly.' And after this took place, immediately the horse got up from the ground and shook himself and stood full of health and unharmed."[20] Service books from the late Byzantine period record prayers that the priest would read for the planting of vines, for the healing of sick olive trees, for the sowing of seeds, and for a bountiful harvest. Within churches in the Byzantine countryside, saints such as Mamas and Tryphon,

Fig. 5.8. St. Mamas. Church of Sts. Peter and Paul, Kalyvia, Attica, Greece. Photo: Sharon E. J. Gerstel.

represented with goats or sheep cradled in their arms and shepherds' staffs resting against their shoulders, offered heavenly intercession on behalf of livestock (fig. 5.8). Within agricultural communities, where parishioners were largely unlettered, the representation of saints such as Polykarpos (literally, "much fruit") may have evoked, through the repetition of their names, a potent wish for healthy crops. The connection between the church and the agricultural cycle was deeply ingrained in the Byzantine mind, and even in the larger cities public ceremonies recalled agricultural activities, such as the harvest of the first grapes. So, too, Byzantine funerary literature used the agricultural cycle as a metaphor for the human life span comparing the deceased to all manners of plants, from cut vines to stalks of wheat ready to be harvested.

Church buildings and services played vital roles in the daily and ritual lives of the Byzantine laity, whether in city or village. The church exerted enormous authority over communal celebration and judicial practices. Preserved sources portray both men and women as deeply religious. However, some texts also suggest that many Byzantines preferred to work or play rather than attend services or adhere to church strictures. It would appear that, as with most aspects of medieval society, the religious life of the average Byzantine was more complicated than we might at first believe. The church provided an alternative space where, for a brief moment or through the duration of the service, the faithful mingled with the holy through participation in the communion rite, interaction with his or her name saint, censing by the priest, or imbibing holy water. The invitation to experience another spatial and temporal world through the medium of faith and the strength of communal belief made the Orthodox church and the church building a potent force in the Byzantine belief system, tightly binding the faithful even after the fall of the empire in 1453.

FOR FURTHER READING

Cormack, Robin. *Byzantine Art.* Oxford: Oxford University Press, 2000.

Gerstel, Sharon E. J. *Beholding the Sacred Mysteries: Programs of the Byzantine Sanctuary.* Seattle: College Art Association and University of Washington Press, 1999.

———. "Painted Sources for Female Piety in Medieval Byzantium." *DOP* 52 (1998): 89–103.

Mathews, Thomas F. *Byzantium: From Antiquity to the Renaissance.* New York: Abrams, 1998.

Ousterhout, Robert. "Holy Space: Architecture and the Liturgy." In Linda Safran, ed., *Heaven on Earth: Art and the Church in Byzantium* (University Park: Pennsylvania State University Press, 2002), 81–120.

Taft, Robert F. "The Frequency of the Eucharist throughout History." In *Beyond East and West: Problems in Liturgical Understanding*, 2nd ed. (Rome: Pontifical Institute, 1997), 87–110.

———. "Women at Church in Byzantium: Where, When—and Why?" *DOP* 52 (1998): 27–87.

DEATH AND DYING
IN BYZANTIUM

NICHOLAS CONSTAS

CHAPTER SIX

The religious nature of much surviving Byzantine literature has ensured that Byzantine funerary practices and attitudes toward death are abundantly documented. Wills and testaments, epitaphs and inscriptions, eulogies and funeral orations, letters of consolation, dirges and laments, magical texts and the literature of dream interpretation, along with the rulings of civil and ecclesiastical law, all witness the realities, both material and metaphysical, of death and dying in the Byzantine world. Hagiographical works, invariably concerned with the final hours of their saintly subjects, and the sermons of popular preachers, especially John Chrysostom, describe a broad range of funerary customs and practices. In addition, a number of treatises deal directly with the rituals of death and burial, such as the sixth-century commentary *On the Burial Service*, by Pseudo-Dionysius the Areopagite, and *On Death and the Burial Service*, written in the fifteenth century by Symeon of Thessalonike. Moreover, a profusion of theological literature deals with the soul's departure from the body, its immediate postmortem experiences, and its prospects for torment or bliss in a life beyond the grave. The evidence of art and iconography, together with artifacts derived from cemeteries, grave sites, funerary chapels, tombs, mausoleums, and sarcophagi, provide additional perspectives. Despite this obvious wealth of material, many aspects of death and dying in Byzantium remain unknown, largely due to the unevenness of the extant sources with respect to gender, social class, geographical region, and historical period.

THE HOUR OF DEATH

When death appeared imminent, those with wealth or property arranged for a notary to prepare a will (*diataxis, diathēkē*), which was drawn up in the presence of witnesses who certified that the signatory was, in a legal formula inherited from Greek antiquity, "of sound mind and body." The services of a priest might also be required, especially if the dying wished to confess sins and receive the sacrament of the eucharist (a separate sacrament of "last rites" being unknown in Byzantium). Others could request monastic tonsure, receive a new name, and go to their graves in the garments of a monk or nun. Those who had not been baptized in infancy, an increasingly rare occurrence after the Late Antique period, could accept initiation into the Christian faith on their deathbed, as was famously the case with the emperor Constantine (Eusebius, *Life of Constantine* 61–63).

For many Byzantines the arrival of the priest was a clear sign that the end was near, and it often provoked cries and lamentations from the members of the household. Symeon of Thessalonike reports that some of the dying refused to receive the eucharist, fearing that it would only hasten their demise (*On Death*, PG 155.672). Others hoped to expire with the sacrament yet in their mouth, believing that it would guarantee entrance into heaven. Throughout these observances, family members and friends would gather around the deathbed, seeking to comfort the dying and to console one another. The dramatic deathbed scene was a major trope in Byzantine sacred and secular literature, and it is not always easy to disentangle historical description from cultural expectations and rhetorical embellishment.[1] Although the Byzantines prayed for a "peaceful end to their lives" (*Liturgy of St. John Chrysostom*), the dying could nonetheless be expected to undergo an agonizing struggle (*psychomachia*), as the soul fought to free itself from the body. It was widely believed that at such moments the dying could see their guardian angel, or a choir of angels, who had come to receive the departing soul. Church paintings of the later period often depict the deceased in the company of the archangel Michael, the "escort of souls" (*psychopomp*). When life finally yielded, the dead were said to have "fallen asleep," a phrase inscribed on numerous Byzantine tombstones. While clearly a comforting euphemism, the notion of death as "sleep" was also a religious concept central to the New Testament (Mark 5:39; John 11:11; 1 Thess. 4:13) that the Byzantines developed at great length.[2]

WASHING AND ANOINTING

With the arrival of death, preparations for the burial began in earnest. The surviving family members had much to do. The care of the dead fell largely upon women, partly as an extension of their domestic responsibilities and partly as a result of their lower social status in a male-dominated society. Nevertheless, there is ample evidence that male members of the family, along with male servants, also participated in the arrangements. The first act was to close the eyes and the mouth of the departed, fold the arms across the chest (or straighten them at the sides), and stretch out the legs. Michael Psellos notes that his nine-year-old daughter, upon sensing the approach of death, folded her own hands across her chest.[3] Psellos was devastated by the loss of his only child, presumably to smallpox. Death was in general a major blow to the Byzantine family, which, in the words of Chrysostom, was thereby "crushed under sorrow as if under the oppressive weight of a dark winter's day" (*Baptismal Catecheses*, PG 49.224).

Despite the tragic atmosphere, work continued with the washing of the body, often lustrated with perfumed, aromatic water (Gregory of Nazianzus, *Letters*, PG 37.64; *Passion of Artemios*, PG 96.1316; see also Mark 16:1; Luke 24:1; John 12:1-7). In the case of the wealthy, expensive unguents could be used in large quantities, overwhelming the cortege with heavy fragrance. An obvious display of wealth, perfumes also served a very practical purpose. In the *Life of Synkletike*, the author notes that in the heat of summer the process of decay could be slowed or at least masked by a mixture of "aloe, myrrh, myrtle, and wine" (PG 28.1556). In the twelfth century, ecclesiastical law condemned the practice of anointing the bodies of the clergy with *myron*, a fragrant, consecrated oil used in baptisms, which indicates that such anointings indeed took place.[4] Perhaps in avoidance of both theological error and worldly ostentation, Symeon of Thessalonike directed that the bodies of monks and clergymen be sponged simply with clean water, making the sign of the cross on their foreheads, eyes, lips, chest, knees, and hands (*On Death,* PG 155.676).

CLOTHING AND SHROUDING

Bathing was followed by dressing the deceased in his or her best clothes, preferably white or a bright color—and thus "white clothing" seen in dreams was a "sign of death" (see Artemidorus, *Dreambook* 2.3). Here a degree of caution was required, for those buried in lavish clothing and expensive jewelry were in danger from grave robbers. In some instances those who died at a young age, before marriage, were buried in bridal costume. The body was then wrapped in a special shroud, the *savanon,* which was also called a "Lazarus" (*Lazároma*) (see John 11:44).[5] These large pieces of cloth, along with longer, gauze-like wrappings containing the head, hands, and feet, recalled the swaddling cloths of infants, a similarity that supported the belief that death was actually a birth into a new life (John Chrysostom, *On Fasting*, PG 60.715; *Hom. on Matt.,* PG 57.348; *Hom. on John*, PG 59.351) (fig. 6.1).

In the Byzantine association of birth and death, the sorrows of the latter were frequently compared to the pangs of childbirth (Basil, *Homily on Psalm 114*). These associations are evident in the iconography of the death of the Virgin Mary, known as the "Dormition" (falling asleep), in which her soul is depicted as a small, swaddled infant, wide awake in the arms of the adult Christ (fig. 6.2). On the day of his own birth, moreover, the infant Christ appears swaddled like a miniature mummy, reclining in a monumental crib. Illustrations of the scriptural verse "The souls of the righteous are in the hand of God" (Wis. 3:1) depict the souls of the departed as small infants, tightly bound in swaddling clothes.[6]

In addition to the practice of shrouding, monks and clergy were buried in their habits and ecclesiastical vestments; royalty were interred in their imperial regalia. With their arms folded across their chest, laypeople would have an icon placed in their hands; monks, the Psalter; and clergy, the book of the Gospels, symbols of their religious stations and devotional practices (Symeon of Thessalonike, *On Death,*

Fig. 6.1. The raising of Lazarus, fresco from the Church of St. Athanasius, Kastoria, Greece, late fourteenth century. Photo: Velis Voutsas.

PG 155.676). The twelfth-century bishop and canonist Theodore Balsamon notes that bishops were given a piece of blessed bread to hold "as an apotropaic device against demons, and as a provision for the journey to heaven" (*Syntagma*, 2/496).

THE RITUAL LAMENT

With the body thus prepared, the elaborate, ritualized process of mourning and lament (*thrēnos*) could begin.[7] It was customary for the female survivors to engage in dramatic expressions of grief and loss, beginning with the loosening of their hair (normally kept pinned or braided and covered), which they then grasped and pulled, often with great violence. These women tore open their clothing and wailed loud laments and sharp ululations, much to the annoyance of the clergy, who frequently complained and considered it demeaning to women. Female servants were expected to participate in these ritual laments,

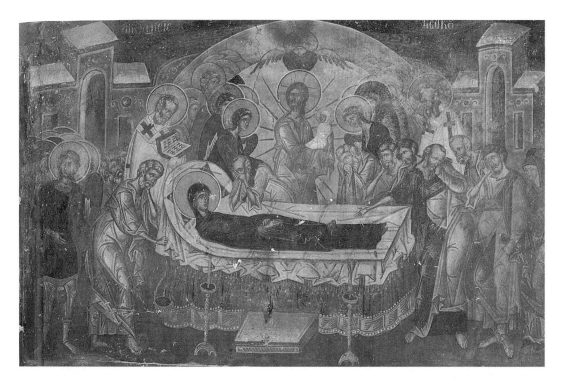

Fig. 6.2. The dormition, or falling asleep, of the Virgin, fresco from the Church of St. Athanasius, Kastoria, late fourteenth century. The bishop on the left holds an open book with the initial words of Psalm 118: "Blessed are the blameless on their way." Photo: Velis Voutsas.

often in place of their wealthy mistress, a practice also condemned by the church as an abuse of the poor (John Chrysostom, *Hom. on John*, PG 59.347–48). Male members of the household participated to a lesser extent, and they likewise pulled on their hair and beards and tore at their clothing (*Life of Neophytos the Recluse*). Related ritual behaviors included falling and sitting on the ground, throwing dirt on one's head and face, striking the head, the arms, and the knees, and in extreme cases creating self-inflicted wounds and bloodletting.[8] Religious leaders were concerned about such practices, which they viewed in part as a lack of faith in the resurrection (John Chrysostom, *Hom. on 1 Cor.*, PG 61.29; *Hom. on 1 Thess.*, PG 62.430, 450). Thus every Byzantine funeral service included a passage from 1 Thessalonians chiding Christians who "grieve as those who have no hope" (1 Thess. 4:13-18), along with the story of Lazarus, whom Christ had raised from the dead (John 11:1-44).

Reinforcing ancient traditions, the Byzantine church developed an elaborate ritual burial service for Christ, conducted on Holy Friday. An outstanding feature of this ceremony was the "lament of the Virgin," in which Mary assumes the role of a Byzantine mother, mourning the tragic loss of her son. Choirs voiced her sorrowful elegies, while icons and monumental paintings depicted her grief (fig. 6.3). With the figure of the dead Christ lying in the foreground on a large stone slab, the Virgin appears falling into a swoon, slumping onto the ground, supported by her female friends, clutching at her tresses, or lamenting in songs the death of her only child.[9]

In addition to family members, friends, and servants, the requiem could be joined, and even conducted, by groups of professional women mourners who were practiced in traditional laments and could improvise as needed, based on the circumstances of death and the requests of their patrons (Gregory of Nyssa, *On Pulcheria*, PG 46.876; John Chrysostom, *Hom. on Matt.*, PG 57.374; *Hom. on John*,

Fig. 6.3. The lament of the Virgin. Church of the Virgin Peribleptos (now St. Kliment), Ohrid, Macedonia. Photo: Erich Lessing/Art Resource, NY.

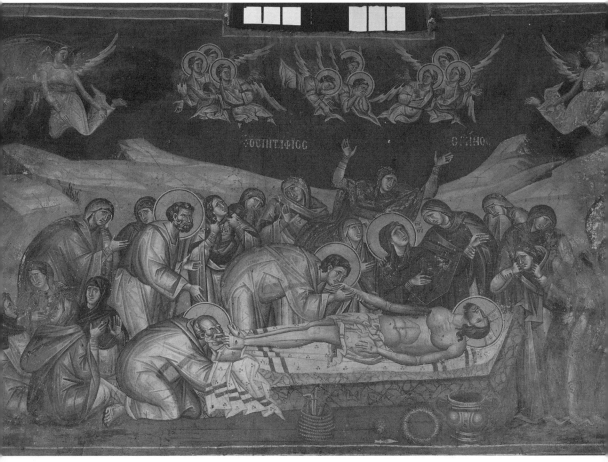

PG 59.467; *On Patience*, 60.726). Distant echoes of these popular dirges survive in the exalted liturgical laments of Holy Friday, in which the departed is intimately addressed as "my soul," "my life," "my light," the "light of my eyes," "my breath," "my sweet springtime," and so on. But what was exemplary in theory was not always appreciated in practice, and the dramatic extremes of which the professional mourners were capable provoked criticisms from church authorities, who considered them troublesome remnants of a pagan culture (John Chrysostom, *Hom. on Matt.,* PG 57.374; Michael Psellos, 5/366). As we might expect, the family continued to grieve long after the burial, and the *Life of Euphrosyne* describes a scene in which the survivors are moved to laments upon finding an article of clothing belonging to the deceased (PG 114.36).

THE CASKET AND FUNERAL SERVICE

The interval between the moment of death and the time of burial varied with the location and time of year. In the summer months, it was not possible for the dead to be waked for more than a few hours, or perhaps a day at most. In the absence of embalming techniques, most people were buried on the first day after their death.[10] During times of famines or earthquakes, when there were large numbers of bodies awaiting burial and only a small number available to dig graves, Byzantine writers comment on the unusual situation in which the bodies of the dead remained unburied for three days or more.[11]

When the laments concluded (or at least subsided), the body was taken to the local church or cemetery chapel for a funeral service. The shrouded corpse, placed on a simple pallet, would be carried to the church upon the shoulders of the relatives and friends of the departed. Caskets, if used, were typically made of plain wood or, in the case of the wealthy, more expensive cedar and cypress. In some areas, simple caskets could be acquired from churches and benevolent societies, who lent them out as needed and received them back after the funeral (Asterios of Amaseia, *Homilies*, PG 40.185; see also 61.787). Funeral expenses varied according to one's means, although cutting corners was considered a disgrace, especially if the family was wealthy. In a papyrus from Byzantine Egypt, a father's dying wish was that "my beloved sons provide me with a funeral worthy of my person."[12] Early Byzantine emperors, beginning with Constantine, sought to regulate the funeral business to enable the poor to bury their loved ones with a basic standard of dignity and decorum. The same laws were repromulgated in the sixth century (Justinian, *Novella* 1.387) and again in the ninth (Leo the Wise, PG 107.449), suggesting that they were not consistently adhered to. In many instances the needs of the poor were met by charitable guilds and societies (Theodore of Stoudios, PG 99.953).

At the church, the body was usually placed in the narthex. Bishops were typically laid out in the nave, close to the altar, although laypeople and monks could also be placed there depending on the circumstances (Symeon of Thessalonike, *On Death,* PG 155.685). The casket remained open, with the face of the departed exposed to view. Viewing the deceased was important. At the funeral of Basil of Caesarea, the eulogist remarked that the crowd pressed round the casket in order to see his face one last time (Gregory of Nazianzus, *Oration on Basil*, PG 36.601). The same was true at the funeral of Basil's sister Macrina, whose face was gazed upon with great devotion by those she left behind (Gregory of Nyssa, *Life of Macrina*, PG 46.993). At the funerals of those considered saints, such as a revered monastic figure, some might try to take a part of the shroud or a piece of the clothing as a blessed relic (*Life of Eusebia*, PG 114.997; *Life of Avramios*, PG 155.77; *Life of Theodore of Stoudios*, PG 99.165). In the *Life of St. Ignatios* the mourners went so far as to break apart the bed frame and tear up the sheets upon which the saint had spent his last hours. At the funeral of St. Eustratios of Augarus the crowd attempted to take not only the saint's clothing but locks of his hair and even his limbs.[13]

The funeral service itself (reckoned by some to be a sacrament) stressed the vanity of worldly pursuits, offered prayers for the repose of the departed, and invited the congregation to approach the body for a final farewell, the ceremonial of the last kiss. Death was presented as a separation both from the body and from the world, but also as a transition to a place of rest, free from all pain, sorrow, and corruption. As a rite of passage, death was said to herald the victory over instability and the transitory nature of human existence, a victory marked in advance by Christ and the martyrs, whom the liturgy constantly invoked. Indeed, the very structure of the service paralleled the ritual burial of Christ on Holy Friday, making every funeral an echo of Christ's, thereby infusing it with the promise of resurrection. At the service's conclusion, the body was taken to the place of burial, preceded by the chanters and flanked by the clergy carrying candles. It was customary to chant the Trisagion ("Holy God, Holy Mighty, Holy Immortal, have mercy on us"); and verses from Psalm 119 ("Blessed are the blameless on the way"; LXX 118). If the procession was lengthy and passed through public streets and squares, the professional mourners resumed their lamentations, although Chrysostom found such behavior disgraceful and feared that it would scandalize the non-Christians who might chance to see it (John Chrysostom, *On Laz.*, PG 48.1020; *Hom. on John*, 59.346; *Hom. on Phil.*, PG 62.203; *Hom. on Heb.*, PG 63.42–44).

Despite the church's efforts to minimize excessive outbursts and dramatic scenes, they were often beyond control. Byzantine law books, for example, note that if a person had died in debt, it was not unusual for the creditors to appear at the home or the cemetery, seeking to seize payment in whatever form was available. Funerals were at times disrupted and processions brought to a halt; one can readily imagine the discomfort this caused the surviving family members (*Pandects* 11.7.38). Against such acts of civil disturbance, the government issued harsh laws, imposing imprisonment and fines, a portion of which was given to the family. Those caught taking bribes were stripped of their rank and fined, and they could even be exiled, degrees of punishment that indicate the severity of the problem (*Code of Justinian* 9.19.6;

A Funeral Hymn of John of Damascus (circa 675–749)

What earthly delight endures unmingled with grief? What earthly glory remains immutable? All things are less than a shadow, more deluding than a dream. In a single moment all these are effaced by death; but in the light of Your countenance, O Christ, and in the enjoyment of Your beauty, grant rest to the one whom You have chosen; for You love mankind.

O what an ordeal must the soul endure when it parts from the body! O how profusely that soul weeps, and there is no one to show it pity. It turns its eyes to the angels and its prayer is in vain. It extends its hands to men and finds no one to help. Therefore, my beloved brethren, considering the brevity of our life, let us beseech from Christ mercy for our souls. . . .

Where is the attachment to the world? Where is the allurement of all that is temporal? Where is silver and gold? Where is the multitude of servants and anxieties? All is dust, all is ashes, all is shadow. Come, let us cry out to the Immortal King: O Lord, deem worthy of Your eternal blessings the one who has departed from us, granting him rest in Your ageless bliss.

—PG 96.1368–69

Pandects 48.6.3; *Novella* 1.450–54, 2.378). While a family was in mourning, it could not be taken to court, and, if currently involved in litigation, the trial was postponed for nine days (*Novella* 2.195).

CEMETERIES AND ASPECTS OF BURIAL

In the ancient Mediterranean the bodies of the dead were considered unclean and buried outside of the city or town. This was also a practical consideration because of the limited availability of space in heavily populated areas, and the practice continued in the early Byzantine period. By the fourth century most cemeteries had churches and chapels, used almost exclusively for burial services, along with various mausoleums and shrines. By the seventh century, however, cemeteries began to be built within urban spaces, such as the site of the city's ancient agora. Constantinople, moreover, had subterranean chambers, called *hypogaea*, which accommodated various tombs, often separated by walls with fresco paintings on them. In ordinary cemeteries the bodies were placed in tile-lined graves that were covered with a mound of dirt, then layered with plaster. Canon law dictated that the dead be buried in individual caskets, but in the event of plague and famine this was not always possible, and at times two or more bodies were placed in a single casket or conveyed on carts or simply wrapped in sheets and placed over horses to be brought to the cemetery (Theodore of Stoudios, PG 99.805). In the case of disease the body would be covered with a layer of lime before the grave was filled with soil. Other restrictions applied as well: laymen, for example, could not be buried in the cemeteries of convents. In some instances there were special graveyards for criminals and especially murderers (*Life of Andrew of Crete*, PG 115.1125).

In general the laity were not interred within churches. Church interments of laypeople were officially banned under Theodosius I (*Theodosian Code* 9.17.1) and likewise anathematized by canon law, although they continued to occur. Among those buried in churches were usually the building's donors (along with their family members), who were almost always from among the wealthiest or most influential strata of society. Aristocratic patrons typically found repose either within an arched niche, in a stone sarcophagus, or beneath the pavement of the church. The arched niche, called an arcosolium, was a feature of Christian burial dating back to the time of the Roman catacombs. It was constructed in front of a wall, into which a cavity had been excavated for the interment of the body. For the late Byzantine period, elaborately carved arcosolia are much in evidence, such as those in the funerary chapel and exonarthex of the Monastery of the Chora in Constantinople (color gallery, plate E).[14] The sarcophagus was a decorated stone coffin carved from expensive materials, often hewn from a single stone. In the late Byzantine period sarcophagi were more typically assembled from marble plaques and panels. Interment could also be in a grave cut into the pavement, generally in the floor of the narthex, which could be reopened for additional burials. In some cases subsidiary chapels were annexed to the nave or narthex and likewise used for burials. However, no single burial type was limited to a particular area of the church, and each can be found in narthexes, naves, porches, side chapels, burial chambers, and crypts.[15]

As the body was about to be buried, the priest anointed it with oil, which he poured on the body in the sign of the cross. Given the virtual equivalence of the words "oil" (*elaion*) and "mercy" (*eleos*), the rite was said to symbolize the church's hope that the departed would meet with God's mercy (Pseudo-Dionysius, *On the Ecclesiastical Hierarchy*, PG 3.565; Symeon of Thessalonike, *On Death*, PG 155.685). Within the casket itself relatives and friends might place various objects, such as ceramic sherds inscribed with the sign of the cross to repel evil spirits. Flasks of oil have also been found within graves, but their use is uncertain. Other, more expensive objects, such as pieces of jewelry and coins, could also be included. Afterwards, the body was placed in the grave, oriented whenever possible with its head toward the west, so that, upon rising, it would be facing east, the direction from which Christ would appear at the time of his second coming (see Matt. 24:27). Bodies were normally buried, cremation being considered a pagan practice. Byzantine cultural memory had not forgotten pagan attempts to burn and thus utterly obliterate the bodies of martyrs, in order to mock their faith in the Resurrection (Eusebius, *Church History* 5.2.62). Finally, Christ himself was buried, which alone, it was reasoned, provided sufficient precedent for his followers.

Burial was thus a strong religious and social obligation, and to leave a body unburied, or to bury it in an inappropriate manner, was considered an act of great impiety and a terrible misfortune for the deceased. Military manuals impressed upon generals the need to see that the fallen were properly buried (*Tactics* 16.13; PG 107.909). According to popular legends, the falcon, if it spotted an unburied body, would cover it with dirt, thus witnessing to the "universal law of nature" regarding the burial of the dead (Eustathios of Antioch, *On the Hexameron*, PG 18.749; compare John Chrysostom, *On Babylas*, PG 50.527; *Hom. on 1 Cor.*, PG 61.305; *Eclogues*, PG 63.642). For those lost at sea, and in other situations in which burial was impossible, the church had annual commemorations known as "Saturdays of the Souls" (*psychosabbata*), when prayers were said for those deprived of a proper funeral. While it did not forbid their burial, the Byzantine church did not perform funeral services for non-Christians (including infants who died before baptism), schismatics, and others under various ecclesiastical anathemas or for those who had taken their own life, provided they were not suffering from mental illness (*Syntagma* 2/12; 6/149). Orthodox Christians had to be buried by Orthodox clergy, although Theodore of Stoudios allowed for a heretical priest to preside in the absence of an Orthodox one (PG 99.1652). After the schism between the Latin church and the Byzantine, Orthodox clergy were not permitted to conduct funeral services for Roman Catholics.

Families were generally buried in the same cemetery, often with a stone plaque (*stele*), which could be either a simple marker or a work of carved marble inscribed with elaborate epitaphs, depending on the resources of the family. Epitaphs could be either in prose or in verse, often written by celebrated poets, such as Manuel Philes, who wrote a large number of epigrams for the tombs of his aristocratic patrons.[16] More prosaic epitaphs gave the name of the deceased, along with the date of their death and a brief supplication for his or her repose. More expansive inscriptions could include detailed information about the life of the deceased, for example, if he or she was married or single, the name of the spouse, and whether children had been left behind. In times of intense theological controversies, which inevitably triggered social divisions, the epitaph could also indicate that the deceased was an Orthodox Christian (Theophylact of Bulgaria, PG 126.188).

Gravestones could also be ornamented with crosses. For those able to afford a mausoleum or arcosolium, family and friends could place inside small oil lamps and icons, some with special inscriptions on them. Painted grave portraits are known from at least the fifth century (John Chrysostom, *On Babylas*, PG 50.556) and were, in the eleventh century, the subject of an epigram by Christopher of Mytilene, who wrote "on the tomb of the patrician Melios, which is painted with images of him both as a layman and as a monk."[17] From the twelfth century we have the detailed account of the crown prince Isaac, the Sebastokrator (born 1093), who designed his own mausoleum. Intended initially for the Monastery of the Chora in Constantinople, Isaac's tomb consisted of a large marble coffin, with silver inlay and revetment, around which was a protective bronze grille or railing. Affixed to the tomb were stands holding mosaic icons in expensive frames, along with portraits of him and his parents, all of which had to be properly lighted and maintained.[18]

After the burial it was customary for the family to return to the home of the deceased for a memorial meal. In addition the church had a series of memorial services (*mnemosyna*), which were conducted on the third, ninth, and fortieth day after death and again on the first anniversary. Byzantine writers offer different explanations for these dates. Some associated them with certain days in the life of Christ. Others believed that the soul, like a bird seeking its nest, remained on earth for three days, hovering about the place of its death, sorrowful at the prospect of leaving the world and the body. Still others understood these services to mark the gradual dissolution of the body, in what was essentially a reversal of the body's original formation in the womb. The human face, for example, was believed to take shape on the third day after conception and thus decompose on the third day after death. The heart was believed to be the material and spiritual core of the self, and, unlike the rest of the body, it survived until the fortieth day, when it too was finally dissolved.[19] As the deceased (body and soul) made his or her gradual transition into another state of existence, the family would gather for prayer, bringing offerings of *kollyva* to the church, a dish of boiled wheat mixed with almonds, nuts, and raisins (*Syntagma*, 2/6; Symeon of Thessalonike, PG 155.688–89). The *mnemosyna* were followed by visits to the grave for additional prayers and on occasion a simple memorial meal.

In many monastic communities the bodies of monks were exhumed after enough time had elapsed to ensure thorough decomposition (usually a few years). Once the bones were recovered, they were cleaned and placed together with any surviving grave goods in a common ossuary. The latter could take the form of a separate structure or a tomb or tombs built into or annexed to the monastery's cemetery chapel. The bones of laypeople were also exhumed and could be reburied with the bones of family members or placed in ossuaries attached to small churches. In some instances monastic ossuaries served as places for informal reflection on the transience of human life.[20]

GRAVE ROBBING

Despite the church's prayers for eternal repose, the sleep of the dead was frequently disturbed. Expensive clothing and other valuables encouraged grave robbing (John Chrysostom, *On Psalms*, PG 55.231; *Homily on the Letter to the Philippians*, PG 61.293), which constituted a major social problem, reflected in the large number of laws repeatedly issued against it. John Chrysostom, for example, repeatedly warns his wealthy congregants that their ostentatious burials provoked rampant grave robbing (*On Psalms*, PG 55.239), and Gregory of Nazianzus gave voice to the affluent who "wished to be buried in utter poverty, so as to escape the notice of grave robbers" (*Epigrams*, PG 38.124; see *Life of Ephrem*, PG 114.1261, 1268). Cemetery wardens were often beaten and killed, and repeat offenders, if armed with weapons, were liable to the death penalty; others were sent into exile (*Basilika* 60.23). Leo the Wise ordered that grave robbers be punished by having one of their hands cut off (PG 107.616). The church took its own measures, and a ruling ascribed to Basil of Caesarea prohibits grave robbers from receiving the eucharist for two years (PG 32.800). John the Almsgiver (died circa 620) limited the excommunication to one year, during which time the offender was required to perform two hundred prostrations every day (*Syntagma*, 4/444). To discourage such crimes, the family may have poured perfumed oils on the clothing, which they may have even torn in order to render it useless for sale (John Chrysostom, *Hom.*

on John, PG 59.465). Like the bodies within them, the grave sites them-selves were considered sacred, and the markers and other objects were protected by law; violators were threatened with harsh punishments, including fines, imprisonment, and exile (*Code of Justinian* 9.191–95; *Theodosian Code* 3.16.1; *Pandects* 47.12). A canon ascribed to Gregory of Nyssa enjoins leniency upon those who simply disturbed markers, but not for those who disturbed the bones of the dead (*Syntagma,* 4/326–27; compare PG 45.233).

THE LIFE OF THE WORLD TO COME

The Byzantines believed rather strongly that death was not the end; there is virtually no evidence of Byzantine disbelief in some form of an afterlife. At the same time the Byzantines recognized that the life of the soul outside the body was perhaps easier for the mystic to experi-ence than for the theologian to define. With their healthy appreciation for the limits of rationalism, thoughtful Byzantines acknowledged that systematic definitions in matters of faith were not only elusive but per-haps undesirable. Thus, apart from the belief in the soul's ability to sur-vive the death of the body and an affirmation of a future resurrection into a status determined by one's earthly actions, the Byzantine church never officially elaborated on the details of life after death. As we might expect, such a lacuna offered an irresistible opportunity for specula-tion, and many questions about death and the afterlife remained open for discussion. What happened at the moment of death? What did the soul experience as it left the body, and where, if anywhere, did it go? What was the world of spirits like? Would family members and friends recognize one another in the altered state of the resurrection?

The soul's departure from the body was understood to be a critical moment of self-discovery, when one's true character would be uncov-ered and revealed.[21] The sixth-century monastic teacher Dorotheus of Gaza, for example, believed that the thoughts and mental images to which the soul had become habituated in life would constitute its new environment and reality as consciousness passed into eternity. In death, therefore, thoughts and memories would have as much power over the self as they had in life, indeed more so, Dorotheus argues,

Prayer of Symeon the Fool upon the death of his mother, from Leontius of Neapolis's *Life of Symeon the Fool,* 640s

Lord, for my, your servant's sake, accept the soul of my good mother. Remember, God, the trouble and distress which she suffered on my account. . . . Grant her angels who will keep her soul safe from the spirits and beasts of the air, evil and unmerciful beings who endeavor to swallow up everything which comes into their midst. Lord, Lord, send out to her mighty guards to rebuke every impure power molesting her, and, my God, command that her soul be separated from her body without pain or torture. And if, being a woman, she sinned in word or deed in this life, forgive her soul on behalf of the sacrifice which she bore and offered to You Master, namely me, your unworthy servant. Yes, Lord, Lord God, righteous judge and lover of humanity, do not carry her from oppression to oppression, from distress to distress, and from groanings to groanings, but instead of grief, which she suffered for the sake of her only child, carry her to joy, instead of tears, to the rejoicing prepared for your saints, God, my God, forever and ever. Amen.

—Translation from Derek Krueger, *Symeon the Holy Fool: Leontius's* Life *and the Late Antique City* (Berkeley: University of California Press, 1996), 147.

for now they can be more or less avoided through the distractions of the body. After death, however, ruling desires and long-buried memories reaffirm themselves, occurring and recurring with massive force and unmitigated intensity, from which there will be no possibility of escape, for there will be no dispassionate point of reference. As a result, vicious souls return eternally to the scenes of their crimes, and they remember only those whom they harmed; murderers, for example, behold only the faces of their victims (*Discourse* 12).

For the Byzantines the survival of memory within the framework of absolute moral accountability was one of the most important features of life after death. Thus the decorative programs of funerary chapels frequently include the scene of the last judgment. Byzantine literature likewise abounds with accounts of the soul's departure from the body, at which time it encounters its own conscience through graphic confrontations with its thoughts, words, and deeds, as its life is critically screened and reviewed. These narratives often take the form of prosecution by angry demons in the charged setting of a courtroom, where angels act as counsels for the defense.

In the eleventh-century *Life of Lazarus of Mount Galesion* a sinful layman sees a vision of his soul being sentenced in a courtroom after death, whereupon he resolves to become a monk. On his way to the local monastery, night falls, and as he sleeps by the side of the road, he is awakened by a figure in the guise of a monk, who leads him to a precipice from where he pushes the unsuspecting man to his death. The episode is revealed in a dream to the abbot, who beholds angels escorting the man's soul to heaven, although demons are also grasping at it, attempting to drag it downward. "Leave him to us," the demons shout, "for he is ours, and was in our employ until the very hour of his death, and you have no grounds to take him." In defense of their claim, the demons produce a detailed catalog of the man's sins arranged under various headings. In response the angels argue that, on the contrary, the man clearly intended to repent, and his intention was accepted by God. The demons object, maintaining that the man "failed to confess his sins and did not truly repent." At that point, the litigation is interrupted by the voice of the heavenly judge, who rules in favor of the defendant: "His desire to repent, to become a monk, and to cease from his evil ways is verified by his deeds. The fact that he failed to arrive at the monastery where he would have confessed and repented was not his fault, but yours, who hindered him on his way. Therefore, in place of the monastic labors that he would have performed, I accept his blood, which was shed unjustly by you." With that, the demons vanish "like smoke," and the angels, rejoicing, escort the soul to heaven.

In addition to the setting of a courtroom, similar scenes are staged at a series of nightmarish, aerial "tollgates" (*telonia*), where souls ascending to heaven are detained by passport control and have their moral baggage ruthlessly inspected by demonic customs officials. In a sermon, Cyril of Alexandria, the fifth-century preacher, describes the soul's harrowing progress through an infernal revenue service staffed by a swarm of "archons, cosmocrats, teloniarchs, logothetes, and *praktopsephistai* [fiscal officials of low rank]." At the first five of these weigh stations each of the bodily senses is closely scrutinized ("from the time of one's youth until the hour of death"), beginning with sins of the mouth, followed by those of the eyes, the ears, the sense of smell, and touch (*On the Departure of the Soul*, PG 77.1073B–1076B). The tenth-century *Life of Basil the Younger* tells of a certain Theodora, a pious though not perfect woman, whose soul passes through a series of twenty-one tollgates arranged in three groups of seven, with a twenty-second being a final examination for general "inhumanity and hardness of heart." The story proved to be quite popular and was known, for instance, to Meletios Galesiotes (circa 1209–1286), who mentions Theodora twice by name in the verses of his *Alphabetalphabetos*.

The Byzantines' quotidian experience of the splintering hierarchies of the church and the corrupt bureaucracy of the state influenced the development of these complex and taxing metaphysical systems. The episode from the *Life of Lazarus of Mount Galesion*, moreover, expresses monastic concern over the problem of penances left incomplete at the time of death. More generally, these popular tales were valued for their power to catalyze moral reform, prompting a salutary fear of punishment and damnation. It seems that the mere thought of rapacious tax collectors and grasping lawyers created great anxiety among the Byzantine populace and thus were considered effective in concretizing a sense of final reckoning and ultimate accountability. The example of Antony the Great is perhaps typical: in consequence of having witnessed an episode similar to the one described in the *Life of Lazarus*, the fourth-century father of Egyptian monasticism is said to have "struggled all the more to advance daily, and shared the vision with others, for whom the account would be beneficial, so that they might learn that discipline bore good fruit" (Athanasius, *Life of Antony* 66).

If Byzantine theologians generally declined to reduce the symbolic forms of pious narratives to dogmatic certainties, they nevertheless remained committed to a robust, realist affirmation of bodily resurrection. At the end of time Christ would "return in majesty, to judge the living and the dead" (*Nicene Creed*). At the "cry of the archangel" (see 1 Thess. 4:16) the bodies of the dead would arise from their graves and be reunited with their souls in a state of unimaginable glory. Faced with this basic doctrine, however, the Byzantines were curious about the precise nature of the resurrected body and expressed deep concern over whether family members and friends would know and recognize each other in heaven.

The problem of "kindred recognition" (*koinos anagnorismos*), as it was termed, appears throughout the sources and was provoked partly by the radical disfigurement of the body in death, but also by familiar biblical lessons, in which the resurrected Christ was unrecognizable even to his most intimate friends and disciples (see Mark 16:12; Luke 24:13-16; John 20:14). These concerns were further complicated by various philosophical and religious dualisms (for example, Platonic, gnostic, Bogomil), which denied the goodness of the material world and denigrated the role of the body. However, a more balanced view was suggested by the exquisitely sensory character of the Byzantine liturgy, including devotion to icons and especially bodily relics, all of which argued for the irreducible place of the body in the definition of human identity. Thus Byzantine thinkers consistently (if not always uniformly) promoted the material continuity of the self as it flowed from life through death to resurrection.

In the late eighth century, for example, belief in "kindred recognition" was championed by Theodore of Stoudios, who refuted the notion that the resurrected body would be "angelomorphic" and thus unrecognizable. At the same time he argued that the regenerated body will not be recognized on the basis of its "corruptible, accidental characteristics," but rather in the "beauty of its incorruption." Any other view, he insisted, was "equal in its impiety to the mythology of Origen" (a Platonizing theologian of the third century). He therefore affirmed that "brother shall know brother, parents shall know their children, wives shall know their husbands, and friends shall know their friends" (*Small Catechism* 22).

Theodore develops a similar view in his *Refutations of the Iconoclasts*, where he argues that the body of the resurrected Christ remained a fully human body, bearing all of its particular, individual characteristics (2.41–47). This would seem to include gender, an argument that went back to the early patristic period. Irenaeus of Lyons, for instance, maintained that "it is only just that in the same body in which the saints toiled and were afflicted, they should receive the reward of their suffering" (*Against Heresies* 2.2.19). In the early fifth century the monk Macarius observed that "all our members will be resurrected, and, as scripture says, 'not a single hair shall be lost' [compare Luke 21:18]; and thus Peter will be Peter and Paul will be Paul" (*Homily* 15.10). Andrew of Caesarea, in the seventh century, similarly replied that it is "foolish to think that the body will be resurrected divorced from its own members, through which it worked good or evil, for it is necessary that the members which glorified God on earth should themselves be glorified in heaven" (fragment 166.12–14).

Michael Glykas, writing in the twelfth century, also dealt with the question of gender in the resurrection but gave a rather different response. Glykas admitted that the question had long puzzled him and that the matter remained greatly disputed. Drawing more directly on the Origenistic sources rejected by Theodore of Stoudios, he suggested that differences in gender are the result of a cosmic fall from a primal, sexually undifferentiated "angelic" state of humanity (*On Ambiguities in Sacred Scripture* 80). Because Glykas believed that the "end will be like the beginning," he concluded that resurrected bodies will return to their original condition and thus will be genderless, like "clear glass vessels, filled with light" (87). As for the resurrected Christ, he was "visible to his disciples only by an act of accommodation" and took food "only to assure them of his rising" (75–76). Glykas nonetheless affirmed the "dogma" of kindred recognition, as he called it, in part because the Rich Man in torment recognized Lazarus and called him by name (Luke 16:19-31). Such recognition, however, would not occur through external signs, but rather through a form of spiritual insight (80).

Seen in their historical contexts, Byzantine concerns about life beyond the grave functioned as a kind of collective, societal epistemology, that is, a means of self-definition shaping and articulating the image that the community had of itself. In times of political crisis, for example, interest in the resurrection could serve to express the hope for the revival and restoration of national life. The widespread concern for "kindred recognition," moreover, suggests that the Byzantines held the social bonds of family and friendship in particular esteem. Concern for the dead was an extension of concern for society as a whole, and honoring the memory of the departed was a way to cherish and celebrate life itself. Byzantine meditation on death, therefore, was not simply a species of medieval morbidity, inasmuch as a sober recognition of one's mortality was seen as the point of entry into a fully human life. St. Antony the Great, who lived to the age of 105, taught his disciples that "it is good to reflect on the words of the Apostle: 'I die every day' [1 Cor. 15:31], for if we live as though dying daily, we shall not sin. And the meaning of the saying is this: as we rise day by day we should think that we shall not abide till evening; and again, when we are about to lie down to sleep, we should think that we shall not rise up. For our life is naturally uncertain, and a gift allotted to us daily" (*Life of Antony* 19).

FOR FURTHER READING

Abrahamse, Dorothy. "Rituals of Death in the Middle Byzantine Period." *Greek Orthodox Theological Review* 29 (1984): 125–34.

Alexiou, Margaret. *The Ritual Lament in Greek Tradition.* Cambridge: Cambridge University Press, 1974.

Constas, Nicholas. "'To Sleep, Perchance to Dream': The Middle State of Souls in Patristic and Byzantine Literature." *DOP* 55 (2001): 91–124.

Dennis, George. "Death in Byzantium." *DOP* 55 (2001): 1–7.

Maguire, Henry. "The Depiction of Sorrow in Middle Byzantine Art." *DOP* 31 (1977): 122–74.

Talbot, Alice-Mary. "Old Age in Byzantium." *Byzantinische Zeitschrift* 77 (1984): 267–78.

DEVOTIONAL LIFE
AND ARTIFACTS

ICONS, PRAYER, AND VISION IN THE ELEVENTH CENTURY

CHARLES BARBER

CHAPTER SEVEN

The icon is one of the most evocative objects bequeathed to us by Byzantine Christianity.[1] Whether it was a painted wooden panel or a wall painting, or rendered in enamel, ivory, steatite, or any other medium, the icon, conveying the likeness of a holy person, promised the presence of holiness to those who looked at it. Such presence was attested by phenomena that embraced but also surpassed the visible; the experience of an icon was more than that of an objective visual record of the given subject. Indeed, accounts of icon devotion introduce all the senses into the experience of holy images.

Through the eyes one can, of course, see the subject, and the bulk of this chapter is devoted to unraveling the complexity of this simple statement. Beyond the eyes, however, we find that all the other senses were embraced by the image. Through the ears one could hear words uttered by the saint represented in the icon. In the *Life* of the fifth-century saint Elisabeth the Wonderworker, written in the post-iconoclastic era, one reads of an icon of St. Glykeria that spoke to Elisabeth's father, Eunomianos. Glykeria's lips were seen to move as she asked Eunomianos to fulfill the vow he had made when he asked her for help in conceiving a child (*Life of Elisabeth the Wonderworker*, 126). Perfumed oils exuded by icons drew the sense of smell toward an affirmation of holy presence. A notable instance is found in the *Life* of the ninth-century saint Theodora of Thessalonike, in which a painter called John had visions of the saint and painted her icon according to what he had seen. After some time "sweet-scented oil was seen to issue forth from the palm of the right hand of this holy image" (*Life of Theodora of Thessalonike*, 211). The oil was found to heal those that rubbed it on themselves. Icons were also tangible things, whether the kissing mouth or the touching hand mediated this tactile piety.[2] An account of the death of the emperor Theophilos (829–842) reports his quiet passing when he finally abandoned his iconoclastic beliefs and kissed the image of Christ found on the encolpion, or reliquary pendant, worn by one of his courtiers (*Life of Theodora the Empress*, 372–73). In so doing, he embraced the veneration of icons and left behind the critique of icons that had dominated the discourse of the second phase of Iconoclasm (815–842).[3] Finally, taste participated when the material surface of the icon was ingested for healing purposes.[4] Perhaps the seventh-century *Miracles of Cosmas and Damian* offers the most notable example: a woman was cured of a fever by scraping down and ingesting the images of the saints she had painted in her bedroom.[5] These examples bring forth an impression of great intimacy and immediacy in the icon. We are looking not simply at the marks on the surface of an object but rather at a thing that mediates a powerful presence to all human senses. Furthermore, these texts, and many like them, indicate that lay and monastic alike participated in the veneration of icons. We might therefore ask whether they saw the same thing when they looked at the icon.

KING DAVID AND THE PRESENCE OF CHRIST

An image such as that seen in figure 7.1 (see also color gallery, plate F) supports the sense of immediacy, of a very real presence in this particular medium of representation. The image appears in the Theodore Psalter, the most profusely illustrated psalmbook to survive from Byzantium.[6] The manuscript was produced in and for the Stoudios monastery in Constantinople. The work is replete with visual encounters between the human and the divine. In this instance David, dressed as a king, is shown standing before an icon of Christ. David's left hand gestures toward this icon. He is also looking at this icon and is speaking to it. The idea of speech is introduced by the text written above David, which can be translated as: "David says . . ." What he says is indicated by a scribal mark that designates text from Ps. 16:13: "and cast them down: deliver my soul from the ungodly; draw thy sword because of the enemies of thine hand" (KJV). Christ can be seen responding to these words. While most of his body remains in a classic frontal pose, Christ's right hand breaks the icon's frame. He points down toward the scene below. Here we can see that David's request has been acted upon. An angel has plunged a spear into the neck of a standing figure. A second figure has already fallen, bleeding, to the ground. The image not only is a testimony to the effectiveness of prayer but also offers a sense of presence in the icon itself. Christ is more than a depiction: he is an animate participant in a conversation with David, who can both see and speak to a Christ who is present to him in this icon.

Attractive as the above prospect might be, we should be wary of considering such presence to be a general condition of icons or a necessary consequence of the prayer directed at them. Indeed, the lengthy and varied history of Byzantine attitudes to their religious images makes any such overarching claim about the icon and the devotion paid to it highly problematic.

Rather than paint a very broad and impressionistic account of praying before icons, I propose a specific understanding of the acts of looking and praying that are found in the Theodore Psalter. While analyzing the context for the reception of this work of art within the Stoudios monastery, I draw attention to the possible problems inherent in the assumption, even in an Orthodox context, of a natural relationship between prayer and the visible aspect of icon veneration. In the image I have presented, the reader or viewer of the manuscript is shown an act of prayer that is clearly linked to the process of seeing. David not only utters words but also directs them and his eyes at a visible object that shows a living Christ responding to his request. The question is, What conditions make it possible for this eleventh-century audience to accept that David indeed sees this icon of Christ become an animate presence? To answer this question, we need to explore two topics. First, we need to understand what it is that is shown in an icon.

Fig. 7.1. King David speaking to an icon of Christ. Detail of folio 15v (see color gallery, plate F), British Library Add. 19.352. By permission of the British Library.

Second, we need to ask what are the particular expectations that frame the act of seeing in this particular manuscript.

ICONS AND THE VISIBLE

The answer to the question of what it is that is shown in an icon is, in theory, relatively simple. In spite of my introductory remarks on the commonplace expectations of presence that have come to embrace the icon, in the eleventh century the prevailing conception was that an icon simply showed that which was visible of its subject. This conception had been defined during the period of Byzantine Iconoclasm and was sustained in the eleventh century on numerous occasions. For example, visible likeness was the criterion for testing the icon of Symeon of Stoudios in the trial of Symeon the New Theologian. The visible was also explored as evidence for the limit of human capabilities in the writings of Michael Psellos. Furthermore, visible form was fundamental to Eustratios of Nicaea's logical account of the relationship between icon and worship in his critique of Leo of Chalcedon's views of the worship owed the work of art.[7] All of these readings depended upon a common assumption that an image can *only* show what is ordinarily visible to the human eye. This was deemed to embrace the external visible forms of a given subject but not their inner living essence. As such, art and artists could only provide inanimate forms to their audiences. Yet, if we look at the manuscript's image of David before the icon, it would appear that such a constraint on vision has been surpassed.

Given that animation is not a product of artistic intervention, we need to ask,

---

Ingesting Images

The seventh-century *Miracles of Cosmas and Damian* tells of a woman who had been healed of various ailments at the saints' shrine on the Golden Horn, just outside Constantinople. When she returned home, she painted images of Cosmas and Damian "on all the walls of her house, being as she was insatiable in her desire of seeing them." Then one night she developed a terrible case of colic while alone in her house: "Perceiving herself to be in danger, she crawled out of bed and, upon reaching the place where those most wise saints were depicted on the wall, she stood up leaning on her faith as upon a stick and scraped off with her fingernails some plaster. This she put into water and, after drinking the mixture, she was immediately cured of her pains by the visitation of the saints."

—Cyril Mango, trans., *Miracles of Cosmas and Damian* 15, in *The Art of the Byzantine Empire: 312–1453* (Englewood Cliffs, N.J.: Prentice-Hall, 1972), 139.

What can bring such life to an image? The predominant answer to this question in the Byzantine world was that such empty forms could only be animated by divine intervention, namely, through the operation of grace. Distinct from both the painter's and the viewer's intervention, such a possibility, potentially available to every icon, became manifest in miraculous images. In eleventh-century Constantinople this would have been confirmed every Tuesday and Friday by the regular public miracles performed by the Hodegetria and Blachernai icons of the Theotokos, two of the most famous images of the Mother of God.[8] There is no evidence to suggest that the image we are discussing had such an identity. While one can never rule out an operation of grace that is no longer evident to us, I suggest that the animation visible in this icon is neither the product of the painter's hand nor the consequence of an act of grace, but is rather consequent upon an act of looking that depends upon the disposition of the one who looks and prays.[9]

In the case of the Theodore Psalter image we can offer a very precise context for understanding this act of looking. The manuscript was completed in February 1066 at the Studios monastery in Constantinople. The book was made for a clearly defined audience and community. The manuscript's patron was Michael, Abbot of the Studios monastery. It was written and designed by Theodore of Caesarea, who lived and worked in the same monastery. The production and possession of the manuscript are thus bound to this institution and so it is reasonable to assume that the Studios context will also inflect the consumption of this work.

We are fortunate to possess texts that can propose a context for this act of seeing and praying. These are to be found in the writings of a monk from the Studios, Niketas Stethatos. He was born circa 1005 and died circa 1090. Toward the end of his life he served as the Abbot of the Studios community. Throughout his life he was an active theologian. He was, for example, engaged in writing against aspects of Latin Catholicism in the 1050s. His greatest renown, however, lay in his editing the works and writing a biography of Symeon the New Theologian (949–1022), who had also been for a brief time in the later tenth century a monk in the Studios monastery. This editorial work perhaps belongs to the 1050s. The *Life of Symeon the New Theologian* certainly belongs to the 1050s.[10] This suggests that both the ideas of

Symeon the New Theologian and those of Niketas Stethatos were available at the Stoudios monastery during the years preceding the production of the Theodore Psalter, the same years that marked the abbacy of Michael, the patron of this work.[11] While Niketas differed in many respects from Symeon's thinking, clear parallels marked his writing on vision.[12] In his *Three Centuries* Niketas, among numerous spiritual topics, provided a sustained discussion of the value of vision for the spiritual life.[13] These drew strongly on the teachings of Symeon. These texts offer a context for understanding the role of vision and prayer in our image and manuscript.

For Niketas prayer was an intellectual activity: "Prayer may be defined as the intellect's unceasing intercourse with God" (PG 120.937B; *Philokalia*, 129). In several chapters that discuss the role of psalmody in the spiritual life, he offers a telling elaboration of this definition:

> We pray with the intellect when, as we say prayers and recite psalms, we perceive the meaning hidden in the Holy Scriptures and thence garner in the heart a harvest of ever more exalted divine thoughts. Rapt spiritually by these thoughts into the regions of light, the soul shines with a clear radiance, is further purified, rises wholly to the heavens, and beholds the beauty of the blessings held in store for the saints. Out of ardent longing for these blessings, tears—the fruit of prayer—at once flow from our eyes, induced by the light-creating energy of the Spirit, their taste so sweet that in experiencing them one may even forget to eat. This is the fruit of prayer, begotten through the quality of their psalmody in the soul of those who pray. (PG 120.933CD; *Philokalia*, 127)

This text introduces a paradox that should be borne in mind as we seek to understand David's visual and verbal address to the icon of Christ. Our modern expectations of vision are shaped by a sense of its unmediated directness, such that vision and truth are commonly bound together.[14] For Niketas, however, the "fruit of prayer" is tears. Tears, of course, impair our vision and so call attention to the limited capacity of human eyes. Nevertheless, Niketas proposes that such tears open the way to a more complete visual experience. As we shall see, he uses this problematic relationship among prayers, tears, and vision to prepare the monk for his escape from the narrow confines of natural sight and for his translation to a new plane of spiritual seeing that surpasses the physical organ of sight.

The following passages taken from the writings of Symeon the New Theologian, Niketas's spiritual model, illustrate the insufficient nature of the natural eye. The texts are from the thirty-sixth homily of his *Catechetical Discourses* and offer an extremely rare example of Symeon discussing an actual use of an icon in his spiritual life. The topic of the *Discourse* is thanksgiving for the gift of illumination. In the tenth section Symeon prepares his listeners for the encounter with an icon by first offering thanks to God for a vision of him:

> When a blind man gradually recovers his sight and notices the features of a man and bit by bit ascertains what he is, it is not the features that are transformed or altered into the visible. Rather, as the vision of that man's eyes becomes clearer, it sees the features as they are. It is as though they wholly imprint themselves on his vision and penetrate through it, impressing and engraving themselves, as on a tablet, on the mind and the memory of the soul. You Yourself became visible in the same manner when You had completely cleaned my mind by the clear light of the Holy Ghost. Thence seeing more clearly and distinctly, You seemed to come forth and shine more brightly, and allowed me to see the features of Your shapeless shape.[15]

Here Symeon proposes that human eyes require divine intervention in order to see more fully. It is they, rather than the object of their vision, that require alteration. Having set up this transformational model, Symeon then introduces an encounter with an icon of the Theotokos:

> Having said these things You became silent and little by little, O sweet and good Lord, You were hidden from my eyes; whether I became distant from You or You departed from me, I know not. I returned once more wholly into myself and entered into my former dwelling, whence I had thought to have left. When I recalled the beauty of Your glory and of Your words, as I walked about, sat down, ate, drank, and prayed, I wept and lived in an indescribable joy, having known You, the Maker of all things. How could I have failed to rejoice? But I again fell into sorrow and so desiring to see You again, I went off to embrace the spotless icon of the one who bore You and having bowed down before it, You became visible to me within my wretched heart before I could stand up, as if You had transformed it into light, and then I knew that I knowingly have You within me. Therefore from then onwards I loved You, not by recollection of You and that which surrounds You, nor for the memory of such things, but I in very truth believed that I had You, Substantial Love, within me. For You, O God, are love indeed. (*Catéchèses*, 350–52; *Discourses*, 375–76)

It is striking that Symeon plays with a very visual sense of the absence or presence of the divine. In seeking to recover the presence of the divine, he addresses worship to an icon, but, notably, it is not the subject of the icon, the Theotokos, who becomes present to him. Rather, it is Christ who appears in his heart. This presents us with a distinction between sight, vision, and object and a seeming disregard for the icon itself. It is an account that underlines that Symeon was seeking to surpass the human in order to receive a vision that was impressed within his body rather than that passed through his eyes.

BEYOND THE VISIBLE: A SPIRITUAL JOURNEY

A return to the writings of Niketas broadens our understanding of this visual gap and deepens our sense of the Stoudite context for the manuscript's depiction of iconic vision. Niketas, like Symeon, does not offer much praise of human visual experience. Above all, the spiritual journey begins with a detachment from "visible things" (PG 120.853A, 869D, 900B, 901B; *Philokalia*, 80, 90, 107, 108). By this, Niketas means the deceptive world that is known to us through the senses alone. One is faced with a dilemma:

> Those engaged in spiritual warfare confront the question of which in us is the more noble: the visible or the intelligible? If it is the visible, there is nothing in us more to be preferred or desired than what is corruptible, nor is the soul more noble than the body. If it is the intelligible, then we must recognize that "God is spirit, and those who worship Him must worship in spirit and in truth" (John 4:24). Thus once the soul is firmly established in spiritual work, freed from the downward pull of the body and rendered entirely spiritual through union with what is superior to it, then bodily discipline is superfluous. (PG 120.972BC; *Philokalia*, 150)

In this hierarchical description, Niketas marks a distinction that returns throughout his chapters. For him the visible is at best a partial form of knowledge that is limited by being bound to the human senses. For a full knowledge of divine things, the monk must ascend from the sensible to the intelligible realm.

Niketas's *Three Centuries* proposes a threefold account of the monk's spiritual ascent. The first stage, discussed in the first *Century* "On the Practice of the Virtues," aims at the monk's purification.

The purgative stage pertains to those newly engaged in spiritual warfare. It is characterized by the rejection of the materialistic self, liberation from material evil, and
investiture with the regenerate self, renewed by the Holy Spirit. It involves hatred
of materiality, the attenuation of the flesh, the avoidance of whatever incites the
mind to passion, repentance for sins committed, the dissolving with tears of the
bitter sediment left by sin, the regulation of our life according to the generosity of
the Spirit, and the cleansing through compunction of the inside of the cup—the
intellect—from every defilement of flesh and spirit, so that it can be filled with the
wine of the Logos that gladdens the heart of the purified and can be brought to
the King of the celestial powers for Him to taste. Its final goal is that we should be
forged in the fire of ascetic struggle, scouring off the rust of sin, and steeled and
tempered in the water of compunction, so that sword-like we may effectively cut
off the passions and the demons. Reaching this point through long ascetic struggle,
we quench the fire within us, muzzle the brute-like passions, become strong in
the Spirit instead of weak, and like another Job conquer the tempter through our
patient endurance. (PG 120.972D–973A; *Philokalia*, 150–51)

Purification is seen, first and foremost, as a cleansing of the intellect
from materialism. Tears play a central role in this process, marking
both the cleansing and the constraint of the passions.

Niketas describes the second stage, that of illumination, in these
terms:

The illuminative stage pertains to those who as a result of their struggles have
attained the first level of dispassion. It is characterized by the spiritual knowledge
of created beings, the contemplation of their inner essences and communion in
the Holy Spirit. It involves the intellect's purification by divine fire, the noetic
opening of the eyes of the heart, and the birth of the Logos accompanied by
sublime intellections of spiritual knowledge. Its final goal is the elucidation of the
nature of created things by the Logos of Wisdom, insight into divine and human
affairs, and the revelation of the mysteries of the kingdom of heaven. He who has
reached this point through the inner activity of the intellect rides, like another
Elijah, in a chariot of fire drawn by the quaternity of the virtues; and while still
living he is raised to the noetic realm and traverses the heavens, since he has risen
above the lowliness of the body. (PG 120.973B; *Philokalia*, 151)

In the second stage, Niketas dwells on the intellect. In particular, he
defines this as the moment when intellect rules the body, and one's
knowledge reaches beyond the surface of things to their essence.

The third and final stage is mystical union. This is achieved when
the monk has become perfected.

The mystical and perfective stage pertains to those who have already passed
through all things and have come to the 'measure of the stature of the fullness

of Christ' (Eph. 4:13). It is characterized by the transcending of the sphere of demonic powers and of all sublunar things, by our attaining to the higher celestial ranks, approaching the primordial light and plumbing the depths of God through the Spirit. It involves immersing our contemplative intellect in the inner principles of providence, justice and truth, and also the interpretation of the arcane symbolism, parables and obscure passages in Holy Scripture. Its final goal is our initiation into the hidden mysteries of God and our being filled with ineffable wisdom through union with the Holy Spirit, so that each becomes a wise theologian in the great Church of God, illuminating others with the inner meaning of theology. He who has reached this point through the deepest humility and compunction has, like another Paul, been caught up into the third heaven of theology, and has heard indescribable things which he who is still dominated by the sense-world is not permitted to hear; and he experiences unutterable blessings, such as no eye has seen or ear heard. He becomes a steward of God's mysteries, for he is God's mouthpiece, and through words he communicates these mysteries to other people; and in this he finds blessed repose. For he is now perfected in the perfect God, united in the company of other theologians with the supreme angelic powers of the Cherubim and Seraphim, in whom dwells the principle of wisdom and spiritual knowledge. (PG 120.973C–976A; *Philokalia*, 151–52)

This union moves beyond vision, as verbal communion becomes the privileged means of knowing.

It would thus appear that the three stages are an escape from the visible, sensible realm. But Niketas does not abandon the senses entirely. Rather, throughout the *Three Centuries* he seeks to redirect them: sensible vision is translated into noetic vision. The link is made early on in the first *Century*, when he names intelligence as the sense within the soul that corresponds to the corporeal sense of vision (PG 120.856BC; *Philokalia*, 81). If the link between the two can be maintained, then corporeal vision can be elevated to a higher spiritual function. Hence: "If your intellect clearly distinguishes the intentions of its thoughts and in its purity gives its assent only to those that are divine; if your reason can interpret the physical movements of the whole of visible creation—that is to say, can clearly elucidate the inner essences of things; if noetically you can perceive heavenly wisdom and spiritual knowledge: then through the light of the Sun of righteousness you have transcended all sense-perception and have attained what lies beyond it, and you savour the delight of things unseen" (PG 120.856CD; *Philokalia*, 81). Thus one aims to look through the immediate sensual data to the essential nature of the thing seen. The monk is invited to transcend the lowly state of visible things. "Open your spiritual eye to the contemplation of God and recognize the delight-fulness of the Lord from the beauty of creation" (PG 120.885CD; *Philokalia*, 98).

To achieve this transition from the corporeal to the spiritual eye, one must purify the eyes. It is tears that do this. These are not ordinary tears, such as might be wept over a loss, but the tears that are granted by God, the tears of compunction (PG 120.884BC; *Philokalia*, 97).

> Those who have not tasted the sweetness of the tears of compunction and are ignorant of its grace and of how it operates, think that such tears differ in no way from those shed for the dead; and they invent all manner of specious reasons and pretexts for thinking this, such as might naturally occur to us. But when what was haughty in our intellect inclines towards humility, and when the soul has closed its eyes to the deceitfulness of visible things and aspires solely to the contemplation of the immaterial, primal light, repudiating all that derives from sense perception and receiving the grace bestowed by the Spirit, then as water from a spring tears at once gush from it and sweeten its senses, filling the mind with all manner of joy and divine light. More than this, they shatter the heart and make the intellect humble in its contemplation of the higher world. These things cannot happen to those who lament and mourn in another way. (PG 120.920C–921A; *Philokalia*, 119)

These tears are thus a gift granted to those who have prepared to receive them. The presence of such a gift is significant as the tears call attention to the eyes, reminding us of their privileged status as a medium of human knowledge. By way of comparison, the ears, for example, are not provided with an equivalent specific tool for their cleansing. The process of cleansing the eyes is twofold. First, the tears begin by obscuring vision, calling attention to the limited quality of this human faculty. Then, having called attention to the natural limits of the eyes, these tears will transform them into a medium fit for the intellect. This is understood to be a restoration of prelapsarian vision, a return that makes it possible to see divine things clearly, directly, and fully (PG 120.944AB; *Philokalia*, 132).

This long excursus on vision in the writings of Niketas suggests a way of reading the visual implications of the Theodore Psalter's image of David addressing a prayer to an icon of Christ (fig. 7.1 and color gallery, plate F). We do not hear Christ's response. Instead, we can see that the Christ who has become visible to him through the icon has answered the prayer. The image would thus fulfill the desire found in the act of prayer before the icon, namely, the coming-into-presence by the one to whom the prayer is directed. As noted above, Christ himself could grant such presence. In this instance, however, one might suggest that the presence has been made possible by the one looking. David was no ordinary viewer. As a prophet and saint, he embodied the perfected human being. Thus, when he is seen to be looking at the icon, he is to be understood as looking with spiritual rather than corporeal eyes. As such, he is not bound by the marks made on the object itself. Rather, he has seen through the icon to the essence of that which lies behind it, the animate Christ.

SPIRITUAL VISION AND THE LAYPERSON

It might be reasonable to assume that, because of David's status, the image in the Psalter offers a model of spiritual vision that pertains only to a distinct and elite category of viewers, such as the saints, prophets, holy men, and monks who inhabit this manuscript. A second page from this manuscript (fig. 7.2), however, can broaden the category of such spiritual viewers to include laypeople. Here we see an image linked to Ps. 70:4 (LXX 69:5): "Let all that seek thee exult and be glad in thee: and let those that love thy salvation say continually, Let God be magnified" (KJV). The image shows four men standing beneath an icon. Their raised arms indicate that they are praying. To the right are two monks; to the left are two laymen, indicated by their distinctive costumes. While none are haloed, these four are labeled as the righteous. Unlike in the first image, Christ is not shown as an animated being. Nonetheless, the image brings laypeople's viewing of icons within the bounds of this text. A third folio shows laymen achieving spiritual vision (fig. 7.3). The image is linked to Ps. 128:1-2 (LXX 127:1-2): "Blessed are all they that fear the Lord; who walk in his ways. Thou shalt eat the labours of thy hand: blessed art thou, and it shall be well with them" (KJV). In the upper part of the image we see a group of laymen praying before an animate Christ who is circumscribed within a golden circle. In this instance they are looking not at an icon but at Christ himself. It

Fig. 7.2. Theodore Psalter. Monks and laymen pray before an icon of Christ. Folio 89r, British Library Add. 19.352. By permission of the British Library.

is a vision that has surpassed the material bounds of the icon and that brings these laypeople within the paradigm of spiritual vision that this manuscript and the texts that we have been examining propose.

These images challenge us to consider whether one can easily draw a distinction between lay and monastic spirituality or between lay and monastic icon piety. Monastic communities were economic, cultural, and spiritual centers with porous boundaries. They provided models for lay piety in eleventh-century Byzantium and guided those who wished to pursue a spiritual life in the lay world. In this regard it is notable that Symeon the New Theologian's first visions occurred before he formally entered the monastery.[16] When he was about fourteen years old, he had begun to study with the Stoudite monk Symeon the Pious. This period of study lasted for perhaps seven years. During this time Symeon devoted himself to ascetic exercises and readings while continuing to work in the household of a patrician. At about age twenty-one he had his first vision. Rather than feeling affirmed in his monastic training, Symeon immediately fled deeper into the world beyond the monastery. Only when he was twenty-nine did Symeon begin to return to the monastic profession. He renewed contact with Symeon the Pious and found inspiration in his family's own copy of the *Ladder* by John of Sinai. The presence of this text in a lay library is a telling instance of the fluid boundaries between lay and monastic space that enabled Symeon to spend so long outside the monastery developing his spiritual life.

This lack of a rigid boundary between lay and monastic spirituality is confirmed by the evidence found in the will of a provincial aristocrat, Eustathios Boilas, dated to April 1059.[17] Among Boilas's possessions were two manuscripts of the *Ladder*, included in a long list of objects already given to the monastery and church founded by Boilas, the Church of the Theotokos tou Salem.[18] The list is remarkable in how it introduces us to the breadth of literature that might be available in a provincial church at the furthest corner of the empire. Beyond the biblical, liturgical, and homiletic sources that one might expect to find, there were romances, dream books,

Fig. 7.3. Theodore Psalter. Three laymen achieve a spiritual vision of Christ. Folio 170v, British Library Add. 19.352. By permission of the British Library.

An Icon in Procession

The Spanish traveler Pero Tafur visited Constantinople in 1437–1438. Here is his account of the weekly procession with the icon of the Virgin Hodegetria in Constantinople:

The next day I went to the church of St. Mary, where the body of Constantine is buried. In this church is a picture of Our Lady the Virgin, made by St. Luke; on the other side is Our Lord crucified. It is painted on stone, and with the frame and stand it weighs, they say, several hundredweight. So heavy is it as a whole that six men cannot lift it. Every Tuesday some twenty men come there, clad in long red linen draperies, which cover the head like a stalking dress. These men come of a special lineage, and by them alone can the office be filled. There is a great procession, and the men who are so clad go one by one to the picture, and he whom it is pleased with take it up as easily as if it weighed only an ounce. The bearer then places it on his shoulder, and they go singing out of the church to a great square, where he who carries the picture walks with it from one end to the other, and fifty times round the square. By fixing one's eyes upon the picture, it appears to be raised high above the ground and completely transfigured. When it is set down again, another comes and takes it up and puts it likewise on his shoulder, and then another, and in that manner some four or five of them pass the day. There is a market in the square on that day, and a great crowd assembles, and the clergy take cotton-wool and touch the picture and distribute it among the people who are there, and then, still in procession, they take it back to its place. While I was at Constantinople I did not miss a single day when this picture was exhibited, since it is certainly a great marvel.

—Pero Tafur,
Travels and Adventures 1435–1439,
trans. Malcolm Letts (New York:
Harper and Brothers, 1926), 141–42.

histories, patristic texts, hagiography, and, most pertinent for this study, a number of monastic spiritual treatises.[19] These included the *Spiritual Meadow* of John Moschos, the *Pandektes* of Antiochos of Mar Saba (PG 89.1420–856), the *Hodegos* of Anastasios of Sinai,[20] and the *Ladder* of John Klimakos from seventh-century Palestine, as well as the eleventh-century *Melissa* of Antonios (PG 136.765–1244). What is notable about these books is that Boilas did not allow them to disappear within the exclusive domain of the monastic library. Rather, these books were to remain the property of the family even while held within the church. Furthermore, they were to be kept so that "my two daughters may have the use and possession of them for chanting, reading, and learning."[21] Boilas thus signals the degree to which monastic spiritual texts might be available to a lay readership.

The evidence for lay spiritual formation presented in Boilas's will and Symeon's biography suggests that the nexus of visual and spiritual desire found in the monastic accounts analyzed in this chapter pervaded lay society in eleventh-century Byzantium. Thanks to these writings and to the Theodore Psalter, it has become apparent that both laypeople and monastics pursued a similar spiritual/visual experience, one that was defined by common texts and common preparation and that allowed them to see beyond the icons that surrounded them.

FOR FURTHER READING

Barber, Charles. *Figure and Likeness: On the Limits of Representation in Byzantine Iconoclasm*. Princeton: Princeton University Press, 2002.

Belting, Hans. *Likeness and Presence: A History of the Image before the Era of Art*. Trans. Edmund Jephcott. Chicago: Chicago University Press, 1994.

Cormack, Robin. *Painting the Soul: Icons, Death Masks and Shrouds*. London: Reaktion Books, 1997.

———. *Writing in Gold: Byzantine Society and Its Icons*. Oxford: Oxford University Press, 1985.

Kartsonis, Anna. "The Responding Icon." In Linda Safran, ed., *Heaven on Earth: Art and the Church in Byzantium*, 58–80. University Park: Pennsylvania State University Press, 2002.

Nelson, Robert S. "To Say and to See: Ekphrasis and Vision in Byzantium." In Robert S. Nelson, ed., *Visuality before and beyond the Renaissance*, 143–68. Cambridge: Cambridge University Press, 2000.

Peers, Glenn. *Sacred Shock: Framing Visual Experience in Byzantium*. University Park: Pennsylvania State University Press, 2004.

Vassilaki, Maria, ed. *Mother of God: Representations of the Virgin in Byzantine Art*. Athens: Benaki Museum, 2000.

OBJECTS OF DEVOTION
AND PROTECTION

BRIGITTE PITARAKIS

CHAPTER EIGHT

The great number and variety of surviving Byzantine jewelry crosses and pendants reflect individual religious practices in a profoundly pious society. The forms of these objects and the images and invocations inscribed on them afforded their wearers protection from the evil spirits that constantly threatened all aspects of daily life. Illness, in particular, and the fear of other misfortunes made such devices necessary, a matter of common sense. Many of these objects, generically called *enkolpia* (hollow breast pendants), held relics, thus adding to their protective power. Ancient magical traditions endured throughout the history of the Byzantine Empire as Christianity assimilated ancient apotropaic imagery, often combining it with explicitly Christian images. Indeed, this Christian iconography was not merely to be venerated but was equally endowed with apotropaic properties. In Byzantium, as is typical in traditional societies, the categories of superstition, magic, and faith intersected. A survey of devotional objects demonstrates how amulets, reliquaries, and crosses could function simultaneously to focus prayer and to ward off evil. Indeed, the functions of veneration and protection meld in these material objects. Even as church leaders struggled to curtail the use of amulets, the people understood that wearing amulets in expectation of protection was itself a devotional practice. Consideration of the objects and their iconography yields insight into the devotional lives of the persons who used them, providing perspective on the motivations for a range of pious practices in Byzantine society.

CROSSES AND AMULETS

The composite nature of a single object illustrates the multiple pieties at work in Byzantine religious jewelry. The woman who owned a sixth- or seventh-century gold pectoral cross suspended it on a necklace between two cylindrical cases (fig. 8.1). An X-ray test of one of its amulet capsules has revealed the edge of what is likely a rolled gold tablet. Although the inscription on this tablet remains unknown, similar extant sheets are inscribed with curses against demons, invocations of angels, and prayers to God.[1] In this exquisite ensemble the use of the cross does not preclude the use of magical amulets. Instead, tablets complement the cross to provide the wearer added protection.

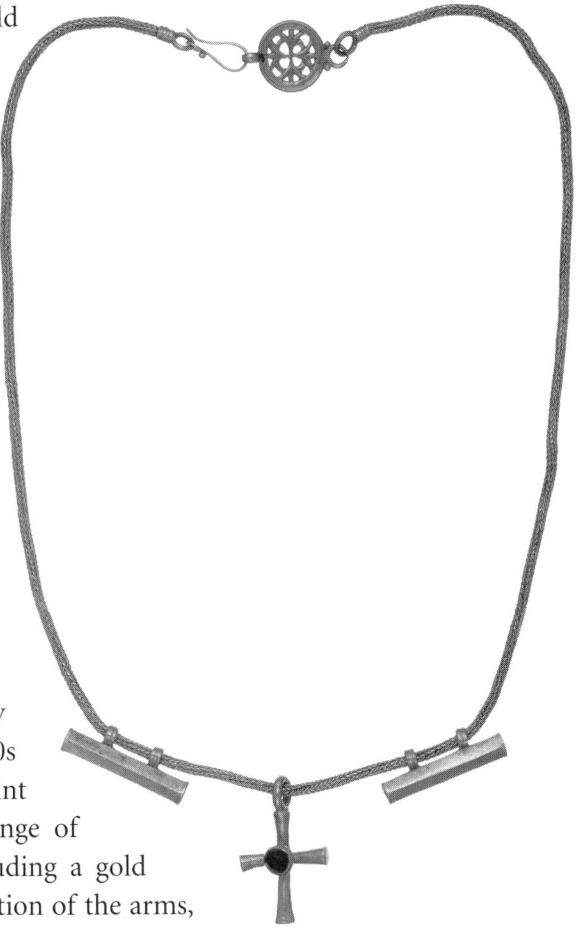

Archaeological contexts provide further evidence for the complementary use of crosses and amulets. For example, sixth- and seventh-century Byzantine houses excavated in the 1970s at Anemurion,[2] at the southernmost point of Asia Minor, have yielded a wide range of utilitarian objects and phylacteria, including a gold cross with glasspaste inset at the intersection of the arms, a bronze cylindrical tube intended to be suspended from the neck containing a silver scroll, and two amuletic medallions, one with the evil eye being assailed by a variety of sharp instruments and animals topped by the generic legend "Lord help" and a second with the Holy Rider (a warrior saint; see figs. 1.3, 9.1, and further discussion below) spearing a female demon. A local coin from the second century was pierced in the seventh for reuse as a charm, a practice strongly condemned by the Church Fathers; however, well into the sixth and seventh centuries Byzantines set coins and secular medallions (or their

Fig. 8.1. Necklace with pectoral cross and phylacteries, fifth to sixth century. Photo: By Michael Cavanagh and Kevin Montague, © 2006 Indiana University Art Museum.

imitations) into precious pectoral necklaces and body chains side by side with crosses and medallions displaying Christian imagery.[3] Coins with religious imagery continued to be reemployed on breast pendants of the middle Byzantine period.

Paralleling their use on the body, amuletic medallions inspired by coin iconography also appear on household objects, including a group of seventh-century copper-alloy jugs.[4] A decorative band composed of medallions stamped in relief encircles their cylindrical necks; the repertory of images includes representations of imperial busts, the personification of Constantinople, and the image of the anonymous Holy Rider (fig. 8.2), one of the most common protective symbols. Differences in the size of these jugs and the archaeological contexts in which they have been found reinforce their identification as domestic objects rather than pilgrimage flasks, as has been earlier suggested. In all likelihood the owners of these jugs wished to ensure that the liquid they contained could be consumed safely.

Fig. 8.2. Copper-alloy flask, seventh century, with protective medallion of the Holy Rider on its neck. Metropolitan Museum of Art, Rogers Fund (67.200.2). Photo: The Metropolitan Museum of Art, all rights reserved.

WARRIOR SAINTS, ROAMING WOMBS, AND OTHER AMULET IMAGES

Although the Holy Rider represented on fifth- and sixth-century amulets was initially anonymous, he progressively assumed the identity of a variety of Byzantine warrior saints. In several instances the nimbed rider is armed with a cross-headed spear, as in a standing warrior saint piercing a serpent, engraved on a small sixth- or seventh-century gold cross (fig. 8.3). The saint on this cross is probably St. George, the namesake saint of the cross's commissioner, a certain "George from Skopelos," identified by the dedicatory inscription.[5]

The iconography of the warrior saint emphasizes the role of the cross as a powerful weapon against evil. Several centuries later, a tenth-century mural painting in Yılanlı Kilise, in the Peristrema (Ihlara) Valley of Cappadocia, depicts the warriors George and Theodore on horseback directing their spears at the two heads of a dragon placed between them, while a staffed cross is staked through the neck of the monster. The accompanying inscription poses the question "Who made you shine?" The monster answers: "It is Christ himself who is planted in me."[6] This Cappadocian composition thus illustrates the survival of an ancient technology of protection in popular religious iconography.

The production of amulets with the anonymous Holy Rider continued well into the medieval period. The motif recurs on a group of lead, copper-alloy, and silver medallions dated between the tenth and the twelfth centuries (fig. 8.4), which characteristically depict on their reverse sides a head with radiating serpents encircled by an inscription containing the word "womb" (*hystera*). The medusa-like head may be the demon Chnoubis but more likely symbolically represents the "roaming womb," which, in both popular belief and Byzantine medicine, was considered to threaten successful childbirth and cause a great variety of ailments—including bleeding, migraine, and fever—by traveling throughout the body. The amulets exorcised the roaming womb and commanded it to return to its proper place. Inscriptions on some of these objects testify that they were occasionally used by men; however, their primary function was to protect women in childbirth and small children.[7] Perhaps surprisingly, the images on these amulets could also serve as the focus of devotion when the medieval *hystera* amulets incorporated more explicitly Christian subjects. In one example the head with radiating serpents is framed by the inscription "Light is Life," an allusion to Christ (fig. 8.5). The reverse of this lead amulet bears a representation of the sainted empress Theophano shown in the *orans* position, with both hands uplifted in prayer. A model of pious behavior, Theophano was canonized some time after her death in 895 or 896, when her body started to perform miracles. But the selection of St. Theophano to decorate an amulet intended to protect women in childbirth may invoke her own miraculous birth. According to the *Life of Theophano*, written shortly after her death,

Fig. 8.3. Gold pectoral cross, sixth century, belonging to a George from Skopelos, with warrior saint, bottom, probably St. George, piercing a serpent. Photo: Copyright the Trustees of the British Museum.

Theophano's birth required the miraculous intervention of the Virgin Mary. Theophano's father had removed a belt from a column in the Church of the Theotokos *Bassou* in Constantinople and tied it around the loins of his wife, Anna, who was having a very difficult labor.[8] The wearer of the amulet thus finds a double protection in both the magical *hystera* and the intercessory role of Theophano through the benevolence of the Virgin.

Another image that appeared on the reverse side of *hystera* amulets contained a metaphoric allusion to women's health: namely, the biblical subject of the woman with the issue of blood (Matt. 9:2-22). This scene recurs on a group of tenth-century intaglios, carved in bloodstone or green jasper, which may have been used for protection in childbirth or in a wider sense for problems related to bleeding.[9] On these objects the woman with the issue of blood appears on one side, while an image of the crucifixion (color gallery, plate G) or the Virgin *orans* appears on the other. Women carrying these luxurious intaglios with Christian imagery were not concerned by clerical condemnation of the use of magical amulets, incorporated in canon 36 of the council of Laodicea (Phrygia), in the late fourth century (Mansi 2.570). An elegantly disguised attack on such magical practices is found in Theodore of Stoudios's praise of his mother. The ninth-century Constantinopolitan abbot stresses that she did not make use of omens, amulets, or spells in childbirth "like other women" (PG 99.884–85). In contrast to Theodore's mother, who does not seem to have suffered infertility, the empress Zoe hoped to bear an heir to Romanos III, leading her to the use of amulets and other magical practices. In his *Chronography* Michael Psellos reports that Zoe fastened pebbles to her body, hung charms about her, wore chains, and decked herself out "with the rest of the nonsense" (*Chronography* 3.5). The empress's "superstitions" did not conflict with her strong devotion to her icon of Christ *Antiphonetes*, "the one who responds." Indeed, Psellos's account of Zoe's relation with her icon offers an interesting insight into Byzantine rites of private piety. Psellos vividly relates how "in moments of great distress [Zoe would] clasp the sacred object in her hands, contemplate it, talk to it as though it were indeed alive, and address it with one sweet term of endearment after another" (*Chronography* 6.66).

USES OF THE GOSPELS:
PHYLACTERIES AND CHRISTOLOGICAL IMAGES

Byzantines also wore phylacteries, amulets containing small scrolls or books, independent of other iconographic symbols. The wearing of small biblical or liturgical texts was an ancient practice. The Syriac monastic history of Thomas, bishop of Marga (840), tells of a monk named Elias, who had been ordained bishop of the town of Mokan. Instead of a pectoral cross, Elias wore a miniature Gospel book around his neck. On the other hand, when he traveled, he took with him a brass cross that he would fix on a wooden staff before praying and singing psalms.[10] This account illustrates the complementary roles of the Gospel book and the cross. Here the former functions as a phylactery, while the latter is an object of devotion serving as a support for prayers. But the role of each of these objects could just as easily be inverted. In the *Life of Nilus the Younger* (died 1004), when the holy man was close to death, he pulled from his chest a *phylacterion* that he had always kept there. He then placed this New Testament anthology on his eyes and lips and breast, and having invoked the Lord, he lost consciousness (PG 120.109).[11]

While in these testimonies wearing Gospel books around the neck is an expression of piety, their use in the early Christian period was decidedly apotropaic, containing the power to ward off evil and misfortune. Jerome criticized the "superstitious little women" of his own day who tied onto themselves little Gospel books or pieces of the wood of the cross, or similar objects. "Like the Pharisees," he reported, these women wore the scriptures on their bodies rather than in their hearts (PL 26.175). Indeed, the amuletic use of miniature Gospel books finds parallels in Jewish and Muslim traditions, in which the sacred writing's use as an amulet continues up to our own day.

In contrast to Judaism and Islam, however, in Byzantium, images could convey the scripture as effectively as words, and the cult of icons affected the practice of wearing amulets. An alternative to the use of Gospel books as phylacteries was the decoration of objects with a cycle of images from the life of Christ. A large group of sixth-century amuletic armbands, for example, combine christological scenes with other religious compositions and magical elements. The apotropaic power of christological scenes is well illustrated by a small gold octagonal box-shaped pendant in the British Museum decorated with the images of the nativity and the adoration of the Magi on the front. The reverse bears an inscription with explicit apotropaic intent: "The sure salvation and averting of all the evils." The edge of this small object is enriched with an additional inscription referring to the medical saints Cosmas and Damian, suggesting that the object was intended to hold the medicinal wax salve (*kērōtē*) that was distributed at their Constantinopolitan sanctuary.[12] The multiple layers of protective devices found on this object display the Byzantines' pressing need for various agents capable of engaging the benevolence of God against the forces of evil.

Aside from christological cycles, Christian amuletic jewelry also introduces other religious compositions, such as the Virgin and child enthroned and the Christ in majesty, corresponding to the major themes found in the decorative programs of early Christian sanctuaries. Placed on the conchs of apses, these are the images at which the faithful gaze during the performance of the liturgy. Thus the power of these images on amulets is strengthened by their visual reference to the sacred place where the life-giving sacrifice of Christ is reenacted. The enthroned Virgin and child engraved on the central medallion of a sixth-century silver bracelet,[13] which, according to its dedicatory inscription, had been commissioned for providing health to a woman named Anna, finds a monumental parallel in the apsidal composition of the Church of the Panagia Kanakaria in Lythrankomi, Cyprus. Similarly, the image of Christ in majesty on two closely related sixth-century bronze amuletic medallions relates to the monumental composition in the apse of the Church of Hosios David in Thessalonike.[14] Several centuries later, in the late twelfth or early thirteenth century, the composition of the Christ in majesty recurs as the central theme of an enameled oval medallion in the Vatopedi monastery on Mount Athos (color gallery, plate H). The youthful figure of the enthroned Christ framed by the symbols of the Evangelists holding his oval mandorla, on the front, is attached to a jasper intaglio with the Virgin and child on the back. The expected power of the medallion is specified in a verse inscription addressing the Virgin, which reads: "You who carry the Word purely, I carry on the breast for health of body."[15] The beneficial value of the medallion derives from the metaphoric assimilation of its recipient to the Virgin, who carries the infant Christ on her lap. But the object also carries a dogmatic message in its representation of Christ both in infancy and in majesty, reminding the bearer of his double nature, both divine and human.

Intaglios and cameos were the amulets of the rich, effective both in averting evil spirits and in attracting heavenly powers. A double-sided late tenth- or early eleventh-century bloodstone cameo probably belonged to a high official or a dignitary. In addition to a finely carved representation of Christ Pantocrator (Almighty) identified as "Jesus Christ the Merciful," the owner added a dedicatory inscription on its reverse that reads: "O Christ our Lord, he who puts his hope in thee will not fail."[16] It is noteworthy that this formula is identical to the one that, according to the *Story of the Image of Edessa* (attributed to the Emperor Constantine VII Porphyrogennetos), King Abgar of Edessa had inscribed on the Mandylion, the Holy Towel he had received from Christ (PG 113.437). That description of the translation of the Mandylion to Constantinople on August 15, 944, was read annually during the commemorative feast of the translation, which coincided with the feast of the Dormition of the Virgin. The inscription engraved on the back of the cameo thus derives its protective value both from its association with the liturgy and from the allusion that it makes to the story of the Mandylion, which had cured King Abgar. The power of the image of the living Christ that had been imprinted on the towel was thus transferred to the image carved on the cameo. Although the original setting of this prestigious object is unknown, its owner no doubt carried it as a protective device. A similar concern governed the selection of two miraculous imprints of Christ's face, the Mandylion and the Keramion, or Holy Brick, for the decoration of an enameled bronze pectoral reliquary-cross in the Vatican Museum that dates from the late eleventh or the twelfth century.[17] Also found in the sanctuary programs of contemporary churches, the combination of the Mandylion and Keramion had powerful protective connotations. The protective power of these images on amulets derived from their widespread appearance in devotional spaces; their social contexts lent authority to their private uses.

PECTORAL CROSSES:
ICONOGRAPHY AND ECONOMICS

More humble members of society employed mass-produced bronze pectoral reliquary-crosses as amulets. Widely distributed in the eleventh century, these crosses include schematic representations of saints shown in the attitude of prayer with both hands uplifted, such as the figure of Theophano previously discussed (fig. 8.5). Such iconography derived from early Christian pilgrimage souvenirs and funerary art, and its ongoing selection into the middle Byzantine period reflects a conservatism in devotional preferences among the populace, with forms, styles, and functions enduring over time. After the Virgin the most popular saint represented on these crosses is St. George, whose prayers averted evil spirits just as his spear attacked the dragon (fig. 8.6). Two other saints frequently found on these crosses are Stephen and Niketas, choices that may be explained in the light of the victorious connotation of their names ("crown" and "victor"). Although these crosses probably enjoyed a great popularity among the troops of the Byzantine army, their allusion to victory must be considered in the wider sense of victory over evil. Indeed, many of their wearers were not soldiers, nor was the iconography necessarily military. In monumental paintings and manuscript illumination the *orans* position is very rare and generally reserved for female saints and male monks. The praying saints on bronze crosses may represent ascetic holy men, models of sanctity more immediate to the social classes using these crosses.

The iconography of the middle Byzantine bronze pectoral crosses did not imitate styles popular at higher levels of society.[18] Rather, their iconographic patterns disseminated horizontally along the broad base of the economic pyramid among the masses. The pictorial language of these objects was common to a large

Fig.8.6. Bronze pectoral reliquary-cross, eleventh century, incised with images of St. George. Photo: Sadberk Hanım Museum, Istanbul, inv. no. H.K.296-4825.

network of workshops scattered throughout the empire. In contrast to the overall tendency in other artistic media, including precious pectoral reliquary-crosses in enamel or niello, the bronze reliquary-crosses make no formal distinction among the categories of saints: the saints engraved on the surfaces are generic images of holy people endowed with protective character. Often the images lack inscriptions identifying the name of the saint. Significantly, busts of similarly anonymous figures were also used on domestic metalware, such as padlocks and stamp seals, the function of which was to place precious objects, documents, or food under saintly protection.[19]

Inquiry into the meaning of wearing a pectoral cross for veneration and protection also raises questions about the economics of cross production. During the early Byzantine period, wealthy Christians wore sumptuous necklaces with a variety of ornamental pendants that displayed a wide range of goldsmithing techniques. Extant stone molds and matrixes used by Byzantine goldsmiths also indicate that pectoral crosses were manufactured simultaneously with jewelry pendants and earrings. A woman who wished to acquire a cross commissioned a goldsmith, just as she might for any other kind of jewelry. The elegant woman depicted on a painted Coptic plaster figurine, for example, proudly displays a large cross, suspended on her bosom as an object of adornment (fig. 8.7).[20]

However, Byzantine pectoral crosses were not usually objects of lavish display: in their role as protective devices, crosses were often hidden under the vestments of their wearer. In Byzantine art, saints are rarely depicted wearing pectoral crosses. An exception are some medieval images of the martyr St. Orestes, a young soldier from Sebasteia who was betrayed to his executioners by the cross hanging around his neck.[21] St. Orestes in military dress wearing a jewelry cross on his chest appears in the lavish eleventh-century fresco decoration of Karanlık Kilise in Cappadocia (fig. 8.8).[22] Aside from this example, in which the cross appears as an expression of its owner's faith, pectoral crosses can also be found in some

Fig. 8.7. Plaster Coptic figurine of a woman wearing a cross around her neck. Gift of Maurice Nahman, 1912 (12.185.4). Photo: Metropolitan Museum of Art, all rights reserved.

representations of monks to emphasize their pious behavior and intercessory power.

Although many wore their crosses concealed, the hierarchy of metals found within a single archaeological context shows that the cross was a privileged, if hidden, object, often larger in size and more costly than other types of jewelry. The metal objects found in a sixth-century house in Golemanovo Kale in Sadovec, near the city of Pleven, Bulgaria, include a small silver cross decorated with an elegant filigree ornament and a glasspaste cabochon at the intersection of the arms. This object stands out from the two plain silver earrings and the bronze fibula with which it was associated.[23]

As a symbolic allusion to the passion of Christ, the cross was endowed with an intrinsic value transcending the media and manner in which it was manufactured. In the *Life of Macrina* Gregory of Nyssa reports that when he visited his sister on her deathbed in 379, he discovered that she wore an iron cross suspended on a slender chain. In this context Gregory's specification of the modest nature of the metal does not seem to have been made haphazardly.

Fig. 8.8. St. Orestes with a jeweled pectoral cross, eleventh century, Karanlık Kilise, Cappadocia. Photo: Catherine Jolivet-Lévy.

Gregory offers this cross to Vetiana, the nun who was preparing his sister's body for burial. To his surprise he also finds that his sister wore a ring with an engraved cross, which, according to Vetiana, contained a fragment of the true cross on which Christ had been crucified. Gregory kept this ring as a legacy (*Life of Macrina*, 30.7–21). This early testimony bears witness to the complementary roles of pectoral crosses and relics of the true cross, which were commonly transmitted to their wearers' heirs. But the concern for salvation meant that metal crosses often accompanied their recipients to their graves.

Several surviving jewelry crosses from the early Christian period served as personal reliquaries for the true cross. Such crosses were objects of desire and admiration both for the materials in which they were manufactured and for their capacity to work miracles. The seventh-century *Life of John the Almsgiver*, patriarch of Alexandria, contains an evocative story on the fate of a gold pectoral cross holding a relic of the true cross. Another John, bishop of Tiberias in Palestine, bequeathed his cross to his heir. John the Almsgiver, who greatly admired this cross, offered twice its value in order to own it. The heir accepted the offer but cheated the patriarch by offering him a replica of the original cross. This unscrupulousness points to widespread counterfeiting in the relics market. Happily, in hagiography, at least, counterfeiters are usually identified and denounced through the intervention of heavenly powers. The man who cheated the patriarch had a dream in which threatening angels forced him to give up the original cross in order to become an honest man (*Life of John the Almsgiver* 11).

Early Byzantine miracle accounts emphasize the power of the cross to combat demonic forces. Another seventh-century miracle story tells of a silver cross enclosing a fragment of the true cross that belonged to Anastasius of Sinai. This cross had the power to release a man suffering from demonic assaults.[24] And an account of the journey of Peter the Iberian to Jerusalem in 431 narrates how bits of the true cross encased in the cover of his Gospel book produced a miraculous oil that provided physical relief to him and his travel companion when they anointed their bodies.[25]

PRIVATE PIETY: RELICS AND WEARABLE ICONS

The expansion of the cult of the saints and the craze for collecting their relics multiplied the types of personal reliquaries in the middle Byzantine period. The owners of such relics encased them in beautiful receptacles. In cases in which the origin of the relic was known, their owners proudly indicated this ostentatiously with decorative inscriptions. The taste for the literary epigram among the twelfth-century aristocracy generated private reliquaries personalized by short poems praising the beauty of their adornment with gold, pearls, and precious stones. A recurring word in these epigrams, emphasizing the piety of their commissioner, is "love" (*pothos*). In this case faith appears to have stimulated effusive acts of reverence. For poorer people driven by the same religious zeal, goldsmiths produced a variety of ready-made dedicatory formulas. Either customized or generic, these inscriptions expressed concerns for heavenly help and salvation, motivations for devotional behavior at all levels of Byzantine society.

The interior of the most precious reliquaries was arranged into compartments separating a multiplicity of relics. However, pectoral reliquaries often incorporated a compound of particles of the true cross and various anonymous relics, including saints' bones, earth, pebbles, or dust from holy places, mixed with balm, incense, and other fragrant substances. These pectoral reliquaries opened to allow physical access to the relics for private devotional practices: the user kissed the relics and anointed himself or herself with the holy oil it contained. Indeed, balm and other kinds of fragrant oils were at the core of the private cult of the relics, as Byzantines anointed their bodies for health and for protection from evil. Such practices featured in the cult of St. Demetrius in Thessalonike, which centered on myrrh that exuded from his tomb and was distributed to the faithful. A thirteenth-century enameled medallion of St. Demetrius in the British Museum attests the benefit of physical contact with the shrine's myrrh. Anointed with the blood and myrrh of the saint, the recipient of the *enkolpion*, probably a high official in the Byzantine army, supplicates him to be his fiery defender in battle.[26]

Because icons and relics shared the same capacities to intercede with God on behalf of humanity and to work miracles, wearing an image responded to the same devotional needs as wearing a relic. The engraved representations of saints that appear on bronze cross *enkolpia* that contained relics, for example, recur on flat crosses that were not reliquaries. These different types of crosses appear to have been used interchangeably, suggesting that they afforded a similar degree of protection. Archaeological excavation of the twelfth-century cemetery in the atrium of the Church of St. Polyeuktos in Constantinople, for example, has yielded several pectoral reliquary-crosses together with a range of flat crosses in various materials including copper-alloy, lead, and steatite. All these objects probably shared the same protective power.[27] The same site also yielded a small *enkolpion* that illustrates the growing role of icons in private devotional practices. This ivory plaque decorated with a bust-length representation of St. Nicholas was probably not initially crafted as a pendant. Instead, its final owner had it adapted by drilling a hole on its upper edge and inserting a wire suspension loop so that the miracle-working saint's image could be worn on the chest like a relic.

From the twelfth century, and especially during the thirteenth and fourteenth, in concert with the developing role of the painted icon as a privileged focus for devotional practices, *enkolpia* of rectangular or circular shape became prevalent in private piety. Although some served as reliquaries, many of them had no cavity for a relic; they were simply icons carried on the body. Their owners carried them tightly on their person and kissed them in veneration, just as they would relics. A group of *enkolpia* dated to the thirteenth or fourteenth century illustrates this shift in devotional practices. Their box-like shape has confused scholars, who initially believed them to be reliquary boxes (fig. 8.9), but their interiors are merely filled with a mixture of resin, wax, brick dust or marble dust, and sulphur intended to reinforce the thin sheets of silver from which they are formed. Their metallic surfaces, usually a rectangular plaque like a miniature icon, are decorated with embossed images that derive from contemporary painted icons. The most widespread type depicts the crucifixion on one side, while the other side shows two or three warrior saints dressed in their armor and standing under arches. These wearable icons also depict other scenes popular in the period, including Daniel in the lions' den and John the Baptist preaching in the desert. Such images, endowed with both a protective and a salvific connotation, were also very popular on cameos, steatites, and other types of breast pendants from the twelfth century onwards.

Fig. 8.9. Silver enkolpion with miniature icon of three military saints, late thirteenth to fourteenth century. Photo: Vatopedi Monastery, Mount Athos. Photo used by permission.

MONETARY VALUES

Crosses and various types of *enkolpia* were not only objects of worship but also financial assets. A good illustration of the prestige associated with pectoral reliquary-crosses is found in a catalog of gifts that the patriarch Nikephoros presented to Pope Leo III upon his enthronement in 811. The envoy included liturgical vestments decorated in gold, but the most important piece was a gold pectoral reliquary-cross composed of two interlocking boxes enclosing pieces of the true cross. The text explains that this prestigious cross was decorated with images in niello and covered with rock crystal (PG 100.200).

What about the value of the cheaper variants that were cast in bronze? It is worth noting that in Byzantine society bronze was a relatively precious material, too expensive for the poor. Excavations of medieval villages turn up such crosses only in the wealthiest households. Our knowledge of the prices of domestic objects and jewelry in Byzantium is limited. However, appraisals included in monastic inventories show that in the fourteenth century, for example, the price of a silver belt could be higher than that of a cow in some regions.[28] In the eyes of the people who used these objects, their monetary value thus played an important role that must be taken into consideration alongside their spiritual value.

A particularly evocative testimony to the multiple meanings and values of metal devotional objects is a silver *enkolpion* found in 1987 during the restoration work conducted on the Byzantine land walls at the Belgrade gate (Xylokerkos Gate) in Istanbul (fig. 8.10 and color gallery, plate I). The object consists of two embossed sheets of silver joined together by a narrow silver band that is soldered on the circumference. One side, probably the back, depicts two standing warrior saints in armor facing each other in profile with their hands uplifted in prayer, while their two shields lie on the ground in front of them. The figure on the right, with a long pointed beard, can be securely identified as Theodore Stratelates, while the one on the left might be Theodore Teron, or possibly George or Demetrius. The other side of the *enkolpion* bears a representation of Daniel in the lions' den, whose association with the two warrior saints may be grounded in the

biblical story of Bel and the Dragon, which describes Daniel's destruc-
tion of a dragon in Babylon (Dan. 14:23-28). The images decorating
both its faces imbue this *enkolpion* with an apotropaic power. The
scene of Daniel in the lions' den, however, also carries strong salvific
connotations. In the decorative programs of Cappadocian churches,
for example, the image of Daniel in the lions' den often occurs both
in funerary contexts and near liturgical bowls of holy water. In some
cases the image appears in close prox-
imity to depictions of Sts. George
and Theodore on horseback spearing a dragon or a serpent.[29] What
makes this silver *enkolpion* (fig. 8.10)
exceptional is that it was discovered
among a large hoard of 2,280 silver
coins dating from the thirteenth and
fourteenth centuries and a collection of medical instruments, all of
which had been hidden in a glazed
one-handled pottery jar.[30] The composition of the hoard is diverse and
includes a complete selection of
the types of silver coins in use in
the imperial capital. It was probably buried during the reconquest
of Constantinople by John V and
his son Manuel (later Manuel II) on
July 1, 1379, together with another
hoard, composed of 1,221 copper
coins, which was found a few meters
away. The presence of medical instru-

Fig. 8.10. Silver *enkolpion*
with praying military saints,
late thirteenth to fourteenth
century. For reverse side see
color gallery, plate I. Photo:
Istanbul Archaeological
Museum, inv. no. H.K.95.278.

ments may suggest that the owner of these two hoards was a doctor,
while the hiding of the *enkolpion* suggests that its owner regarded it as
a valuable financial asset.

This overview of pious practice in Byzantium through the study
of small devotional objects has articulated a range of social behaviors
that can be inferred from the pieces themselves. In general, these

objects reflect central Byzantine Christian concerns with concrete daily problems like health and salvation. The comparative study of objects from different periods of the empire illustrates the evolution of these private devotional practices as well as a strong tendency toward conservatism with respect to both form and function. Pre-Christian amuletic images intended to ward off evil survive from all periods, at the same time that their Christian counterparts were endowed with multivalent functions, both apotropaic and devotional. The iconography demonstrates that military saints dominated popular faith in Byzantium, from the Holy Rider of Late Antiquity to middle and late Byzantine depictions of Demetrius, George, and Theodore in armor. The cult of relics carried around the neck reached its climax during the eleventh century, when it pervaded all levels of society. Whether precious works smithed in gold or objects mass-produced in base metal, the shape and decoration of these small objects tended to be standardized. Their use in daily life involved rituals of touching, kissing, looking at, and venerating the images and relics. The hinged reliquaries, which allowed access to the relics within, imply practices for storing and accessing curative substances, like balm or fragrance, or facilitating contact with relics. Although often performed privately, the commissioning, purchase, veneration, and wearing of these pieces indicate that such devotional practices were collective practices engaged in widely. Amulets, pectoral crosses, and *enkolpia* point to religious practices and sensibilities shared by the whole spectrum of Byzantine society. Venerating objects and using them for protection were deeply entwined forms of Byzantine Christian piety.

FOR FURTHER READING

Kalavrezou, Ioli, ed. *Byzantine Women and Their World*. New Haven: Yale University Press, 2003.

Kartsonis, Anna. "Protection against All Evil: Function, Use and Operation of Byzantine Historiated Phylacteries." *Byzantinische Forschungen* 20 (1994): 73–102.

Maguire, Eunice Dautermann, Henry P. Maguire, and Marjorie J. Duncan-Flowers. *Art and Holy Powers in the Early Christian House*. Urbana: Krannert Art Museum and University of Illinois Press, 1989.

Pitarakis, Brigitte. "Female Piety in Context: Understanding Developments in Private Devotional Practices." In Maria Vassilaki, ed., *Images of the Mother of God*: *Perceptions of the Theotokos in Byzantium*, 153–66. London: Ashgate, 2005.

Spier, Jeffrey. "Medieval Byzantine Magical Amulets and Their Tradition." *Journal of the Warburg and Courtauld Institutes* 56 (1993): 25–62.

THE RELIGIOUS LIVES OF
CHILDREN AND ADOLESCENTS

PETER HATLIE

CHAPTER NINE

Early Byzantine young people are best known historically in their role as sporting fans with a penchant for hooliganism. Byzantine historians, poets, and artists give a fairly full account of events at the circus, and modern historians have followed the games and their predominantly young adult male crowd of fans quite closely. As interesting as these young men may be, their rowdy behavior at the circus should not be regarded as typical or characteristic, since what took place there constituted only a part of their upbringing and life experience. Nor should it be forgotten that although such circusgoers stole the headlines, they still represented only a small minority of all Byzantine young people—male and female, urban and rural, sporting fans and not. The aim of this chapter is to go beyond the well-studied circus-going youth and begin to retrace, through a variety of written and material sources, the more ordinary experience of growing up and coming of age in the early Byzantine centuries, notably with respect to the religious experiences of young people. The chronological focus is on the fourth through ninth centuries, an age marking the definitive transition from Greco-Roman Antiquity to the Byzantine Middle Ages. One of the most popular types of literature in circulation during this age was the saint's life (or hagiography), whose accounts of childhood and young adult experiences constitute an important source of information for examining typical patterns of religious behavior as well as prevailing attitudes and expectations. What emerges from this and other sources of the period is a sense of the enormous influence of religion on childhood, adolescent, and young adult development, together with a clear understanding of how deeply indebted the Byzantines were in this regard to both their early Christian and their Greco-Roman forebears.

INFANCY AND CHILDHOOD

Giving birth to healthy children and bringing them safely through infancy were highly uncertain prospects in early Byzantium, just as they were in all preindustrial societies. Infertility, high rates of infant mortality, and inadequate or troubled parenting were all factors that could, and frequently did, compromise a successful childbirth. In response to these challenges, religion—in all of its various forms of expression—promised help. Problems with conception prompted couples to pray to particular saints and visit special shrines, to attend their local church more regularly, and to seek the intervention of charismatic, miracle-working holy men.[1] The actual conception itself, if and when it occurred, was considered a wondrous work that God performed either directly or through holy intermediaries. It might even come quite suddenly during an intense moment of prayer (*Life of Stephen the Younger* 92–93). The successful birth of a wanted child, by whatever means, brought joy and temporary relief to expectant parents. Before long, however, a number of new and frightening dangers to the child's welfare presented themselves. The employment of a variety of apotropaic and healing aids, some officially embraced by the church and others not, constituted one of the young parents' predictable responses to these dangers. For life-threatening cases baptism was naturally of the utmost urgency and could be administered in extremis even if the normal waiting period of eight to forty days after birth had not yet passed. In addition, priests might be summoned to bring the sick and dying into direct physical contact with sanctified materials, such as blessed oil, the cross, or an icon.[2]

On their own initiative, and probably at some distance from official church authority, parents also turned to a range of quasi-magical devices to safeguard themselves and their children against sickness and evil. Such devices included amulets, jewelry, silks, bells, and other objects that were believed to be invested with special powers against Satan and his various demons, breeders of ill fortune that they were. The Byzantine use of such folk-based remedies had deep, demonstrable links to the pagan past, although Judeo-Christian symbolism prevailed at the level of mere recognition. A handful of early Christian bishops, led by John Chrysostom, remained unconvinced: they demanded that their congregations do away with such objects, together with the traditions that accompanied them. The evidence from later centuries suggests that only a minority of individuals followed their warnings. In the later eighth century a pious young mother in Constantinople named Theoktiste was the exception proving the rule.

> After giving birth [she] avoided doing what other wives were accustomed to do on behalf of their infants, when they employ omens and amulets and certain other enchantments to neutralize the assault of demons. They deploy these items on couches and beds. They use necklaces and other charms too. She, on the contrary, contented herself with the seal of the life-giving Cross alone as her armor and shield of protection. In sum: whereas all other women believe in the instructive, mystical and practical power of such devices, she alone stayed away from them, neither inclining her head to them, nor invoking them, nor participating in superstitious rites. And as a consequence, she often drew criticism from those who were experts in such matters. (*Life of Theoktiste of Constantinople* 844b–45a, PG 99)

The rich store of surviving religious clothing and objects connected with childbirth and neonatal care proves the ubiquity of such practices. Visual references to Solomon, St. Sissinios, and other supposed forces of good figured prominently here often depicted on horseback (fig. 9.1). A demon by the name of Gellō (or Gyllou) was one of any number of evil forces against which these objects were supposed to work, her dreaded specialty being the suffocation of infant children by night. Sometimes she came in person, while at others she possessed older women to do her business. The ancient Greek poet Sappho knew of her hundreds of years before the Byzantines did, and until recently modern Greeks still feared her dark powers.[3]

Fig. 9.1. Amulet with Holy Rider and Evil Eye, made of two thin, embossed copper sheets, fifth to seventh century. Photo: Walters Art Museum, Baltimore.

In response to anxieties about the future and the need to make a number of practical decisions, some parents turned to astrology for guidance—a tradition that went back to the religious sciences of Greco-Roman antiquity. In commissioning nativity horoscopes, Byzantines perpetuated the ancient belief that the stars and planets could reveal the child's life span, future physical appearance and temperament, place in the family scheme, character, wealth and honors, state of marriage, and even condition at death (*On the Ages of Humankind* 456–57).[4]

These same people no doubt turned to the official church for more secure guidance when the allure of esoteric and folk wisdom waned. In principle, the church took a positive and sympathetic interest in the very young. From the famous passage of Matt. 19:13-15 ("Suffer the little children") to numerous other scriptural and patristic teachings, the message was that God valued children and cared about their fate. Early Christian authorities recognized the young child's faults and vulnerabilities, and attended to parental calls for help.[5] A cycle of sixth-century mosaics from the Church of St. Demetrius in Thessalonike (figs. 9.2, 9.3, 9.4) reminds us that the support of officially sanctioned religion remained close at hand, as parents turned their attention to their child's upbringing. The mosaics depict a young girl named Maria at three different moments in her childhood: shortly after birth when she is being presented to the saint's shrine; upon taking her first steps; and as a growing child. In keeping with fairly common practice, Maria's parents made a donation to Demetrius's shrine—in this case a large one—in the hopes of gaining the saint's protection and favor.[6]

The same mosaics may indicate another practice, namely, the pledging of an infant or small child to a church or monastery, what is commonly referred to as

Figs. 9.2, 3, 4. Three scenes from the life of the child Maria, from a sixth-century mosaic (destroyed by fire in 1917) in the Church of St. Demetrius in Thessalonike. The first scene shows the presentation of the infant Maria to St. Demetrius. The second shows Maria as a child, offering candles to St. Demetrius. The third shows her as an older child next to the saint. Photos: The British School at Athens.

"oblation" in its more developed Western medieval form. Even if Maria's status as an oblate cannot be firmly established, the practice is fairly well documented for other infants of the Byzantine centuries. Sometimes the practice served as an alternative to the child's abandonment and enslavement. At other times it was offered as an expression of the parents' gratitude to God for the child's birth.[7] A sense of familial necessity may have combined with religious idealism in many such cases. Indeed, the sense of necessity proved strong among the poor and stronger still when young girls were involved, since prevailing social conventions dictated that male children had greater value within the family scheme than females did. But whatever the sex of the child and the motivations of parents, the act of oblation itself deprived children of the eventual right to choose their fate, and in turn could lead later to some awkward difficulties. If one child within a family was earmarked for the church and another for marriage, it could happen that they changed their minds and sought to switch roles as they grew older and became aware of the arrangement. Religious officials had difficulty giving satisfactory answers to this quandary (Theodore of Stoudios, *Letters* 738–40). Nor were they much clearer about the related problem of establishing minimum age thresholds at which children with a living parent or guardian could be handed over to a religious institution. There is significant evidence of child oblates and very young vocations, both those well under sixteen years of age and in some cases mere infants.[8]

In all of these scenes of adoption and oblation the experience of infants and young children themselves remains almost entirely unknown because of the absence of first-person accounts. The same is true for those boys and girls who reportedly entered monasteries of their own accord as mere infants. One of the few things that can be ascertained concerns the long-term fate of such children, specifically whether they had the right to finalize their vocation later in life or whether, on the contrary, their initial vocation was irrevocable. Some religious authorities called for a second and final vocational pledge, toward age sixteen and the coming of reason, for candidates wishing to remain in the religious life. No absolute consensus developed on this issue, however, and so it seems probable that considerable numbers of children remained bound by pledges made by them or for them in infancy or childhood (Theodore of Stoudios, *Letters* 721). One is tempted to link the high incidence of instability that is known to have plagued early Byzantine monasticism with this life-course problem: young people often tried to undo religious promises taken earlier in life without their full consent by simply running away. Along the same lines, and indeed better documented, was the young person's attempt to achieve a better fit within a vocation made at a young age. The pledged monk might end up being a member of the clergy, or conversely the cleric might gravitate over the years to the monastic life. Rather than fleeing the religious world within which they found themselves, some found it more agreeable to make a lateral move.[9]

EDUCATION, AMUSEMENTS, AND THE INNOCENCE OF THE YOUNG CHILD

Most children passed their infant years in more ordinary circumstances than the oblates and early vocations just discussed. The number of young orphans was evidently high, yet even they could expect to grow up more or less normally under the direction of an extended family member or a legally appointed guardian. For most of these children, except the acutely disadvantaged, two activities dominated the years leading up to adolescence: play and schooling. Early Byzantine church authorities such as John Chrysostom and Basil of Caesarea stressed the importance of one or both activities for proper religious development, devoting influential treatises to the subject.

Basil framed the challenge of childhood education in this way: "Everything we do is nothing but a preparation for the other life. Therefore we declare that whatever may bring us to this end is to be loved and pursued with all our strength, whereas those things that draw us away from it must be passed over as useless" (Basil, *Young Men* 380). Basil used this benchmark—later to become a standard in Byzantine education—for deciding which books should be included in the young Christian's curriculum, which behaviors in children should be reinforced and which discouraged, and what distractions and pleasures should be conceded. Chrysostom's treatise followed a similar line of argument, albeit with a greater emphasis on strict

behavioral conditioning. Whereas Basil hoped to channel a youngster's flow of energies and curiosity, Chrysostom typically tried to dam
it up (*On Vainglory*).

One notable thing about both of these works is that part of their
target audience was parents themselves. This makes perfect sense,
since parents normally provided elementary instruction in reading,
writing, and religion at home. Homeschooling continued until the
child reached about age seven, and it could even be prolonged by
some years in the event that private tutors were either distant or unaf-
fordable.[10] Mothers played a prominent role in the homeschool environment compared to their counterparts in the Greco-Roman world;
this shift went hand in hand with a number of new familial rights and
responsibilities claimed by early Christian and Byzantine mothers,
including their stronger claim to retain family property and act as
guardians over children upon their husband's death. But regardless of
whether a child's first teacher was the mother, the father, a close family
member, or a tutor, the subject taught was often referred to as "sacred
letters," a term that probably indicates a form of elementary education
conducted on the basis of scriptural readings and lessons.[11]

When parents were steeped in religious conservatism, they might
insist on a separate and more intensive series of lessons in reading
scripture and reciting the Psalms at a very young age. Holy men and
monasteries provided such instruction, occasionally for mere infants
but more commonly for children approaching age ten and older who
were no longer being educated in the household (John of Ephesus,
Lives 89–90; *Life of Anthony II Kauleas* 414). Indeed, once a child's
education at home had run its course, the world changed for parents
and children alike. In the case of young girls, plans for marriage began
at a very young age, consequently removing the need for further education in most instances. As for boys, marriage plans became urgent
only some years later, normally in adolescence or early adulthood.
Depending on the family's economic status, boys now either went
to work in some profession or trade or embarked upon a course of
secular studies. Some parents and guardians evidently took seriously
this potential decrease in familial influences and controls, and sought
a remedy by enrolling their male children in religiously based schools,
both monastic and episcopal.[12]

Faced with the prospect of young people within their walls, religious institutions themselves came forth with fledgling programs of study and boarding facilities to meet their needs. Many young men entered churches or monasteries around age ten to receive a blend of religious and practical instruction (*Life of John of Psichon* 108–10; *Life of Nicholas of Stoudios* 869c–72c). Their presence within monasteries in particular, and the apparent uncertainty of their status there—pupil or monk?—constituted yet another reason for the debate over age thresholds. For young girls of ten or so who entered convents, the debate over age thresholds was even more urgent because for them and their parents the choice was not between religious schooling in the monastery or secular schooling in the world—with any final decisions about marriage and profession or vocation to be taken later—but rather the more stark choice between a life in the monastery or a life in marriage. Whereas boys consigned to such institutions might emerge later to do something else in life (see *Life of Anthony II Kauleas* 414–15; *Life of Eutychios of Constantinople* 10), for girls this was highly unlikely.

Pious biographies are quick to point out that children themselves often made the decision to join a monastery or seek a church office at a young age. Sometimes this act contradicted the will of parents and had less to do with obtaining an education than it did with answering an inner religious call that would eventually lead them to sainthood. This kind of child, whom scholars have come to call the *puer senex* ("elderly child"), was exceptional from birth, exhibiting mature behaviors and acute spiritual sensibilities long before adulthood. Dreams, visions, and divine signs courted such children at an early age as they charted a course for themselves that excluded the experiences of average children, such as love and obedience to family, or indulgence in childhood games and amusements.[13] Where real biography ends and pious fiction begins in these

> **In Praise of a Young Cleric**
>
> In the *Life of Theodore of Sykeon*, the saint speaks to the young Patriarch of Constantinople, Sergios I (early seventh century), who has protested that he was too young for the office: "God chose you because of your young age. He wanted you to possess that particular sense of resolve typical of youth so that you might endure and nobly bear the many trials and tribulations that are bound to visit our kingdom. Older people cannot manage this sort of thing."
>
> —George the Monk, *Life of Theodore of Sykeon (BHG 1748)*, ed. and trans. André-Jean Festugière (Brussels: Société des Bollandistes, 1970), 1:108–9.

accounts of spiritually precocious children is difficult to say. Generally speaking, however, it is clear that these narratives juxtapose the high ideals of childhood religious development of a chosen few over against the common (or perhaps even purposely low) expectations written into the script of other children mentioned in the biography.

Among the most precocious of all Byzantines was Theodore of Sykeon, a late sixth- and early seventh-century saint from Asia Minor who at age twelve outlived a major plague and received a vision from God telling him to take up the ascetic life. By age thirteen he had confined himself to a cell for two weeks of fasting and prayer without speaking to anyone, and by age fourteen he had officially severed ties with his friends and family in order to become a full-time hermit (*Life of Theodore of Sykeon* 1.7–13). Of a similar stamp to Theodore was the fifth- or sixth-century Constantinopolitan ascetic John Kalybites, who at age twelve took incredible pains to elude his wealthy parents and renounce the world, only to return to his family home some eight years later, now a successful ascetic dressed up in the guise of a poor, withered, and entirely unrecognizable beggar (*Life of John Kalybites* 262–71). These remarkable and rich childhood stories share two significant themes: first, because they are exceptional youth, neither John nor Theodore indulge in the amusements of other children, such as running, jumping, dancing, singing, silly games, and vain childish tricks; and second, the childhood games that both heroes do engage in specifically advance their religious vocations and ultimately serve the will of God. In John's case the tricks involve a series of white lies, sleights of hand, and disappearing acts that he used to extricate himself from family ties (*Life of John Kalybites* 263–66). More intriguing is the case of Theodore's first act of exorcism. He was about fourteen at the time and initially as perplexed as he was reluctant to take the matter on. Once involved, however, he engaged in a protracted series of exchanges with the demon, lasting three days and cast in the form of a game, something between hide-and-seek and infantile mimicry. Terribly annoyed throughout, the demon denounced Theodore as "son of the whore" and "a mere kid." Ultimately Theodore broke the demon's will, causing it to flee in utter shame at having been defeated by a youngster rather than by an accomplished holy man (*Life of Theodore of Sykeon* 1.15–16). This story of Theodore's first exorcism looks similar to that of John's escape and renunciation insofar as it, too, makes the point that even exceptional children are inclined to engage in play. More to the point: the play of such saintly children is inspired with divine purpose, whereas that of ordinary children is frivolous.

In everyday life there was, of course, a middle way between these contrasting models of ordinary children with base amusements and the *puer senex* with a form of spiritually enlightened play. In his treatise on children John Chrysostom begins to plot that middle ground, rejecting the ordinary amusements of youth, including the theater, but proposing instead that "we devise harmless pleasures for children, that we lead them to saintly lives and give them recreation, that we show our regard for them by many gifts so that their soul may patiently bear our rejection of the theater. In place of those spectacles let us introduce pleasing stories, flowery meadows, and fair buildings" (*On Vainglory* 180). Basil of Caesarea had already introduced such fair spectacles into the curriculum of his boarding school for children. Among the regular activities planned there was a memorization game in which students won recognition for recalling names and events from the book of Proverbs. As Basil explains it, the game was designed to be relaxing and pleasurable so as to allow students to learn scripture more easily (Basil, *Rule* 953c–56a). Ordinary children of all ages must have engaged in comparable forms of religious recreation, even though available sources yield very little on the subject. Among the few surviving artifacts of religious interest to survive is an early Byzantine wooden doll from Egypt, rendered in the shape of a cross and resembling contemporary ex-voto offerings (fig. 9.5). Was this a religious toy? It may well have been an object that average children found both edifying and amusing, similar to and yet different from the more mundane sources of amusement that occupied their attention. Even future saints played with such objects if they were raised in a normal

Fig. 9.5. Wooden doll in the shape of a cross. Coptic Egypt, sixth to seventh centuries (?). Photo: Benaki Museum, Athens, inv. no. 10750.

childhood setting, as was sometimes the case. Instead of criticizing their heroes for not adopting a sterner disposition at an early age, their biographers simply described their early childhood experiences as innocent and without grave sin (*Life of Theophanes 1* 4; *Life of Euthymios of Sardis* 21–23).

In fact, innocence was the trademark of all good children. In a few children the quality laid the foundations for a later spiritual awakening leading to sainthood; for most, its appearance simply meant that demons had not taken charge of matters. Among all human beings young children were alone presumed capable of living in a state approaching complete innocence, and it was perhaps because of their possession of this rare gift that adults occasionally invested them with an unusual degree of spiritual authority. The use of children in divination ceremonies employing hypnosis, sleep deprivation, suggestive incantations, and other psychosomatic inducements reflected a belief in their special ability to act as vessels for visiting spirits both good and evil.[14] The official church condemned such rituals outright, as black magic.

At the same time children featured in the authorized rituals of the church. The festival of Palm Sunday commemorated Jesus' entry into Jerusalem on the way to his passion and death. In Byzantine art Jesus enters Jerusalem led by a procession of joyous children: the message seems to be that children alone can truly revel in the moment because they alone remain ignorant of and detached from the gravity

Fig. 9.6. Jesus' entry into Jerusalem, welcomed enthusiastically by children. Rossano Gospels, early sixth century. Photo: Scala/Art Resource, NY.

of the occasion (fig. 9.6). Or, to put it another way, only children can usher in the last bloody days of passion and death with a completely clean conscience, and paradoxically they remain close if unwitting collaborators in God's plan for doing so. The important role given to children in these scenes of Jesus' entry into Jerusalem was not in the first instance biblically inspired, but rather grew out of early Christian exegesis linking the entry (Matt. 21:1-9) to Jesus' subsequent cleansing of the Temple (Matt. 21:15-16). By the late fourth century Palm Sunday liturgical traditions in Jerusalem had already adopted this interpretation of the entrance, and from there the custom took firm root in the rest of the Byzantine world (*Egeria's Travels* 31). Special rites and prayers confirm the central role of children in the various Palm Sunday liturgies (*L' Eucologio Barbarini gr. 336* 220–21, 204–5), attesting to a long-standing tradition that not only welcomed the very young into the church through baptism and "suffered" them thereafter, but also required something of them that was integral to its own proper standing.

ADOLESCENCE: RESTLESSNESS AND RESPONSIBILITIES

In adolescence the young person's experience of becoming an adult predominated over his or her full participation in adulthood. The timing of biological and social changes was neither coordinated nor the same for everyone, nor indeed were most of the dramatic personal changes and rites of passage that took place during the transition from childhood to adulthood under the young person's own control. A mix of anticipation and frustration was thus characteristic of the experience of this age group. Depending upon when various social thresholds were finally crossed, the sweep of one's adolescent years could be as great as the years between fifteen and thirty or as narrowly defined as the years between the arrival of puberty at age fourteen (or so) and the end of the next seven-year block of time at age twenty. The terminologies for what constituted adolescence were likewise flexible, underscoring how fluid this transitional phase of life was considered to be. Some modern scholars have put undue emphasis on this point, proposing accordingly that adolescence as such simply did not exist for people of the ancient or medieval past. This proposition is difficult to accept in view of the consistent catalog of behaviors and adult expectations that sources attached to people of this general age group.[15]

Restlessness was one of the most common problems associated with adolescence and young adulthood. As they looked on, adults could admire the emerging strength and physical beauty of the adolescent, but they were equally troubled by the seemingly uncontrollable emotional impulses that went along with this phase of life. Sexual urges were a principal problem and thus became a focus of concern for parents and guardians. A commitment to marriage now pressed hard upon those who had not been betrothed in childhood. For those who had entered religious life earlier or were now doing so, on the other hand, strict controls on their sexual activity greeted them on their arrival.[16] Concerns about a youth's sexual fallibility were rooted in a much broader series of doubts and misgivings about the character of adolescents and young people. One early Byzantine author generalized: "When people are in the bloom of youth, they are as opposed to embracing the good as they are keen on things that are out of bounds. They are simply unable to perceive what is useful and to reach higher goals because of the fact that puberty has not been completed" (*Life of Nikephoros of Sebaze* 20).

> ### The Development of a Pious Child
>
> From the *vita* of the ninth-century bishop Euthymios of Sardis: "As with well-bred plants, infants signal their progress toward the Lord by growing upright and upward. Watching them grow tall and beautiful, the gardener feels assured of the good fruits to come and gladdened by a sense of hope awakened to the changes ahead."
>
> —Methodios the Patriarch, *Life of Euthymios, Bishop of Sardis* 2, ed. J. Gouillard, *Travaux et Mémoires* 10 (1987): 23.

The case histories of numerous individuals from the early Byzantine period testify to the unwillingness of youth to follow the dictates, wise or not, of their parents and guardians. The stories range from marriage plans gone awry to sudden flights from hometown and profession, and much in between. Many of these actions were premeditated, though there is also reason to believe that some young people with big ideas were simply acting out an adolescent whim. Either way one can understand why adults labeled such behavior as unstable, because it typically put young people at odds with parental plans for their future. There was nothing so very new in this pattern of intergenerational relations. Conflicts between young and old had been strongly felt in Greek and Roman society on certain key issues, such as marriage, career, and the general question of obedience to parents and elders, and they were no less so in the early Byzantine centuries.[17]

Something important had changed, however, with respect to religiously motivated conflicts between young and old. Unlike their counterparts in the ancient world, early Byzantine adolescents and young adults with a burning passion for religious conversion could justify discord with their elders—along with other eccentric conduct undertaken in the name of the Lord—on higher scriptural grounds. Both Luke 14:26-27 on the cost of discipleship and Matt. 10:34-39 or Luke 12:51-53 regarding family loyalties were clear enough on the need for everyone to pursue a higher religious calling at any price, and "everyone" included young people. Indeed, several of the followers of Jesus were themselves known to have been young when they made the radical decision to take up discipleship, and they in turn came to serve as models for religiously restless youth of a later age.[18]

Weighing the influence of these scriptural lessons on early Byzantine youth may help to explain why so much intergenerational conflict surfaced during their adolescent years. One might suggest, in fact, that there were a greater variety of pretexts at hand for such conflicts to develop than ever before, notably in comparison to the earlier Greek and Roman worlds, where a movement toward religious or philosophical conversion indeed existed among the young, though only for a small minority of the population and rarely in such radical terms as to constitute a life-changing event.[19] The religiously motivated rebellion of early Byzantine youth, found within a surprisingly broad range of social groups and situations, was instead deeply consequential.

Among the most dramatic stories preserved are those of young people who abruptly left promising careers in church, government, or business to become ascetics, often far from home; those who refused to marry or suddenly decided to sever existing bonds, preferring a life of religious celibacy instead; those whose dreams and visions summoned them unexpectedly to the monastery; and those who were determined to tear themselves away from the thick net of family and friends, or perhaps even existing monastic ties, in order to go on a pilgrimage or seek out a more challenging ascetic regime.[20] Numerous others answered the call to a life in the church or monastery at about the same age but in more regular fashion, without the drama and difficulty attested above. For them embracing one form of religious life or another was more the realization of earlier plans rather than the result of a sudden spiritual awakening. Often it was a decision that parents and friends supported rather than something that disrupted well-laid plans. What they shared with their more highly charged peers, however, was the understanding that important decisions in life could not ripen forever. Most evidence points to the ages between sixteen and twenty as the time when the pressure to settle into the various responsibilities of adulthood was at its heaviest. This pattern was no less true for the timing of major religious choices in general and the question of initiating or changing a religious vocation in particular.

The church waited until the late seventh century before attempting to set universal minimum age requirements for entrance into the ranks of regular and monastic clergy. At the Council of Trullo (692) bishops required that candidates for the office of subdeacon be at least age twenty, that of deacon twenty-five, and that of priest thirty. Male and female candidates to the monastic life needed to have reached an absolute minimum of age ten but could still be turned away until seventeen or eighteen for lack of maturity. The bishops set these standards with the full knowledge that the church's treatment of this issue had been inconsistent in the past. At the same time it is not clear that they expected to have the last word on this matter, since the canons on age requirements were not detailed and comprehensive, nor without loopholes.[21] Most ambiguous of all was the question of how much could be expected of young men in their middle and later teens. The bishops at Trullo steered clear of well-known discussions regarding the age at which young people gained full powers of reason and thus could be expected to assume adult responsibilities, including the taking of serious religious vows (Basil, *The Longer Rules* 956ab; Justinian, *Novels* 123.13, 604). They also said nothing either for or against the office of lector, an entry-level clerical function that had long been reserved for teenage males of around eighteen as a kind of gateway to higher clerical orders and furthermore had acquired a special symbolic significance because of the association between the first two letters of Jesus' given name (IH) and the number eighteen.

These matters would attract attention once again in the eighth century in the letters of Theodore of Stoudios and at the Second Council of Nicaea.[22] Nevertheless, in light of the somewhat elusive approach of the fathers at Trullo, it seems reasonable to conclude that as of the seventh century the church was uninterested in drawing up overly specific guidelines about the issue of youth and office holding. They allowed that the monastic vocation could begin early in the teen years but did not insist, and similarly they allowed that formal service to the church could start at age twenty but did not exclude that it might come sooner. Various episodes from the lives of aspiring monks and clergy suggest a similar logic to that of Trullo, namely, that teenagers with a religious calling remained an uncertain investment—promising yet problematic—because of the significantly uneven rates of maturity that were typical of people within this age group.[23] Care and proper timing were thus required if they were to be converted into a true asset for a monastery or the church. This meant that the vocational track for good prospects might be accelerated a year or two beyond what the guidelines called for, just as a troubled or unfit adolescent's progress might be delayed.

> ### St. Nikephoros of Sebaze as a Child
>
> After putting off his attachment to his mother's milk, he now entered that tender and unseasonable age of life, when the child grows rapidly and rejects the noble things in life, while also being drawn to every base impulse. Almost nothing good or noble can come out of someone who has not yet reached adulthood. Except in his case: for he would have nothing to do with the meaner side of life, nor did he occupy his mind with the kind of vanities that destroy the beauty of the soul.
>
> —*Life of Nikephoros of Sebaze* 2, ed. F. Halkin, *Byzantion* 23 (1953–1954): 20.

As church and monastic authorities were pondering how and when best to integrate incoming adolescents and young adults into their midst, it must be said that they concerned themselves much more with men than with women. Although a number of socially constructed gender roles had already emerged over the course of childhood years, during adolescence the expectation of gender differences increased. For women coming of age, this meant having to come to terms with male-dominated church and monastic establishments, which, in effect, circumscribed the role of women within public religious life. As far as monasticism was concerned, young women could enter monasteries at roughly the same age as men, but their experience of the monastic life was plainly different. For example, there were proportionally fewer female recruits than male, far fewer female institutions in existence than male, perhaps stricter rules for entrance, and likely, too, much less choice and control as to where female houses could be founded and how their internal life was structured. Recognition of the fact that women were denied an experience of the monastic life on par with men seems to be preserved in the cycle of early Byzantine saints' *Lives* dedicated to cross-dressing nuns, some of whom took the decision to dress up like men and enter male monasteries while still young and virgins in order to pursue a superior form of asceticism.[24] But if young women were forced to accept a number of restrictions on their liberty and power of choice upon entering the monastic world, they were handed an even more unsatisfactory and restricted role within the official church; for the only real office a woman could hope to hold was that of deaconess, and the minimum age for this position was finally set at forty in the later seventh century (*Council in Trullo* 40). Such rules amounted to the complete exclusion of adolescent and young adult women from ordination of any kind within the official church.

Whether and how they reacted is frankly difficult to judge owing to a lack of information. Some scholars have reasonably argued that women's reaction to their exclusion from ordination and the limitations placed on their religious freedoms outside the confines of marriage manifested itself in their devotion to icons. In other words, an intense devotion to icons, practiced especially within the domestic sphere, came to be the laywoman's only way to compensate—emotionally and spiritually—for the lack of meaningful religious opportunities in the world.[25] Young women must have internalized this lesson quite early in life, as they followed the examples of their female elders and came to terms with the gendered world in which they lived. Afterwards, in the two vocations that lay open to them, a small minority of women entered the cloister while the rest lived as laywomen. Among the latter group who then went on to marry, their devotion to icons was no doubt reinforced with the advent of every pregnancy. For them icons and religious amulets acted as a special guarantee of health and protection, in addition to serving as a necessary reminder of their essential value as human beings in the eyes of God.

THE ROLE OF RELIGION THROUGHOUT LIFE

The topic of women and childbirth returns us to the very beginnings of the life cycle with which this chapter began. To summarize the findings of this brief and selective survey, three observations about youth and religious experience seem appropriate. First, it is clear that the religious impulse, in the many forms of expression it took, was a strong and constant presence within the growing child's life. Although the present state of evidence allows only a limited perspective on the realities of childhood, it still points to a nexus of religious demands, assurances, questions, rites, and practices that forever framed the experience of youth, while also giving certain experiences of childhood their essential shape. Worthy of note was the experience of a child's first weeks of life, which seem hardly conceivable without the presence of priests, prayers, prophecies, and religious objects to ensure its survival. Second, much of what was accepted as Christian tradition in regard to youth had deeper roots in the Greco-Roman world, while much of what was thought to be dubious from a Christian point of view prevailed anyhow. In other words, and not surprisingly, there were any number of historical constants and continuities over the long term, including the notion that adult-like children (or the *puer senex*) were rare and contrary to nature, though worth prizing for their special gifts. Third, and finally, Eastern Christianity certainly left its own peculiar imprints on the attitudes of both parents and elders as well as on children themselves. Perhaps the most important of these involved the youth's right, in accordance with scripture and the emerging Christian tradition, to dissolve bonds with parents and family in response to a religious calling. The impact of this Christian mandate was tangibly felt over time, from parents taking the liberty to pledge children to religious institutions, to children and teens themselves deciding to abandon home for the religious life.

FOR FURTHER READING

Abrahamse, Dorothy. "Images of Childhood in Early Byzantine Hagiography." *Journal of Psychohistory* 6 (1979): 497–518.

Baun, Jane. "The Fate of Babies Dying before Baptism in Byzantium." In Diane Wood, ed., *The Church and Childhood*, 115–25. Oxford: Blackwell, 1994.

Clark, Gillian. "The Fathers and the Children." In *The Church and Childhood*, 1–27.

Eyben, Emiel. "Sozialgeschichte des Kindes im römischen Altertum." In Jochen Marten and Augustus Nitschke, eds., *Zur Sozialgeschichte der Kindheit*, 317–64. Freiburg: Alber, 1986.

Gould, Graham. "Childhood in Eastern Patristic Thought: Some Problems of Theology and Theological Anthropology." In *The Church and Childhood*, 39–52.

Hennessy, Cecily. *Images of Children of Byzantium.* Aldershot: Ashgate, 2006.

Kalogeras, Nikos. "What Do They Think about Children? Perceptions of Childhood in Early Byzantine Literature." *BMGS* 25 (2001): 2–19.

Miller, Timothy S. *The Orphans of Byzantium: Child Welfare in the Christian Empire.* Washington, D.C.: Catholic University of America Press, 2003.

Patlagean, Evelyne. "L'Enfant et son avenir dans la famille byzantine (ivème–xiième siècles)." *Annales de démographie historique* (1973): 85–93. Reprinted in *Structure sociale, famille, chrétienté à Byzance.* London: Variorum, 1981.

Wiedemann, Thomas. *Adults and Children in the Roman Empire.* London: Routledge, 1989.

Wood, Diane, ed. *Church and Childhood.* Oxford: Blackwell, 1994.

THE DEVOTIONAL LIFE OF LAYWOMEN

ALICE-MARY TALBOT

Religious faith and devotional practices played a significant part in the lives of Byzantine women, especially those of the middle and upper classes whose daily life was quite circumscribed. Prayer, Bible study, and the veneration of icons at home offered spiritual comfort, while attendance at church services, participation in religious processions, visits to holy shrines, and charitable activities provided socially approved opportunities to leave the confines of the house. The most important events of women's lives, such as marriage, childbirth, and funerals, were inextricably linked with religious rituals in which they played an active role.

THE SOURCES

I have chosen to begin my discussion with the middle of the ninth century not only because the end of Iconoclasm and restoration of image veneration in 843 ushered in a new phase in the history of Eastern Orthodoxy, but also because new types of sources appear in the ninth century and there is a significant increase in the amount of evidence on women's spirituality in Byzantium. These written texts supplement and complement the evidence of material objects presented in chapter 8 by Brigitte Pitarakis.[1] While we must constantly bear in mind the dangers of using evidence from hagiographic texts, the lives of female saints are one major font of information for the religious life of women. Although most Byzantine holy women were nuns, their biographies can still provide insights into the spiritual life of laywomen. We need not believe every detail of every text, but if there is repeated hagiographic evidence for women's home worship, attendance at church services, visitation of shrines, and charitable activities, one may safely conclude that such activities were indeed typical for Byzantine women. These saints' lives often describe the childhood of a future nun or her mother's personal devotions, or they may introduce laywomen seeking a blessing or healing from a living holy woman, or laywomen on pilgrimage to the saint's tomb. Particularly helpful are the biographies of three female saints of the late ninth and tenth centuries who never entered the convent but attained sanctity despite their status as married women. These three saints, the empress Theophano (died 895 or 896), Mary the Younger of Bizye (died 903?), and Thomaïs of Lesbos (who lived in the tenth century), form a group that is sometimes characterized as "pious housewives" or "pious matrons."[2] All three attained sanctity while remaining laywomen; they were all distinguished for their charitable activity, for leading an ascetic life devoted to prayer and other spiritual exercises, and for enduring without complaint verbal and physical abuse from their husbands. These sources provide important evidence that in Byzantium sanctity was possible without adoption of the monastic habit, and they offer a tantalizing glimpse into the spirituality of laywomen.

Monastic *typika*, the foundation documents for Byzantine monasteries, despite their focus on the regulation of communal and liturgical life within the cloister, can also provide insights into laywomen's piety, since they describe the close ties developed by aristocratic laywomen with monastic institutions, as founders, patrons, or future residents. The sixty or so preserved monastic *typika*, dating from the ninth to the fifteenth centuries, offer autobiographies of female founders, lists of donations to monasteries, and provisions for the liturgical commemoration of deceased lay benefactors.

An underused source for female religious life is the acts of the synod of Constantinople, particularly those for the last two centuries of the empire, between 1261 and 1453. A number of these acts, which recount cases brought before the synod of the patriarchate, provide incidental information on the relations between laywomen and monasteries that is not available elsewhere.

Monastic archives, especially those from Mount Athos, also offer evidence on women's attitudes toward the monasteries of the Holy Mountain, and their concern for their salvation in the afterlife. Despite the fact that women were forbidden ever to visit the peninsula of Athos, they made lavish donations to the monasteries, especially of estates, in return for the commitment of the monks to pray for their souls or the souls of their husbands after their death.[3]

Women's last testaments, which sometimes list personal possessions such as icons and books, can also provide valuable evidence for private lay devotion. Other sources include funeral orations (such as those of the historian Michael Psellos for his daughter and his mother), narrative histories, and dedicatory poems.

When analyzing the primary sources for the religious life of Byzantine women, one must keep in mind that the information almost invariably comes to us through the filter of a man's perspective. Compared to their sisters in the West, the women of Byzantium were extremely silent, one might even say mute. One can count on the fingers of one hand texts of the ninth to the fifteenth centuries that can be attributed with assurance to a female author. None of the biographies of female saints of this era can be proved to have been written by a woman; these either are anonymous or were composed by a male hagiographer.

Even the *typika* for women's convents that were ostensibly drafted in the first person by their female founders may in fact have been composed or revised by male "ghostwriters" trained in the standard formulas of monastic foundation charters.[4] Women founders are more likely to be responsible for the autobiographical portions of the documents, and no doubt they expressed their wishes on the main provisions of the rule but may have left the details of composition to secretaries or notaries.

To take yet another genre of literature, a woman who made a pious donation of an icon or a liturgical vessel or textile to a church or monastery might on occasion commission a poet to write verses in her name to be inscribed on the object. The sentiments expressed may have been hers, but the wording is that of a man.

One of the few texts penned by a woman that have come down to us from this period is the *Alexiad*, the twelfth-century princess Anna Komnene's history of the reign of her father Alexios I Komnenos (1081–1118). It is a lengthy book written in a high style that reflects Anna's classical and rhetorical education, virtually unparalleled among other women of her era. Anna's history is of course more interested in diplomacy, battles, and court intrigue than matters of the spirit; nevertheless, some passages shed light on the religious practices of the women in her family.

THE SPIRITUAL LIFE OF LAYWOMEN

Let me now attempt to sum up what we can learn from these varied and scattered sources about the devotional life of Byzantine laywomen.

Bible Study and Worship in the Home

Relatively few women, even of the elite class, were literate; if they did learn to read, their education was closely linked with religious training, since young girls, like boys, learned their letters by reading the Psalter. There is no evidence that girls attended school; instead they were taught by their parents or by a private tutor.[5] If they continued their education, they would advance to reading other texts of scripture and the lives of saints. Girls almost never had access to classical texts or training in grammar, rhetoric, and philosophy, the customary secondary curriculum for young men. Girls who had no schooling at all would still gain some familiarity with the scriptures and saints' lives by hearing the texts read aloud during church services, by seeing images on icons or on church walls, or by listening to stories told by their parents.

Daily devotions at home, whether in the form of spiritual reading, veneration of icons, private prayer, or attendance at services in a private chapel, played a vital role in the lives of Byzantine women, who for the most part led a secluded existence in their homes and may have derived little emotional satisfaction from their arranged marriages. The princess Anna Komnene provides a rare glimpse into the domestic life of a family with well-educated women, in this case the imperial family, commenting that "many a time when a meal was already served I remember seeing my mother with a book in her hands, diligently reading the dogmatic pronouncements of the Holy Fathers, especially of the philosopher and martyr Maximus [the Confessor]." In another passage Anna describes her mother as "reading the books of the saints."[6]

Women who could afford it, like the future saint Mary the Younger of Bizye, kept an icon in their bedroom. As we shall see later, Mary performed her private devotions before this icon; we also learn from her biography that a lamp burned all night long before her icon of the Virgin, giving a faint light to her bedroom (*Life of Mary of Bizye* 9). The anonymous account of miracles at the Pege shrine in Constantinople relates an incident of the late ninth century that demonstrates the potentially disastrous consequences of excessive veneration of icons. A noblewoman named Helena Artavasdina was particularly devoted to two images of the Virgin and the archangel Gabriel at the church of Pege. When they fell to the ground in the earthquake of 869, she asked the abbot for permission to take the images home with her for safekeeping. She then placed them in her bedroom, where she burned candles and incense before them. Eventually she lit such a profusion of lamps and candles that her house caught on fire (*AASS* III.882D–83A)!

Relevant here is the well-known passage from the *Chronographia* of Michael Psellos, describing the passionate devotion of the eleventh-century empress Zoe to an icon of Christ Antiphonetes ("the one who responds"):

> She had made for herself an image of Jesus, fashioning it with as much accuracy as she could. . . . The little figure, embellished with bright metal, appeared to be

---

The Education of the Young Theophano, Future Bride of Leo VI

When she [Theophano] was weaned and arrived at the age of six, her father . . . began to educate her in the sacred letters. And when she was introduced to learning, she eagerly approached the study of the sacred letters, and in a short while learned by heart the psalter and the vespers and matins hymns, and spent her days in reading and study.

—*Life of Theophano* 5, trans. Alice-Mary Talbot, from Eduard Kurtz, *Zwei griechische Texte über die heilige Theophano, die Gemahlin Kaisers Leo VI* (St. Petersburg: Commissionaires de l'Académie Impériale des Sciences, 1898), 3.

almost living. . . . When she had met with some good fortune, or when some trouble had befallen her, she would at once consult her image, in the one case to acknowledge her gratitude, in the other to beg its favour. I myself (writes Psellos) have often seen her, in moments of great distress, clasp the sacred object in her hands, contemplate it, talk to it as though it were indeed alive, and address it with one sweet term of endearment after another. Then at other times I have seen her lying on the ground, her tears bathing the earth, while she beat her breasts over and over again, tearing at them with her hands. If she saw the image turn pale, she would go away crestfallen, but if it took on a fiery red colour, its halo lustrous with a beautiful radiant light, she would lose no time in telling the emperor and prophesying what the future was to bring forth.[7]

Rituals of Birth and Death

The procreation of children was one of women's most important functions, and barrenness was a great sorrow. Sterile women or women who were pregnant but subject to miscarriage might wear protective amulets in the form of inscribed prayers rolled up and placed in a tube or stone pendants inscribed with prayers or images of apotropaic motifs such as the Holy Rider (a warrior saint) or Chnoubis (a demon, the "roaring womb"). Other such pendants were intended to protect women from menstrual disorders or to ensure successful childbirth. Some women also owned small icons or pendants depicting female saints, such as Marina and Theophano, thought to be intercessors for safe pregnancy and childbearing.[8] As we shall see later, barren women often had recourse to living holy men or women or visited saints' shrines to pray for the gift of a child.

If successful in conception, a woman's next hurdle was the delivery of the baby. Some women would make confession and take Holy Communion when they first began to suffer labor pains.[9] Normally women gave birth with the aid of a midwife. Sometimes, however, in the case of prolonged labor or an abnormal breech presentation a woman or a family member would seek divine aid to facilitate the delivery of the child. Thus, when Anna, the mother of the future St. Theophano, had undergone hours of agonizing labor without results, her husband ran to the church of the Virgin at the Bassos Monastery in Constantinople and brought back a girdle that was hanging on one of the church columns and apparently had miraculous powers. As soon as he applied the piece of cloth to his wife's abdomen, her pains eased, and the baby was born with a smile on her face (*Life of Theophano* 3). In another case a woman in labor was unable to deliver the infant because it was trying to emerge feetfirst. In desperation doctors were summoned to cut up the fetus while it was still in the womb in order to save the mother's life. Before they began the operation, however, someone remembered that he had a piece of the cloak of the recently deceased patriarch Ignatios, which had been distributed to the faithful at the time of his funeral. As soon as the holy relic was pressed against the woman's abdomen, the baby turned to a headfirst presentation and was safely delivered (*Life of Patriarch Ignatios*, PG 105:564A–C).

Women also played an important role in funeral ceremonies, washing the corpse and preparing it for burial as well as accompanying the funeral cortege to the cemetery, wailing and singing laments. They also would faithfully attend commemorative services for the recently deceased on the third, ninth, and fortieth day following death and prepare the traditional *kollyva*, a confection of sweetened boiled wheat, dried fruits, and nuts distributed in remembrance of the dead on anniversaries.[10]

Church Attendance

Visiting churches filled a spiritual need and enabled women to leave their homes for a socially approved purpose. Many girls and women went to church services on a daily basis (see *Life of Thomaïs of Lesbos* 8), some even twice a day, like the nine-year-old Styliane, daughter of Michael Psellos: "She would attend vespers readily, taking part in the doxology and in the chanting of hymns. Nor did she ever miss devotional services, participating and worshipping with joy. She would stand there quietly with deep emotion, expressing her reverence for all that was chanted, listening attentively and not letting any detail escape her. Then she would sing the Psalms of David along with the choir. . . . [She also went] to chant the matins, taking part in the choir of psalmodists."[11] St. Thomaïs, we are told, visited churches regularly and rejoiced in the all-night hymnody; one of her favorite sanctuaries was the famous Church of the Virgin at the Hodegoi monastery, where she used to pray before an icon of the Mother of God (*Life of Thomaïs of Lesbos* 12).

The ninth-century pious matron Mary the Younger was also noted for her assiduous church attendance, walking to services twice a day, in all sorts of weather, even though she had to cross a stream to reach the church. Her biographer seems to suggest, however, that there may have been some stigma attached to public worship for women: he almost apologizes for the fact that Mary had no private chapel at home in which to say her prayers but had to go to a church, and he notes that during the course of her devotions she took care to remain in the darkest part of the church, where she performed genuflections until the sweat dripped from her body. When Mary moved to the larger city of Bizye, she stopped going to church and began to worship at home, "prostrating herself before an icon of the Mother of God and chanting the appropriate prayers, along with the book of Psalms, which she understood perfectly. The change was due neither to indolence nor to sloth, but to a prudent reticence and, since she was in a populous city, to a reluctance to come into the sight of one and all, native and foreign."[12]

There is very little textual evidence about the churchgoing habits of village women. Every village, however, had a church where a weekly liturgy was probably held.[13] These churches were supported by modest donations from the local community, as can be seen from surviving inscriptions. In 1265, for example, the inhabitants of the village of Kepoula (in the Mesa Mani) funded the construction of the church of the Hagioi Anargyroi with gifts of cash, ranging normally from one-quarter to one *nomisma* (a gold coin sufficient to purchase an olive tree or two sheep). In most cases the wife's name is listed alongside her husband's. On the island of Naxos in 1288/89 each of the nave frescoes in the bema of the Panagia "stēs Giallous" at Hagiassos was funded by a different couple from the village or, in one case, by a mother and her son.[14]

The ambiguous position of women at public worship services was symbolized by their relegation to certain limited areas of the church. Women were often separated from male worshippers, restricted to a narthex, an upper gallery, or a side aisle, depending on the size and plan of the church structure.[15] Menstruating women and women who had recently given birth were not permitted to enter the church proper but were relegated to an outer narthex or vestibule.

Menstruating women were allowed to come to the church precincts to pray but could not receive communion. The segregation of women at church services may have been motivated by a desire for preservation of order and decorum; elegantly dressed and perfumed women could be a distraction for male worshippers. The early fourteenth-century patriarch Athanasios I criticized noblewomen who came to Hagia Sophia not out of piety but to show off their jewels and finery and painted faces. Later in the century a Russian pilgrim described how at the same church the women stood behind translucent silken draperies in the galleries so that they could observe the services but could not be seen by the men in the congregation. Sometimes male congregants behaved badly, pushing and shoving and using abusive language. For this reason, it was safer for women and children to have their own separate area in the church. Indeed, portraits of female saints are found on the north or left side of metropolitan churches, confirming the presence of women congregants in the north aisle of such churches.[16]

Participation in
Religious Processions

In addition to attendance at regularly scheduled church services, extremely pious women, like Thomaïs the Younger, would also attend nocturnal vigils and processions through the streets.[17] Among such events were the weekly Friday procession in Constantinople from the Church of the Virgin at Blachernai to another church of the Virgin at Chalkoprateia, and the ritual procession that took place each Friday evening at the Blachernai to witness the "usual miracle" of the supernatural lifting of the veil that covered an icon of the Mother of God. At the Hodegoi monastery every Tuesday morning the famous icon of the Virgin Hodegetria, reputedly painted by St. Luke, would be carried outside the church in procession and perform miracles that healed men and women alike. We also know of an annual Constantinopolitan festival procession of Agathe (May 12) in which female spinners, weavers, and wool carders participated; although details of the ceremonies are unclear, they seem to have involved solemn entrance into a church, offering of ornaments to icons, and the singing of religious songs.[18] Women were also members of confraternities, such as the one in Thebes devoted to the veneration of the icon of the Theotokos of Naupaktos. Each month the devotees of the icon, clergy and laity alike, would carry the icon in procession, with holy hymns, to a different church, where it would remain for the next month.[19]

At Eastertide breads decorated with birds' eggs were baked, presumably by women, and might be offered to the local village priest as a gift. At this time of joyous celebration entire families carrying lanterns assembled in the streets singing hymns and even danced before the church doors on the evening of Holy Saturday.[20]

Visitation of Shrines
and Pilgrimage

Women would also make excursions to local shrines, either in family groups on feast days or as individuals, seeking to be cured from sterility or illness or praying for the recovery of a loved one. They would seek the intercession of a saint or holy personage by the veneration of relics or an icon, such as that of St. Anastasia Pharmakolytria ("she who cures poisoning") (fig. 10.1). Chapel spaces decorated with images of female saints, especially St. Anna (mother of the Virgin Mary), may well have been intended for extra-liturgical devotions by female worshippers, such as prayers for fertility and the well-being of children.[21] A particularly vivid description of a barren woman in fervent prayer to the Virgin for fertility is found in the early ninth-century *Life of St. Stephen the Younger*. Stephen's mother, named Anna, produced two daughters early in her married life but failed to conceive again. Desperate for a son as she approached menopause, she visited many churches dedicated to the Virgin, especially the shrine at Blachernai, where she went daily, in addition attending without fail the Friday evening vigil service, in which "she offered supplications and prayers: standing before the holy image of the Mother of God, in which She is represented carrying in her arms her son and God." Three times she repeated a prayer to the Virgin to be freed from the bonds of sterility, reminding the Virgin of her own mother, Anna, who had also been afflicted with childlessness. Accompanying her prayers with genuflection, she fell asleep and saw a vision of the Virgin telling her that as of that moment she has conceived. Anna awoke to find the vigil service over and went home chanting hymns of thanksgiving. After the baby's birth and the requisite forty days of confinement at home, Anna went with her husband and newborn child to the Blachernai church, and there, with tears flowing fast, she made a prayer of thanksgiving before the same icon of the Virgin. At one point she raised the child in a position of prostration and pressed his head against the icon, dedicating Stephen to the Virgin. Then she and her husband bowed their heads before the icon and prostrated themselves at full length on the floor of the church (*Life of Stephen the Younger* 4–6). This is one of the fullest surviving descriptions of a Byzantine woman at prayer.

Although many of the examples cited describe women's devotion to the Virgin Mary, they prayed with equal fervor to Christ and to saints of both sexes. Female pilgrims frequented healing shrines dedicated to male and female saints alike. Even women afflicted with typically feminine complaints like sterility, failure to lactate, or excessive uterine bleeding might seek help from holy men as well as women, or from their relics.[22] Women seem to have had relatively free access to the tombs of saints, even when the relics were deposited at male monasteries; at those monastic complexes where entrance was denied to members of the female sex, women might send a servant to fetch for them a vial of holy oil or holy water, or on occasion they might resort to disguising themselves as eunuchs! Women also seem to have freely approached holy men in the streets, seeking their verbal blessing or a laying on of hands.

Although in the early Christian centuries female pilgrims made the long and arduous

Fig. 10.1. Fresco of St. Anastasia Pharmakolytria with donor, Anastasia Saramalina, from the Church of Panagia Phorbiotissa, Asinou, Cyprus, 1333. Photo: Dumbarton Oaks Byzantine Photograph and Fieldwork Archive, Washington, D.C.

**A Barren Woman's Prayer
to the Virgin**

Mother of God, the shelter of those who have recourse to Thee, and anchor and protectress of those who seek Thee in their grief, the safest harbor for those who are sinking in the sea of life on account of despondency and most ready helper of those who in their despair call upon Thee for assistance, the glory of mothers and the adornment of daughters, who through Thy giving birth to the God-Man transformed the reproachful condemnation of the entire female sex on account of our foremother Eve into joyful confidence, have mercy upon me and hearken unto me and break the bond [of sterility] that is in me, just as Thou didst with Thy mother Anna through her giving birth to Thee, and through Thy maternal intercession bring it about that I give birth to a male child so that I may offer him as a gift to Thy Son and God.

—*Life of St. Stephen the Younger* 4, trans. Alice-Mary Talbot; Marie-France Auzépy, *La Vie d'Étienne le Jeune par Étienne le Diacre* (Aldershot: Ashgate, 1997), 92.

journey to the Holy Land, after the seventh century there is no evidence for long-distance pilgrimage by women.[23] The exception that proves the rule is to be found in the biography of the eleventh-century St. Lazarus of Mount Galesion, which tells the tale of a Constantinopolitan nun who disguised herself as a man with the intention of going to Jerusalem. She joined a group of pilgrims traveling via Ephesus and along with them made a detour to visit the holy man on his pillar on the nearby holy mountain and to hear his homily. Lazarus immediately saw through her disguise and scolded her, saying that women should not travel all about in this fashion and opposing pilgrimage in general with the words, "Wherever anyone does good, there is the true Jerusalem."[24] There is some evidence for what might be termed "middle-distance" pilgrimage. Miracle accounts which provide such information attest women's journeys of up to seventy-five or one hundred miles; we read, for example, of female pilgrims traveling from Nicaea or Prousa to Constantinople, from Verroia to Thessalonike, from Chios to Ephesus.[25]

Women from all levels of society visited healing shrines and holy men. Tombs with miraculous relics and saintly individuals with charismatic powers would be approached with fervor by women from imperial and aristocratic families, as well as by prostitutes, maidservants, beggars, and peasant women. In fact faith healing was often the only recourse for poor people who could not afford to consult physicians trained in traditional Greco-Roman medicine. In thanksgiving for miraculous cures, women would make cash donations or ex-voto offerings to a shrine, ranging from humble gifts of oil or wax to expensive illustrated manuscripts or liturgical furnishings; miracle accounts preserve the records of such pious gifts, as do some epigrams originally engraved on icon frames or embroidered on a liturgical cloth.[26]

Pilgrimages to saints' tombs and living holy men were not only made for the purpose of obtaining miraculous cures. Pious laywomen might visit a holy man to request advice, confess their sins, or seek intercession, as can be seen from the stories of the numerous female visitors to the stylite saint Lazarus on the holy mountain of Galesion near Ephesus.[27] Some pilgrimages could also acquire a festive and recreational aspect, especially if they coincided with a saint's annual feast day and a *panegyris* or fair. A particularly vivid description of the pleasure experienced by a female pilgrim in her visit to a rural shrine is to be found in a fourteenth-century text on the miracles of St. Eugenios of Trebizond. It relates how a certain Barbara, wife of a court official, "cherished what one might call a divine and boundless affection for the famous church of the . . . great martyr Prokopios and the surrounding area. Westerly winds come from the so-called Mountain of Mithras which rises above, and especially in spring people come there and enjoy the flowers and plants and take great delight in the sight of their bloom and in the thick grass."[28]

Verses of Thanksgiving on Votive Offerings

A poem of Manuel Philes (fourteenth century) written on behalf of a noblewoman, Maria Kasiane, whose prayers to the Virgin had brought about the miraculous recovery of her newborn child, and inscribed upon a thank-offering to the Theotokos of the Source, probably an icon frame:

> O Thou who delivered Eve from her intense suffering
> And dost sympathetically watch over my birth pangs
> (For God [was born] of Thee without the natural pain of childbirth),
> Accept this thank-offering, holy Virgin,
> Thou, through whom my infant child who all but died
> Lives and breathes beyond [all] hope.
> For Thou art life and the source of miracles,
> Washing away the mud of sin.
> Maria Kasiane, the daughter of Raoul, of the lineage of the Komnenoi,
> Has spoken these words to Thee in gratitude.

A second poem by Philes, addressed to the Mother of God, was apparently woven into a textile icon of the Virgin commissioned by a certain noblewoman named Irene who had been cured of a terrible headache.

> Thy world-saving dew relieves,
> O maiden, the pain in my head,
> Which resisted the drugs of physicians.
> Appearing in a vision at night and bedazzling me,
> Thou didst prefigure the representation of the miracle. . . .
> Therefore I repay now Thy crowning grace
> With a woven fabric of Thy picture.
> Besprinkle me again with Thy protection,
> And comfort the anguish of my soul.
> These words are as if by Irene the archontissa.

—Alice-Mary Talbot, trans., "Epigrams of Manuel Philes on the Theotokos tes Peges and Its Art," *DOP* 48 (1994): 153, 155.

THE PRACTICE OF CHARITY

Charitable activity was another manifestation of female piety.[29] As in so many cultures, good works on behalf of the less fortunate members of society were a socially acceptable outlet for the energies of middle-class and aristocratic women. For Byzantine women, philanthropy was a direct expression of their Christian faith: in ministering to the poor, they believed they were serving Christ; in feeding the hungry or clothing the naked, they were feeding and clothing Christ (Matt. 25:31-46). Some women expressed their concern for the needy by making donations of money and property to charitable institutions, such as hospitals, poorhouses, and orphanages, or to convents and monasteries whose mission included the provision of food to the poor. Others engaged in "hands-on" activity, handing out alms to individual beggars, weaving cloth to sell to raise money for charitable purposes, or visiting the sick or prisoners. Some women might even go to a public bathhouse to bathe and feed poor people (as did the mother of the author of Empress Theophano's biography; see *Life of Theophano* 18) or wander around the marketplace seeking out homeless people so as to pay their debts (*Life of Thomaïs of Lesbos* 15). These pious benefactors were primarily motivated by their concern for the afterlife; they believed that the performance of charitable works on earth would help ensure their salvation in heaven.

The Ideal Pious Laywoman Who Practices Charity

[Mary] had dedicated herself to God ever since she was a baby, out of her own free will, and had become a dwelling place for all the virtues that delight the Lord of all. Who could possibly describe . . . her kindness and philanthropy toward all in need, . . . saving nothing for herself and furnishing everything to the poor? How many girls do you think she gave away in marriage, providing dowries from her own property? How many young men did she restore who had been ruined by being orphaned? How many widows enjoyed consolation from her generous donations? How many were the hungry whom she fed? The naked whom she clothed? The thirsty whom she filled full of sweetest drink? The poor breathed her rather than air, those who suffered from the ice and froze from the cold were warmed by her clothes. Those who could not even obtain water because of the paralysis of their limbs found her a constant supplier of their needs. . . . As for her journeys to holy churches, and her care and attention for their adornment, her night-long prayers, her all-night standing vigils, her untold genuflections and the sweat that, resulting from this, flowed from her like rivers, the continuous and constant tears, who could have the power to relate them?

—*Life of St. Mary the Younger* 32, trans. Angeliki E. Laiou, in Alice-Mary Talbot, ed., *Holy Women of Byzantium* (Washington, D.C.: Dumbarton Oaks, 1996), 286–87.

VISIONS OF THE AFTERLIFE

And just how did Byzantine women imagine the afterlife? Several texts survive that purport to present a female vision of purgatory and heaven. I refer, for example, to the eleventh-century *Apocalypse of Anastasia*,[30] to the vision of Theodora embedded in the *Life of Basil the Younger*,[31] and to the deathbed visions of Psellos's young daughter Styliane. Alas, all these visions were in actuality penned by men, and we cannot tell whether there is any specifically feminine element in the images conjured up of the afterlife. Nonetheless, since we have no better evidence, let us look at excerpts from one of these visions, Styliane's dream of paradise, ten days before her death, as recounted to her mother and reported by her father:

> When the man with the keys [i.e., St. Peter] opened [the gate], we entered. We were in a garden filled with trees and fruit, also with plants that had thick branches and were joyous to see. There were furthermore all kinds of roses, lilies and many other fragrant flowers. As I stood there gladdened by the loveliness of the garden, I saw, a little further on, a man sitting. He was of such enormous height that he reached the sky, while all around him in a circle stood his servants, dressed in white [i.e., the angels].[32]

The girl then saw two angels hand to God a tiny sickly baby that recovered its health after being placed in God's bosom; Psellos tells us that the infant was a symbol of his daughter's soul. The girl had a second dream-vision of the Virgin entering her bedroom, carrying the baby Jesus in her arms. She then handed the girl the shorter of two branches that she held in her hand, symbolizing her imminent death.[33]

RELATIONS BETWEEN LAYWOMEN AND MONASTERIES

Although issues of spirituality within women's convents fall outside the purview of this chapter, I should like to end with some observations on the often close relationships between laywomen and monasteries. First of all, it is important to remember that many Byzantines, both men and women, took monastic vows at a later stage of life. A frequent pattern was for a woman to enter a convent after she was widowed; less often a married couple might decide to separate once their children were grown and to take the habit in separate monastic communities. A third option was for men and women to take the monastic habit on their deathbed. Sometimes entrance into a monastery in middle or old age was a practical decision, since the monastic community would take care of its ailing members in their final years and arrange for proper burial and commemorative services after death. Thus laypeople often lived with the intention of eventually taking monastic vows, and they might associate themselves with a local monastery well in advance of taking this step.[34]

I have already alluded to one type of connection, that of lay visitation to holy shrines at monasteries in search of healing from disease or barrenness, for prayers for the physical safety or spiritual salvation of relatives, or in fulfillment of a vow of thanksgiving. These female pilgrims often brought with them ex-voto gifts, such as lamp oil or candle wax, and took away various sorts of pious souvenirs, such as vials filled with holy oil or water and clay or lead tokens impressed with the image of the saint.

Laywomen might be engaged with monasteries in other ways as well, as patrons and donors. At the highest levels of society, empresses and other female members of the imperial family or wealthy noble-women might offer large sums of cash and property to support the establishment of a new monastery or nunnery (fig. 10.2) or to restore one that had fallen into disrepair.[35] The motivations for donations on such a lavish scale were multiple: foundation of a nunnery where the donor and her female relatives might spend their declining years; provision for highly desired burial within the sacred space of the monastic church; insurance that prayers would be said in perpetuity for the salvation of the donor and her relatives; expiation of sins and thanksgiving for a prosperous and blessed life on earth; or, on a more mundane level, creation of a tax haven, since properties donated to a monastery were immune from taxation.

Such founders might also contribute the essentials for liturgical observance: eucharistic vessels, vestments, liturgical books, and textiles, as well as icons with frames of precious metal (color gallery, plate J). Other lay donors made offerings expressly in exchange for commemorative services on the anniversary of their death. On the days of memorial services for benefactors of the monastery, donations ensured that the illumination of the church was more extensive

Fig. 10.2. Miniature from the Lincoln College Typikon (Lincoln College, Oxford, gr. 35, fol. 11r) with portrait of the founder of the Bebaias Elpidos nunnery in Constantinople, Theodora Synadene (the nun Theodoule), and her daughter Euphrosyne. Photo: Lincoln College Library, Oxford.

than usual, the nuns were offered special dishes in the refectory, and distributions of bread and wine were made to beggars at the convent gates.

At the lower end of the economic spectrum, poor women might work as servants at a convent or accompany their mistresses who took monastic vows later in life, while some impoverished widows took the monastic habit to ensure food and nursing care in their old age. A typical case is that of Zoe Syropoulina, who in 1271 found herself a widow with no living family members to help support her. She made an agreement with the convent of Nea Petra in Thessaly to donate to the monastery her ancestral property, including three vineyards and four fields, on condition that she be admitted as a nun without any entrance fee, receive the tonsure, and be maintained for the rest of her life. It was further understood that at the time of her death Zoe was to receive proper burial and be commemorated at the convent with requiem liturgies.[36]

Strange as it may seem at first sight, some laywomen became benefactors of monasteries on Mount Athos, even though they were prohibited from setting foot themselves on the Holy Mountain. Women made such donations for two primary reasons: one was practical, to receive an *adelphaton*, or annuity, that included provision of basic foodstuffs for life—wheat, cheese, oil, wine, and legumes. The second and more common purpose was the receipt of spiritual benefits, the prayers of the monks for the salvation of one's soul and/or the souls of relatives. Several women donors specified that they made these donations, so-called *psychika* or "spiritual gifts," as a way of establishing spiritual links with the Holy Mountain that they yearned to visit. One woman wrote wistfully in her act of donation, "When I heard about the Holy Mountain, my soul thirsted for the living God, whether I too might have a share in the Holy Mountain . . . and I too wanted to be commemorated on the Holy Mountain."[37] Another female donor of property and cash to the Great Lavra on Mount Athos noted that she and two co-owners offered this gift so that they might "be commemorated as brethren of the monastery both while living and after our death."[38] It has been suggested that this alludes to membership in an honorary confraternity, such as is attested at other monasteries, that would ensure commemoration by the monks in perpetuity.

THE EVIDENCE FOR WOMEN'S RELIGIOUS LIVES

Let me first sum up certain defining characteristics of the religious life of Byzantine women. Family and religious faith were the essential aspects of life for Byzantine women that emerge from the surviving evidence, primarily literary. For some the bonds of monastic community came to replace the ties of lineage, but prayer and other spiritual exercises were a constant for all women throughout their existence on earth. The desire for salvation was a prime motivating factor in many of women's daily activities, such as private prayer, veneration of icons, attendance at church services, and charitable works. The focus on the afterlife also led women to face death with equanimity but to be concerned about their proper burial and commemoration after death; those who had the means would make donations to monastic communities to ensure memorial services on the anniversary of their death. I suspect that much the same could be said of the spirituality of Byzantine men.[39] It may be, however, that women displayed a more personal devotion to icons and were more involved in good works. On the other hand, they no longer engaged in long-distance pilgrimage, especially to the Holy Land.[40]

There is still much, however, that we do not know about women's personal religious beliefs, since the sources are virtually all written by male authors, and the surviving evidence is scanty and fragmented. We are poorly informed about such issues as how often women attended church services or partook of holy communion and the nature of their devotions within the home. The sources also privilege upper-class and urban women; it is to be hoped that in-depth study of the inscriptions and painted decoration of small rural churches will shed further light on lay piety in the village context.[41] Likewise, future archaeological excavation (of women's tombs, for example) and more intense study of material culture should provide additional evidence for objects associated with female devotional life, especially for women of the lower classes, who have left little trace in the written record.

FOR FURTHER READING

Connor, Carolyn L. *Women of Byzantium.* New Haven: Yale University Press, 2004.

Gerstel, Sharon E. J. "Painted Sources for Female Piety in Medieval Byzantium." *DOP* 52 (1998): 89–103.

Herrin, Judith. "Women and the Faith in Icons in Early Christianity." In Raphael Samuel and Gareth Stedman Jones, eds., *Culture, Ideology and Politics: Essays for Eric Hobsbawm,* 56–83. London: Routledge and Kegan Paul, 1982.

Kalavrezou, Ioli, ed. *Byzantine Women and Their World.* New Haven: Yale University Press, 2003.

Taft, Robert F. "Women at Church in Byzantium: Where, When—and Why?" *DOP* 52 (1998): 27–87.

Talbot, Alice-Mary. *Women and Religious Life in Byzantium.* Aldershot: Ashgate, 2001.

———, ed. *Holy Women of Byzantium.* Washington, D.C.: Dumbarton Oaks, 1996.

ABBREVIATIONS

AASS	*Acta sanctorum*, 71 vols., Paris, 1863–1940
ACW	Ancient Christian Writers
Against Jud.	John Chrysostom, *Against Judaizing Christians*, PG 48
Ap. Const.	*Apostolic Constitutions*, SC 329
BHG	*Bibliotheca hagiographica graeca*, 3 vols., 3rd ed., Brussels: Société des Bollandistes, 1957
BMGS	*Byzantine and Modern Greek Studies*
Catech. Hom.	John Chrysostom, *Catechetical Homilies*, SC 50, 366; English translation: ACW 31
DOP	*Dumbarton Oaks Papers*
Ep.	*Epistles*
FC	Fathers of the Church
Hom. on 1 Cor.	John Chrysostom, *Homilies on 1 Corinthians*, PG 61; English translation NPNF 1.12
Hom. on 1 Thess.	John Chrysostom, *Homilies on 1 Thessalonians*, PG 62

Hom. on Heb.	John Chrysostom, *Homilies on Hebrews*, PG 63
Hom. on John	John Chrysostom, *Homilies on John*, PG 59
Hom. on Matt.	John Chrysostom, *Homilies on Matthew*, PG 57–58
JECS	*Journal of Early Christian Studies*
JRS	*Journal of Roman Studies*
KJV	King James Version of the Bible
LCL	Loeb Classical Library
LXX	Septuagint
Mansi	*Sacrorum conciliorum nova et amplissima collectio.* Edited by J. D. Mansi. Paris: Bibliopolis, 1903.
NPNF	Nicene and Post-Nicene Fathers
On Anna	John Chrysostom, *On Anna*, PG 54
On Kal.	John Chrysostom, *On the Kalends*, PG 48
On Laz.	John Chrysostom, *On Lazarus*. PG 48; English translation: *In St. John Chrysostom: On Wealth and Poverty*. Trans. Catharine Roth. Crestwood, N.Y.: St. Vladimir's Seminary Press, 1984.
On Repent.	John Chrysostom, *On Repentence*, PG 49; English translation: FC 96
On Stat.	John Chrysostom, *On the Statues*, PG 49
On Vainglory	John Chrysostom, *Address on Vainglory and the Right Way to Bring Up Children*, SC 188
PG	*Patrologia graeca*. Edited by J.-P. Migne. 162 vols. Paris, 1857–86.
SC	Sources chrétiennes
StP	*Studia patristica* (Papers of the International Conference on Patristic Studies)

NOTES

Introduction. The Practice of Christianity in Byzantium

1. Cyril of Scythopolis, *Life of Sabas,* 80; *Miracles of Artemios* 5; Theodore of Studios, *Life of Theoktiste of Constantinople*, 884b–845a.

2. Symeon of Thessalonike, PG 155.688–89.

3. For a reassessment of icon veneration and iconoclasm, see Leslie Brubaker, "Icons before Iconoclasm?" in *Morfologie sociali e culturali in Europa fra tarda antichità e alto Medioevo* (Spoleto: Presso La sede del Centro, 1998), 2:1215–54, and Leslie Brubaker and John F. Haldon, *Byzantium in the Iconoclast Era (ca. 680–850): A History* (Cambridge: Cambridge University Press, 2003).

4. For an excellent overview, see John Binns, *An Introduction to the Christian Orthodox Churches* (Cambridge: Cambridge University Press, 2002).

5. John Tzetzes, *Ep.* 104; ed. P. L. M. Leone, *Ioannis Tzetzae epistulae* (Leipzig: Teubner, 1972); trans. in Paul Magdalino, "The Byzantine Holy Man in the Twelfth Century," in *The Byzantine Saint,* ed. Sergei Hackel (San Bernardino, Calif.: Borgo, 1983), 54.

6. David Brakke, *Athanasius and the Politics of Asceticism*, Oxford Early Christian Studies (Oxford: Clarendon, 1995), 182–98.

7. Robert F. Taft, "The Frequency of the Eucharist throughout History," in *Beyond East and West: Problems in Liturgical Understanding*, 2nd ed. (Rome: Pontifical Oriental Institute, 1997), 87–110; Béatrice Caseau, "L'abandon de la communion dans la main (IVᵉ–XIIᵉ siècles)," *Travaux et mémoires* 14 (2002): 79–94.

Chapter One. Lay Piety in the Sermons of John Chrysostom

1. Although the ability of the laity to understand the sermons of highly educated Church Fathers has been doubted, in recent years scholars have emphasized the accessibility of Christian oratory. See Philip Rousseau, "'The Preacher's Audience': A More Optimistic View," in T. W. Hillard et al., eds., *Ancient History in a Modern University: Proceedings of a Conference Held at Macquarie University, 8-13 July, 1993*, vol. 2: *Early Christianity, Late Antiquity, and Beyond* (Grand Rapids: Eerdmans, 1998), 391–400.

2. In Pierre Bourdieu's terms, Chrysostom and his contemporaries were attempting to inculcate a Christian habitus: the core of ideas that underlies the choices and attitudes of commonsense behaviors. See Pierre Bourdieu, *Distinction: A Social Critique of the Judgement of Taste,* trans. Richard Nice (Cambridge: Harvard University Press, 1984), and idem, *The Logic of Practice*, trans. Richard Nice (Stanford: Stanford University Press, 1990).

3. Theodoret of Cyrrhus's *Religious History* (written circa 440) indicates that many Syrian monks rarely or never celebrated communion (SC 257.66–68).

4. Frans van de Paverd, *St. John Chrysostom: The Homilies on the Statues: An Introduction* (Rome: Pontificum. Institutum Studiorum Orientalium, 1991), 161–201.

5. On praying before and after eating: *On Anna* 2 (PG 54.650); *On Laz.* 1 (PG 48. 974–75). On singing, see J. C. B. Petropoulos, "The Church Father as Social Informant: St John Chrysostom on Folk Songs," *StP* 22 (1989): 159–64.

6. In Jewish communities alms were distributed to the poor from a money chest (*quppah*) kept in the synagogue. Gildas Hamel, *Poverty and Charity in Roman Palestine, First Three Centuries C.E.* (Berkeley: University of California Press, 1989), 216–19.

7. On the extent of literacy, see Robert Browning, "Literacy in the Byzantine World," *BMGS* 4 (1978): 39–54.

8. Georgia Frank, *The Memory of the Eyes: Pilgrims to Living Saints in Christian Late Antiquity* (Berkeley: University of California Press, 2000).

9. On miniature codices and magical use of Christian books, see Harry Y. Gamble, *Books and Readers in the Early Church: A History of Early Christian Texts* (New Haven: Yale University Press, 1995), 235–41.

10. Some Christians in Antioch also fasted on the Jewish Day of Atonement; see *Against Jud.* 2 and 4 (PG 48.857–62, 871–82). On Late Antique views of fasting, see Veronika E. Grimm, *From Feasting to Fasting, the Evolution of a Sin: Attitudes to Food in Late Antiquity* (New York: Routledge, 1996).

11. See also *Ap. Const.* 6.27.1–3, SC 329.378. On issues of purity, see David Brakke, "The Problematization of Nocturnal Emissions in Early Christian Syria, Egypt and Gaul," *JECS* 3 (1995): 419–60.

12. For interactions between Jews and Christians in Antioch, see Robert Wilken, *John Chrysostom and the Jews: Rhetoric and Reality in the Late Fourth Century* (Berkeley: University of California Press, 1983); Marcel Simon, *Verus Israel: A Study of the Relations between Christians and Jews in the Roman Empire (135–425)*, trans. H. McKeating (Oxford: Oxford University Press, 1986), 217–23.

13. Compare *Ap. Const.* 5.11–12.6, SC 329.242–46; 6.23.4, SC 329.370; 7.3.4, SC 336.32. Not all church leaders condemned the use of oaths: Theodoret, *Religious History* 3.1,8 SC 234.281–84; 15.5, SC 257.23–25; and 24.8, SC 257.148–51.

14. Compare *Hom. on Gen.* 21, PG 53.179; *On Anna* 1, PG 54.642; *On Vainglory* 48, SC 188.146.

15. For a detailed description of the festivities that took place during the Kalends of January in fourth-century Antioch, see Maud W. Gleason, "Festive Satire: Julian's *Misopogon* and the New Year at Antioch," *JRS* 76 (1986): 106–19.

16. On traditional Roman wedding ceremonies, see Susan Treggiari, *Roman*

Marriage: Iusti Coniuges from the Time of Cicero to the Time of Ulpian (Oxford: Clarendon, 1991), 161–70. By the ninth century in the Byzantine Empire marriage required a priest's benediction. In the West, however, marriage never lost its fundamental connection with civil law. See Philip Lyndon Reynolds, *Marriage in the Western Church: The Christianization of Marriage during the Patristic and Early Medieval Periods* (Leiden: Brill, 1994).

17. On Eastern Church Fathers' condemnations of traditional funeral rituals, see Margaret Alexiou, *The Ritual Lament in Greek Tradition* (Cambridge: Cambridge University Press, 1994), 24–35.

18. *Hom. on Gen.* 45, PG 54.416; *On Stat.* 5, PG 49.70–78; 6, PG 49.85; and 7, PG 49.91.

19. Compare *Hom. on 1 Cor.* 28, PG 61.235. Here Chrysostom acknowledged that many women grieved over lost children.

Chapter Two. The Cult of the Martyrs and the Cappadocian Fathers

1. Martin Esper, "Enkomiastik und Christianismos in Gregors epideiktischer Rede auf den Heiligen Theodor," in Andreas Spiras, ed., *The Biographical Works of Gregory of Nyssa* (Cambridge: Philadelphia Patristics Foundation, 1984), 145; Jean Bernardi, *La Prédication des pères cappadociens* (Montpelier: Presses Universitaires de France, 1968), 85.

2. Johan Leemans, Wendy Mayer, Pauline Allen, and Boudewijn Dehandschutter, *'Let Us Die That We May Live': Greek Homilies on Christian Martyrs from Asia Minor, Palestine, and Syria (c. AD 350–AD 45)* (London: Routledge, 2003), 15.

3. Esper, "Enkomiastik," 151.

4. Leemans et al., *'Let Us Die that We May Live,'* 15.

5. Vasiliki Limberis, "The Eyes Infected by Evil," *Harvard Theological Review* 84 (1991): 176.

6. Ibid., 178.

7. Ibid., 175.

8. Derek Krueger, "Writing and the Liturgy of Memory in Gregory of Nyssa's *Life of Macrina*," *JECS* 8 (2000): 497–505.

9. Ibid., 501.

10. Monique Alexandre, "Les nouveaux martyrs: Motifs maryrologiques dans la vie de saints et thèmes hagiographiques dans l'éloge des martyrs chez Grégoire de Nysse," in Spiras, *The Biographical Works of Gregory of Nyssa*, 39.

Chapter Three. Romanos and the Night Vigil in the Sixth Century

1. Arundhati Roy, *The God of Small Things* (New York: Random House, 1997), 218.

2. *Egeria's Diary*, for example, 4.3–4; 10.4–7. From *Egeria's Travels to the Holy Land*, trans. John Wilkinson (rev. ed.; Warminster, U.K..: Aris & Phillips, 1981). Jonathan Z. Smith's astute analysis of these patterns appears in his *To Take Place: Toward Theory in Ritual* (Chicago: University of Chicago Press, 1987), 89–95.

3. Theodore of Mopsuestia, *Catechetical Homily* 5, in A. Mingana, ed., *Woodbrooke Studies vol. 6: Commentary of Theodore of Mopsuestia on the Lord's Prayer and on the Sacraments of Baptism and the Eucharist* (Cambridge: Heffer and Sons, 1933), 86. See also Georgia Frank, "'Taste and See': The Eucharist and the Eyes of Faith in the Fourth Century," *Church History* 70 (2001): 638–40.

4. Roy, *The God of Small Things*, 218. For this analysis I have found helpful studies on the performative dimensions of Hindu ritual dramas, especially Philip Lutgendorf, *The Life of a Text: Performing the Ramcaritmānas of Tulsidas* (Berkeley: University of California Press, 1991).

5. This summary is based on the magisterial analysis of the literary evidence in Robert Taft, *The Liturgy of the Hours in East and West* (Collegeville, Minn.: Liturgical, 1986), 165–90.

6. Basil, *Letters* 207 (LCL 187–88). On men's and women's choirs in the Syriac churches, see Susan Ashbrook Harvey, "Spoken Words, Voiced Silence: Biblical Women in Syriac Tradition," *JECS* 9 (2001): 105–31, esp. 107–9.

7. Arietta Papaconstantinou, *Le Culte des saints en Égypte des Byzantins aux Abbassides: L'Apport des inscriptions et des papyrus grecs et coptes* (Paris: Éditions du Centre National de la Recherche Scientifique, 2001), 317–22.

8. On the call to imitate saints as a reaction to this exuberance, see Peter Brown, "Enjoying the Saints in Late Antiquity," in Stephen Lamia and Elizabeth Valdez del Álamo, eds., *Decorations for the Holy Dead: Visual Embellishments on Tombs and Shrines of Saints* (Turnhout: Brepols, 2002), 3–17.

9. John Chrysostom, "A Homily on Martyrs," PG 550.661–66, esp. 664; English translation: Wendy Mayer and Pauline Allen, *John Chrysostom* (London: Routledge, 2000), 96.

10. John Chrysostom, *Priesthood* 13.69, SC 272.217. On legislation prohibiting women from attending all-night vigils, see Robert F. Taft, "Women at Church in Byzantium," *DOP* 52 (1998): 27–87, esp. 72–74, and idem, *Liturgy of the Hours*, 166, 171–74.

11. *Life of Matrona of Perge* 3 (*BHG* 1221), trans. Jeffrey Featherstone, in Alice-Mary Talbot, ed., *Holy Women of Byzantium* (Washington, D.C.: Dumbarton Oaks, 1996), 18–64, see esp. 20.

12. This section draws from José Grosdidier de Matons, *Romanos le Mélode et les origines de la poésie religieuse à Byzance* (Paris: Éditions Beauchesne, 1977), esp. 37–47, 103–8. Citations refer to Romanos le Mélode; *Hymnes*, ed. José Grosdidier de Matons, 5 vols. (Paris: Éditions du Cerf, 1964–1981). I provide the corresponding hymn number from Paul Maas and C. A. Trypanis, eds., *Sancti Romani Melodi Cantica: Cantica Genuina* (Oxford: Clarendon, 1963), in brackets in the first citation of any given hymn. For other editions, consult the table in Grosdidiers, *Romanos le Mélode et les origines*, 329–32. Wherever possible, I have used the fine translation by Ephrem Lash in St. Romanos the Melodist, *On the Life of Christ: Kontakia* (San Francisco: HarperCollins, 1995).

13. "On the Man Possessed with Devils" 22 [11].2 (SC 114.54–56), trans. Derek Krueger, *Writing and Holiness: The Practice of Authorship in the Early Christian East* (Philadelphia: University of Pennsylvania Press, 2004), 167.

14. Grosdidier, *Hymns* (SC 128), 4:369–70.

15. Robert Taft, *The Great Entrance: A History of the Transfer of Gifts and Other Pre-anaphoral Rites of the Liturgy of St. John Chrysostom*, Orientalia Christiana analecta 200 (2nd ed.; Rome: Pontificium Institutum Studiorum Orientalium, 1978), 11–12, 405–16.

16. I borrow the term "community poetry" from Eva Stehle's *Performance and Gender in Ancient Greece* (Princeton: Princeton University Press, 1997).

17. See John 13:4-5, which makes no mention of celestial spectators; this element appears in foot-washing rites outlined in a twelfth-century *typikon*, or foundation document for a Byzantine monastery, from Jerusalem. See Papadopoulos-Kerameus, ed., *Analekta hieras stachyologias* 2:108–16, discussed in S. Petrides, "Le lavement des pieds le jeudi-saint dans l'église grecque," *Echos d'Orient* 3 (1899–1900): 321–36, esp. 325. I thank Derek Krueger for this reference. Apart from references to foot washing following adult baptism in fourth-century Gaul and Milan and foot-washing rites in Syria and Armenia, there is no evidence for actual foot washings as part of Holy Week ceremonies in Constantinople during the sixth century (see Petrides, "Le lavement," 321).

18. Margaret Alexiou, *The Ritual Lament in Greek Tradition* (Cambridge: Cambridge University Press, 1974), 142–44; on patterns of lament, see 62–78, 131–84. Others (for example, Gail Holst-Warhaft and Gregory Dobrov) have noted Romanos's appropriation of women's laments, but I am aware of none who explore Romanos's adoption of the genre for male characters.

19. In addition to "On Judas," Peter figures prominently in "On the Pentecost" (49 [33]) and "Peter's Healing of the Lame" (60 [39]). On the political context, see Eva Topping, "The Apostle Peter, Justinian and Romanos the Melodos," *BMGS* 2 (1976): 1–15.

20. M. D. Usher, *Homeric Stitchings: The Homeric Centos of the Empress Eudocia* (Lanham, Md.: Rowman & Littlefield, 1998), esp. 113–29. Text: André-Louis Rey, ed. *Patricius, Eudocie, Optimus, Côme de Jérusalem: Centons Homériques (Homerocentra)*, SC 437 (Paris: Cerf, 1998), 61–68.

21. Robert Taft, "The Liturgy of the Great Church: An Initial Synthesis of Structure and Interpretation on the Eve of Iconoclasm," *DOP* 34–35 (1980–81): 45–75, esp. 72.

Chapter Four. Shrines, Festivals, and the "Undistinguished Mob"

1. Manuel Komnenos, *Novel III*, in Ruth Macrides, "Justice under Manuel I Komnenos: Four Novels on Court Business and Murder," in *Forschungen zur Byzantinischen Rechtsgeschichte*, vol. 11: *Fontes Minores VI* (1984): 149.

2. Symeon the New Theologian, *On the Feasts and Their Celebration*, in Alexander Golitzin, trans., *St. Symeon the New Theologian, On the Mystical Life: The Ethical Discourses*, Vol. 1: *The Church and the Last Things* (Crestwood, N.Y.: St. Vladimir's Seminary Press, 1995), 173.

3. Pierre Maraval, *Lieux saints et pèlerinages d'orient: Histoire et géographie des origines à la conquête arabe* (Paris: Cerf, 1985), 401–10.

4. Dominic Montserrat, "Pilgrimage to the Shrine of SS Cyrus and John at Menouthis in Late Antiquity," in David Frankfurter, ed., *Pilgrimage and Holy Space in Late Antique Egypt* (Leiden: Brill, 1998), 266–67.

5. Sophronius, *Miracles of Sts. Cyrus and John* 51, quoted in Montserrat, "Pilgrimage to the Shrine of SS Cyrus and John," 257.

6. Peter Grossman, "The Pilgrimage Center of Abû Mînâ," in Frankfurter, *Pilgrimage and Holy Space*, 281–302.

7. E. D. Hunt, *Holy Land Pilgrimage in the Later Roman Empire, AD 312–460* (Oxford: Clarendon, 1982), 10–14.

8. *The Piacenza Pilgrim* 18, quoted in John Wilkinson, *Jerusalem Pilgrims before the Crusades* (Warminster, U.K.: Aris and Phillips, 1977), 83.

9. Alice-Mary Talbot, "Byzantine Pilgrimage to the Holy Land from the Eighth to the Fifteenth Century," in Joseph Patrich, ed., *The Sabaite Heritage in the Orthodox Church from the Fifth Century to the Present,* Orientalia Lovaniensia Analecta 98 (Leuven: Peeters, 2001), 98.

10. Andrew Jotischky, "History and Memory as Factors in Greek Orthodox Pilgrimage to the Holy Land under Crusader Rule," in R. N. Swanson, ed., *The Holy Land, Holy Lands, and Christian History: Papers Read at the 1998 Summer Meeting and the 1999 Winter Meeting of the Ecclesiastical History Society* (Rochester, N.Y.: Boydell, 2000), 116.

11. Elizabeth Key Fowden, *The Barbarian Plain: Saint Sergius between Rome and Iran* (Berkeley: University of California Press, 1999).

12. *The Chronicle of Muntaner*, trans. Lady Goodenough, Hakluyt Society, Series 2, 50 (London, 1921), chap. 206, quoted in Clive Foss, "Pilgrimage in Medieval Asia Minor," *DOP* 56 (2002): 141.

13. For a catalog of Byzantine holy sites up to the Arab invasions of the seventh century, see Maraval, *Lieux saints et pèlerinages d'orient*, 251–410.

14. John of Damascus, *On the Divine Images* 3.34.

15. Cynthia Hahn, "Loca Sancta Souvenirs: Sealing the Pilgrim's Experience," in Robert Ousterhout, ed., *The Blessings of Pilgrimage* (Urbana: University of Illinois Press, 1990), 86.

16. Theodoret of Cyrrhus, *Religious History* 26.26.

17. Charlambos Bakirtzis, "Byzantine Ampullae from Thessaloniki," in Ousterhout, *The Blessings of Pilgrimage*, 140–49.

18. John Staurakios, *Oration on the Miracles of St. Demetrius* 37.3–17; ed. J. Iberites, *Makedonika* 1 (1940): 334–76.

19. Choricius of Gaza, *In Praise of Marcian* 1.14 quoted in Fowden, *The Barbarian Plain*, 97.

20. See Speros Vryonis, "The Panegyris of the Byzantine Saint," in Serge Hackel, ed., *The Byzantine Saint: Fourteenth Spring Symposium of Byzantine Studies, University of Birmingham* (San Bernardino, Calif.: Borgo, 1981), 196–226.

21. See Stephen J. Davis, *The Cult of St. Thecla: A Tradition of Women's Piety in Late Antiquity* (Oxford: Oxford University Press, 2001), 37–39.

22. G. Dagron, ed., *Vie et miracles de Sainte Thècle: Texte grec, traduction et commentaire* (Brussels: Société des Bollandistes, 1978), 378.

23. Basil of Caesarea, *Longer Rules* 40 (English translation: W. K. L. Clarke).

24. *Life of St. Elisabeth the Wonderworker*, trans. Valerie Karras, in Alice-Mary Talbot, ed., *Holy Women of Byzantium: Ten Saints' Lives in English Translation* (Washington, D.C.: Dumbarton Oaks Research Library and Collection, 1996), 124.

25. *Timarion* 5, in Barry Baldwin, ed. and trans., *Timarion* (Detroit: Wayne State University Press, 1984), 44.

26. *Timarion* 6.

27. *Timarion* 10.

28. Gregory of Nyssa, *On Pilgrimages*, NPNF 2.5.383.

29. *Life of St. Ioannikios* 43, trans. Denis F. Sullivan, in Alice-Mary Talbot, ed., *Byzantine Defenders of Images: Eight Saints' Lives in English Translation* (Washington, D.C.: Dumbarton Oaks Research Library and Collection, 1998), 300–301.

30. *Miracles of St. Demetrios*, 1.3 §36, in Paul Lemerle, ed., *Les plus anciens recueils des Miracles de saint Démétrius*, vol. 1: *Le texte* (Paris: Éditions du Centre National de la Recherche Scientifique, 1979). *Life of St. Loukas the Younger* 82, in Carolyn L. Connor and Robert Connor, trans., *The Life and Miracles of St. Luke* (Brookline, Mass.: Hellenic College Press, 1994), 137.

31. *Life of Theodore of Sykeon* 71.

32. Jan Olof Rosenquist, ed., *The Hagiographic Dossier of St. Eugenios of Trebizond* (Uppsala, Sweden: Uppsala Universitet, 1996), 225.

33. Maraval, *Lieux saints et pèlerinages d'orient*, 221–43.

Chapter Five. The Layperson in Church

1. See, for example, Alexander Sideras, *Die byzantinischen Grabreden: Prosopographie, Datierung, Überlieferung, 142 Epitaphien und Monodien aus dem byzantinischen Jahrtausend*, Wiener byzantinische Studien 19 (Vienna: Verlag der Österreichischen Akademie der Wissenschaften, 1994); idem, *25 Unedierte byzantinische Grabreden* (Thessalonike: Parateretes, 1990).

2. For an English translation of the text, see Speros Vryonis Jr., "The Will of a Provincial Magnate, Eustathios Boilas (1059)," *DOP* 11 (1957): 263–77. For an analysis of the objects listed in the will, see Maria Parani, Brigitte Pitarakis, and Jean-Michel Spieser, "Un exemple d'inventaire d'objects liturgiques de testament d'Eustathios Boïlas [avril 1059]," *Revue des études byzantines* 61 (2003): 143–65.

3. Denis Sullivan, ed. and trans., *The Life of Saint Nikon: Text, Translation, and Commentary* (Brookline, Mass.: Hellenic College Press, 1987).

4. Angeliki Laiou, "Peasant Names in Fourteenth-Century Macedonia," *BMGS* 1 (1975): 71–95.

5. Manolis Chatzidakis, "Hē mnēmeiakē zōgraphikē stēn Hellada. Posotikes prosengiseis," *Praktika tēs Akadēmias Athēnōn* 56, no. 3 (1981): 380–84.

6. See, for example, Nicholas Stephen Weber, "Saint Gregory Palamas' Homily for Palm Sunday," *Greek Orthodox Theological Review* 34, no. 3 (1989): 263–82, for an English translation of a sermon delivered in Thessalonike.

7. Cyril Mango, *The Art of the Byzantine Empire, 312–1453* (Toronto: Medieval Academy of America, 1986 [1972]), 254.

8. Otto Demus, *Byzantine Mosaic Decoration: Aspects of Monumental Art in Byzantium* (New Rochelle, N.Y.: Caratzas Brothers, 1976 [1948]), 3–39.

9. Alice-Mary Talbot, ed. and trans., *The Correspondence of Athanasius I, Patriarch of Constantinople: Letters to the Emperor Andronicus II, Members of the Imperial Family,*

and Officials, Dumbarton Oaks Texts 3 (Washington, D.C.: Dumbarton Oaks Center for Byzantine Studies, 1975), 86–91.

10. Sharon E. J. Gerstel, "Painted Sources for Female Piety in Medieval Byzantium," *DOP* 52 (1998): 89–103; Robert F. Taft, "Women at Church in Byzantium: Where, When—and Why?" *DOP* 52 (1998): 27–87.

11. Panagiotes N. Trempelas, *Mikron Euchologiōn*, 2 vols. (Athens, 1950–1955), 1:7–40; John Meyendorff, "Christian Marriage in Byzantium: The Canonical and Liturgical Tradition," *DOP* 44 (1990): 99–107.

12. Symeon of Thessalonike, "De matrimonio," PG 155:508A.

13. Trempelas, *Mikron Euchologiōn*, 1:41–96.

14. P. A. Drosoyianni, "A Pair of Byzantine Crowns," *Jahrbuch der Österreichischen Byzantinistik* 32/3 (1982): 529–38; Maria G. Parani, "Byzantine Bridal Costume," in *Dōrēma: A Tribute to the A. G. Leventis Foundation on the Occasion of Its 20th Anniversary* (Nicosia: A. G. Leventis Foundation, 2000), 185–216.

15. Panagiotes N. Trempelas, *Mikron Euchologiōn,* 2:42.

16. Sergei P. Karpov, "Chto i Kak pzazdnovali v Kaffe v XV veke," *Srednie veka* 56 (1993), 226–32.

17. Trempelas, *Mikron Euchologiōn*, 2:47–74.

18. Aleksej Dmitrievskij, *Opisanie liturgitseskich rukopisej*, II, *Euchologia* (Hildesheim: G. Olms, 1965 [1901]), 993, 1051–52.

19. Trempelas, *Mikron Euchologiōn*, 2:52.

20. *AASS*, September, III, 872–73, para. 61.

Chapter Six. Death and Dying in Byzantium

1. The death of monks, including monastic saints, closely follows the patterns and practices described above. Dorothy Abrahamse, "Rituals of Death in the Middle Byzantine Period," *Greek Orthodox Theological Review* 29 (1984): 125–34.

2. For discussion, see Nicholas Constas, "'To Sleep, Perchance to Dream': The Middle State of Souls in Patristic and Byzantine Literature," *DOP* 55 (2001): 91–124.

3. Michael Psellos, *Funeral Oration on His Daughter, Styliane*, in Konstantinos N. Sathas, ed., *Mesaionikē Bibliothēkē* (Hildesheim: Olms, 1972 [1876]), 5:80. The mortality rate for the first five years of life seems to have been about 50 percent, and the average life expectancy has been estimated to be around thirty-five years. George Dennis, "Death in Byzantium," *DOP* 55 (2001): 3; and Alice-Mary Talbot, "Old Age in Byzantium," *Byzantinische Zeitschrift* 77 (1984): 268.

4. *Syntagma tōn theiōn kai hierōn kanonōn*, ed. G.A. Ralles and M. Potles, 6 vols. (Athens: G. Chartophylakos, 1852–1859), 4:467 (cited hereafter as *Syntagma*, followed by volume and page number). Other canons condemn the practice of giving the eucharist to the deceased: Council in Trullo, canon 83, and the comments of Zonaras and Balsamon, in *Syntagma*, 6:495.

5. Immanuel Bekker, ed., *Theophanes Continuatus* (Bonn: Weber, 1838), 280, 468.

6. On the illustrations, see Sirarpie Der Nersessian, "Program and Iconography of the Frescoes of the Parecclesion," in Paul A. Underwood, ed., *The Kariye Djami*, vol.

4 (Princeton: Princeton University Press, 1975), 331–32 (= "The Souls of the Righteous in the Hand of God").

7. The Byzantine ritual lament has been studied by anthropologists and folklorists of modern Greece: see Robert and Eva Blum, *The Dangerous Hour* (London: Chatto and Windus, 1971); Margaret Alexiou, *The Ritual Lament in Greek Tradition* (Cambridge: Cambridge University Press, 1974); and Loring Danforth, *Rituals of Death in Rural Greece* (Princeton: Princeton University Press, 1982).

8. Face: John Chrysostom, *Against the Opponents of the Monastic Life*, PG 47.334; John Chrysostom, *On the Widow's Son*, PG 61.792; John Moschus, *Spiritual Meadow*, PG 87.2956. Knees: *Life of Theodora of Thessalonike*. Self-inflicted wounds: John Climacus, *Ladder of Divine Ascent*, PG 88.816.

9. English translations of the Holy Friday lamentations can be found in *The Lenten Triodion*, trans. Mother Mary and Kallistos Ware (London: Faber & Faber, 1977); see Demetrios Pallas, *Die Passion und Bestattung Christi im Byzanz* (Munich: Institut für Byzantinistik und neugriechische Philologie der Universität, 1965); and Henry Maguire, "The Depiction of Sorrow in Middle Byzantine Art," *DOP* 31 (1977): 122–74.

10. There is some evidence for the mummification and display of deceased Christians in Late Antique Egypt, but see Athanasius, *Life of Antony* 90 (PG 26.969), where the practice is criticized.

11. George Cedrenos, *Historical Digest*, ed. Immanuel Bekker (Bonn: Weber, 1839), 2:675.

12. J. Maspero, *Papyrus grecs d'époque byzantine* (Cairo: Institut français d'archéologie orientale, 1911–1916), no. 67151, line 160.

13. Nicetas of Paphlagonia, *Life of Ignatius of Constantinople*, PG 105.560; *Life of Eustratius of Augarus*, in A. Papadopoulos-Kerameus, ed., *Analekta Hierosolymitikēs stachyologias* (St. Petersburg: Kirvaoum, 1898), 4:399.

14. See Nersessian, "Program and Iconography," 305–49, and Øystein Hjort, "The Sculpture of the Kariye Camii," *DOP* 33 (1979): 248–55.

15. See Natalia Teteriatnikov, "Burial Places in Cappadocian Churches," *Greek Orthodox Theological Review* 29 (1984): 141–57; and Gordana Babić, *Les chapelles annexes des églises byzantines, fonction liturgique et programmes iconographiques* (Paris: Klincksieck, 1969).

16. See Nicholas Constas, "Gregory the Theologian and a Byzantine Epigram on the Resurrection by Manuel Philes," in N. M. Vaporis, ed., *Rightly Teaching the Word of Truth* (Brookline, Mass.: Holy Cross Orthodox Press, 1995), 253–71.

17. E. Kurz, ed., *Die Gedichte des Christophoros Mitylenaios* (Leipzig: Neumann, 1903), no. 16.

18. Nancy Ševčenko, "The Tomb of Isaak Komnenos at Pherrai," *Greek Orthodox Theological Review* 29 (1984): 135–39.

19. See Constas, "To Sleep," 103–4.

20. For an archaeological study of a late Byzantine ossuary, see D. Makropoulou, "To byzantino koimeterio tes mones Blatadon," in *Christianikē Thessalonikē: Stauropēgiakes kai enoriakes Monēs* (Thessalonike: Kentro Historias Thessalonikēs, 1955), 237–44; and eadem, "Apo to usterobyzantino nekrotapheio tēs Monēs Blatadon," *Hē Thessalonikē* 1 (1985): 255–309. On the contemplation of death in late Byzantine art and iconography,

see Rainer Stichel, *Studien zum Verhältnis von Text und Bild spät-und nachbyzantinischer Vergänglichkeitsdarstellungen* (Vienna: Böhlau,1971).

21. For a detailed discussion of the following material, see Constas, "To Sleep."

Chapter Seven. Icons, Prayer, and Vision in the Eleventh Century

1. Notable recent discussions of the icon include Hans Belting, *Likeness and Presence: A History of the Image before the Era of Art*, trans. Edmund Jephcott (Chicago: Chicago University Press, 1994); Robin Cormack, *Painting the Soul: Icons, Death Masks and Shrouds* (London: Reaktion Books, 1997); Oleg Tarasov, *Icon and Devotion: Sacred Spaces in Imperial Russia*, trans. Robin Milner-Gulland (London: Reaktion Books, 2002).

2. Vision and touch are connected by the Patriarch Photios in the ninth century: Vasilios Laourdas, *Photiou Homiliai* (Thessalonike: Hetaireia Makedonikōn Spoudōn, 1959), 167. See the discussion in Robert S. Nelson, "To Say and to See: Ekphrasis and Vision in Byzantium," in Robert S. Nelson, ed., *Visuality before and beyond the Renaissance* (Cambridge: Cambridge University Press, 2000), 143–68.

3. This is clearly signaled in the letter sent in 824 by the emperors Michael II and Theophilos to Louis the Pious: "By common consent they [the iconoclastic synod of 815] forbade such things [veneration of icons] to be done anywhere; and they caused images to be removed from the lower places, and allowed those which were located in more lofty places to remain in their places, so that the picture itself might serve as scripture, [and] so that they might not be adored by the untaught and the infirm." *Monumenta Germaniae historica, Concilia aevi karolini* 1.2 (Hannover: Impensis Bibliopolii Hahniani, 1906), 479.

4. Examples can be found in Gary Vikan, "Ruminations on Edible Icons: Originals and Copies in the Art of Byzantium," *Studies in the History of Art* 20 (1989): 47–59.

5. Ludwig Deubner, *Kosmas und Damian* (Leipzig-Berlin, 1907), 137–38.

6. For the Theodore Psalter see Charles Barber, ed., *Theodore Psalter: Electronic Facsimile* (Urbana: University of Illinois Press, 2000).

7. Irénée Hausherr, ed., *Un grand mystique byzantin: Vie de Syméon le Nouveau Théologien (949–1022) par Nicétas Stéthatos*, Orientalia Christiana Analecta 45 (Rome: Pontificium Institutum Orientalium Studiorum, 1928), 120; Michael Psellos, *Orationes hagiographicae*, ed. Elizabeth A. Fisher (Stuttgart: Teubner, 1994), 195.843–197.879; Andronikos Demetrakopulos, *Bibliotheca Ecclesiastica* (Hildesheim: Olms, 1965), 132–34.

8. For the Hodegetria icon see Christine Angelidi and Titos Papamastorakis, "The Veneration of the Virgin Hodegetria and the Hodegon Monastery," in Maria Vassilaki, ed., *Mother of God: Representations of the Virgin in Byzantine Art* (Athens: Benaki Museum, 2000), 373–87. For the Blachernae icon see Bissera V. Pentcheva, "Rhetorical Images of the Virgin: The Icon of the 'Usual Miracle' at the Blachernai," *Revue des études slaves* 38 (2000): 35–54; Eustratios N. Papaioannou, "The 'Usual Miracle' and an Unusual Image: Psellos and the Icons of Blachernai," *Jahrbuch der Österreichischen Byzantinistik* 51 (2001): 177–88.

9. Recent scholarly accounts of viewing in Byzantium include Robin Cormack, *Writing in Gold: Byzantine Society and Its Icons* (Oxford: Oxford University Press, 1985); Robert S. Nelson, "The Discourse of Icons, Then and Now," *Art History* 12 (1989): 144–57; Liz

James and Ruth Webb, "'To Understand Ultimate Things and Enter Secret Places': Ekphrasis and Art in Byzantium," *Art History* 14 (1991): 1–17; Nelson, "To Say and to See."

10. Hausherr, *Un grand mystique byzantin*, xv–xxi.

11. An Abbot Michael of the Studios is named in the colophon of a Sinai manuscript that dates to 1048; Ihor Ševčenko, "Kosinitza 27: A Temporarily Lost Studite Manuscript Found Again," *Texte und Untersuchungen* 124 (1977): 434 n. 4. In 1053–1054 an Abbot Michael of the Studios was also involved in a dispute with the Patriarch of Constantinople, Michael Keroularios; John Skylitzes, *Synopsis Historiarum*, ed. H. Thurn, Corpus Fontium Historiae Byzantinae 5 (Berlin: de Gruyter, 1973), 433.40–434.50.

12. For example, his discussion of hierarchy: see John van Rossum, "Reflections on Byzantine Ecclesiology: Nicetas Stethatos' 'On the Hierarchy,'" *St. Vladimir's Theological Quarterly* 25 (1981): 75–83.

13. PG 120.851–1009. The text is translated into English in Gerald Palmer, Philip Sherrard, and Kallistos Ware, eds. and trans., *The Philokalia: The Complete Text* (London: Faber and Faber, 1995), 4:76–173.

14. Notable recent discussions of the broad issues in the correlation of vision and modernism can be found in David Levin, *The Opening of Vision: Nihilism and the Postmodern Situation* (New York: Routledge, 1988), and Martin Jay, *Downcast Eyes: The Denigration of Vision in Twentieth-Century French Thought* (Berkeley: University of California Press, 1993).

15. Symeon the New Theologian, *Catéchèses 23–34, Actions de Grâces 1–2*, SC 113 (Paris: Cerf, 1965): 346–48; Symeon the New Theologian, *The Discourses* (New York: Paulist, 1980), 374.

16. Symeon's biographical details are drawn from the *Life* written by Niketas Stethatos (Hausherr, *Un grand mystique byzantin*, 2–18).

17. An edition of and commentary on this text can be found in Paul Lemerle, *Cinq études sur le XIe siècle byzantin* (Paris: Centre National de la Recherche Scientifique, 1977), 15–63. An English translation can be found in Speros Vryonis Jr., "The Will of a Provincial Magnate, Eustathius Boïlas (1059)," *DOP* 11 (1957): 263–77.

18. Boïlas generally refers to the clergy and deacons of the church. Its monastic identity is underlined by the identification of the scribe of the Klimakos manuscript that contains the will as Theodoulos, the monk and priest of the Theotokos Salem: Lemerle, *Cinq etudes*, 38–44 and 61–63. He is also named at the end of the will: Lemerle, *Cinq études*: 29.283–84. There are brief references to monks in the body of the will: Lemerle, *Cinq etudes*, 28.254–57, 29.281–82.

19. Lemerle, *Cinq études*, 24.141–25.165.

20. Karl Heinz Uthemann, ed., *Anastasii Sinaitae Opera, Viae Dux*, Corpus Christianorum Series Graeca 8 (Turnhout: Brepols, 1981).

21. Lemerle, *Cinq études,* 25.167–68; Vryonis, "Will," 270. Note also Judith Waring, "Monastic Reading in the Eleventh and Twelfth Centuries: Divine Ascent or Byzantine Fall?" in Margaret Mullett and Anthony Kirby, eds., *Work and Worship at the Theotokos Evergetis 1050–1200*, Belfast Byzantine Texts and Translations 6, 2 (Belfast: Belfast Byzantine Enterprises, 1997), 409. This library is also understood to be a resource for the education of the sons of Boïlas's freedmen, who are to be educated in the church and raised to become clergy (Lemerle, *Cinq études*, 27.219–21).

Chapter Eight. Objects of Devotion and Protection

1. Ioli Kalavrezou, ed., *Byzantine Women and Their World* (New Haven: Yale University Press, 2003), no. 176, 295; Eunice Dautermann Maguire, Henry P. Maguire, and Marjorie J. Duncan-Flowers, *Art and Holy Powers in the Early Christian House* (Urbana: Krannert Art Museum and University of Illinois Press, 1989), no. 90, 165.

2. James Russel, "Byzantine Instrumenta Domestica from Anemurium: The Significance of Context," in R. L. Hohfelder, ed., *City, Town and Countryside in the Early Byzantine Era* (New York: Columbia University Press, 1982), 136–37.

3. Henry Maguire, "Magic and Money in the Early Middle Ages," *Speculum* 72 (1997): 1037–54.

4. Brigitte Pitarakis, "Une production caractéristique de cruches en alliage cuivreux (VIᵉ–VIIIᵉ siècles): Typologie, technique et diffusion," *Antiquité Tardive* (forthcoming): fig. 16.

5. Ormonde M. Dalton, *Catalogue of Early Christian Antiquities and Objects from the Christian East in the Department of British and Mediaeval Antiquities and Ethnography of the British Museum* (London: Trustees of the British Museum, 1901), no. 287, pl. IV.

6. Nicole Thierry, "Aux limites du sacré et du magique, un programme d'entrée d'une église en Cappadoce," in *La science des cieux: Sages, mages, astrologues*, *Res Orientales* XII (1999): 233–47.

7. Jeffrey Spier, "Medieval Byzantine Magical Amulets and Their Tradition," *Journal of the Warburg and Courtauld Institutes* 56 (1993): 25–62.

8. Eduard Kurtz, ed., *Zwei griechische Texte über die heilige Theophano, die Gemahlin Kaiser Leo VI* (St. Petersburg: Commissionaires de l'Académie Impériale des Sciences, 1898), 2, lines 25–35; Kalavrezou, ed., *Byzantine Women and Their World*, no. 172, 291–92 and 279.

9. Spier, "Medieval Byzantine Magical Amulets," 44.

10. Ernest Alfred Wallis Budge, *The Historia Monastica of Thomas Bishop of Marga* (London: Paul, Trench, Trübner, 1893), 2:506.

11. The passage is translated and commented on in Anna Kartsonis, "Protection against All Evil: Function, Use and Operation of Byzantine Historiated Phylacteries," *Byzantinische Forschungen* 20 (1994): 90–91.

12. Cyril Mango, "On the Cult of Saints Cosmas and Damian at Constantinople," in *Thymiama: stē mnēmē tēs Laskarinas Boura* (Athens: Mouseio Benakē, 1994), 189–92.

13. Gary Vikan, "Two Byzantine Amuletic Armbands and the Group to Which They Belong," *The Journal of the Walters Art Gallery* 49–50 (1991–1992): no. 22, fig. 5, 46.

14. For the medallions see Maguire, Maguire, and Duncan-Flowers, et al., *Art and Holy Powers*, no. 134 (Kelsey Museum of Archaeology, University of Michigan); Marvin Ross, *Metalwork, Ceramics, Glass, Glyptics, Painting, Catalogue of the Byzantine and Early Mediaeval Antiquities in the Dumbarton Oaks Collection*, vol. 1 (Washington, D.C.: Dumbarton Oaks, 1962), no. 60, p. 53, plate 38.

15. Yota Ikonomaki-Papadopoulos, Brigitte Pitarakis, and Katia Loverdou-Tsigarida, *The Holy and Great Monastery of Vatopaidi, Enkolpia* (Mount Athos: The Monastery, 2001), no. 22, 74–75.

16. *The Glory of Byzantium: Art and Culture of the Middle Byzantine Era A.D. 843–1261*, ed. Helen C. Evans and William D. Wixom (New York: Metropolitan Museum of Art, 1997), no. 128.

17. *Splendori di Bisanzio: Testimonianze e riflessi d'arte e cultura Bizantina nelle chiese d'Italia*, exhibition catalog (Milan: Fabbri, 1990), no. 58.

18. Brigitte Pitarakis, *Les croix-reliquaires pectorales byzantines en bronze*, ed. J. Durand, Bibliothèque des Cahiers archéologiques (Paris: Picard, 2006).

19. Gary Vikan and John Nesbitt, *Security in Byzantium: Locking, Sealing and Weighing* (Washington, D.C.: Dumbarton Oaks, 1980), fig. 10, 46.

20. Karl Sandin, "Liturgy, Pilgrimage and Devotion in Byzantine Objects," *Bulletin of the Detroit Institute of Arts*, 67, no. 4 (1993): 53, fig. 14.

21. *Synaxarium ecclesiae Constantinopolitanae: Propylaeum ad Acta Sanctorum*, ed. Hippolyte Delehaye (Brussels: Bollandists, 1902), col. 305–6; discussion in Theano Chatzidakis-Bacharas, *Les peintures murales de Hosios Loukas: Les chapelles orientales* (Athens: Christianikē Archaiologikē Hetaireia, 1982), 79.

22. Catherine Jolivet-Lévy, *La Cappadoce médiévale: Images et spiritualité* (Paris: Zodiaque, 2001), 343.

23. Syna Uenze, *Die spätantike Befestigungen von Sadovec (Bulgaria)* (Munich: Beck, 1992), 478, plates 124, 126.

24. François Nau, "Le texte grec des récits utiles à l'âme d'Anastase (le Sinaïte)," *Oriens Christianus* 3 (1903): 45, 65–66.

25. John Rufus, *Petrus der Iberer*, ed. P. Raabe (Leipzig: Hinrichs, 1895), 29–30, 40–41.

26. Charalambos Bakirtzis, "Pilgrimage to Thessalonike: The Tomb of St. Demetrios," *DOP* 56 (2002): 175–92 (esp. 182), with earlier bibliography.

27. R. M. Harrison, *Excavations at Saraçhane in Istanbul*, vol. 1 (Princeton: Princeton University Press, 1986), nos. 58, 621–38.

28. See Cécile Morrison and Jean-Claude Cheynet, "Prices and Wages in the Byzantine World," in Angeliki E. Laiou, ed., *The Economic History of Byzantium: From the Seventh through the Fifteenth Century* (Washington, D.C.: Dumbarton Oaks, 2002), tables 11, 15.

29. See Catherine Jolivet-Lévy, *Les églises byzantines de Cappadoce: Le programme iconographique de l'abside et de ses abords* (Paris: Éditions du Centre National de la Recherche Scientifique, 1991), 219–20, 247, 304.

30. Turan Gökyıldırım, "The Hoard of Belgratkapı—1987," *The Turkish Numismatic Society Bulletin* 31 (1992): 8–20 (in Turkish with English summary); Julian Baker, "Later Medieval Monetary Life in Constantinople," *Anatolian Archaeology* 9 (2003): 35–36.

Chapter Nine. The Religious Lives of Children and Adolescents

My thanks to Garth Fowden, Sharon Gerstel, and Alice-Mary Talbot for bibliographic assistance with this chapter.

1. *Life of Elisabeth the Wonderworker* 252–56; *Life of Nicholas of Sion* 68–70; John Moschus, *Spiritual Meadow* 94–95.

2. *Life of Eutychios of Constantinople* 41–43, 49–56. Phaidōnos Koukoulōs, *Life and Customs of the Byzantines* (in Greek) (Athens: Institut Français d'Athènes,

1948–1957), 4.9–69; Marie-Hélène Congourdeau, "Regards sur l'enfant nouveau-né à Byzance," *Revue des études byzantines* 51 (1993): 161–69.

3. For demons, Richard Greenfield, *Traditions of Belief in Byzantine Demonology* (Amsterdam: Hakkert, 1988), 182–87; Irène Sorlin, "Striges et Géloudes: Histoire d'une croyance et d'une tradition," *Travaux et mémoires* 11 (1991): 411–36. For magical devices, Gary Vikan, "Art, Medicine, and Magic in Early Byzantium," *DOP* 38 (1984): 65–86, esp. 77–80; James Russell, "The Archaeological Context of Magic in the Early Byzantine Period," in Henry Maguire, ed., *Byzantine Magic* (Washington, D.C.: Dumbarton Oaks, 1995), 42–43 and plates; Henry Maguire, "Magic and the Rise of Christian Imagery," in *Byzantine Magic,* 60–61, 70–71.

4. David Pingree, "The Horoscope of Constantine VII Porphyrogenitus," *DOP* 27 (1973): 219–31; Elizabeth Sears, *The Ages of Man: Medieval Interpretations of the Life Cycle* (Princeton: Princeton University Press, 1986), 47–50; Gilbert Dagron, "Troisième, neuvième et quarantième jours dans la tradition byzantine: Temps chrétien et anthro-pologie," in *Le Temps chrétien de la fin de l'antiquité au moyen âge iiie–xiiie siècles* (Paris: Éditions du Centre National de la Recherche Scientifique, 1984), 420–23.

5. Thomas Wiedemann, *Adults and Children in the Roman Empire* (London: Routledge, 1989), 100–105, 175–86; Congourdeau, "L'Enfant," 164–65; Gillian Clark, "The Fathers and the Children," in Diane Wood, ed., *Church and Childhood* (Oxford: Blackwell, 1994), 22–25; Geoffrey S. Nathan, *The Family in Late Antiquity: The Rise of Christianity and the Endurance of Tradition* (London: Routledge, 2000), 133–59.

6. Henry Maguire, *The Icons of Their Bodies: Saints and Their Images in Byzantium* (Princeton: Princeton University Press, 1996), 101–3; Cecily Hennessy, "Children as Iconic Images in S. Demetrios, Thessaloniki," in Anthony Eastmond and Liz James, eds., *Icon and Word: The Power of Images in Byzantium* (Aldershot: Ashgate, 2003), 157–72.

7. *Life of Theodore of Sykeon* 1.160–61; *Life of Michael the Synkellos* 46. John Boswell, *The Kindness of Strangers: The Abandonment of Children in Western Europe from Late Antiquity to the Renaissance* (New York: Pantheon, 1988); Timothy S. Miller, *The Orphans of Byzantium: Child Welfare in the Christian Empire* (Washington, D.C.: Catholic University of America Press, 2003), 141–42, 153–54; John Doran, "Oblation or Obligation? A Canonical Ambiguity," in Wood, *Church and Childhood,* 127–28.

8. Evelyne Patlagean, "L'Enfant et son avenir dans la famille byzantine (ivème–xiième siècles)," *Annales de démographie historique* (1973): 86–90; idem, *Pauvreté économique et pauvreté sociale à Byzance, 4e–7e siècles* (Paris: Mouton, 1977), 144–45; Miller, *Orphans,* 153–61.

9. *Life of Theoktiste of Paros* 206; *Life of Michael the Synkellos* 48–50; *Life of Peter of Atroa* 73–77.

10. *Life of Patapios* 1213c–16a; *Life of Nikephoros of Medikion* 405–7; see also *Life of Elisabeth the Wonderworker* 256.

11. On maternal rights see Miller, *Orphans,* 69–107. On the curriculum see Ann Moffat, "Schooling in the Iconoclast Centuries," in Anthony Bryer and Judith Herrin, eds., *Iconoclasm: Papers Given at the Ninth Annual Spring Symposium of Byzantine Studies at the University of Birmingham* (Birmingham: Center for Byzantine Studies, 1977), 88–90.

12. Patlagean, "L'Enfant et son avenir," 86–93; idem, "Sur la limitation de la fécon-dité dans la haute époque byzantine," *Annales* 6 (1969): 1361–69.

13. *Life of Sabas,* 87–90; *Life of Niketas* 19. Christian Gnilka, *Aetas Spiritalis: Die Überwindung der natürlichen Altersstufen als Ideal frühchristlichen Lebens* (Bonn: Hanstein, 1972); Emiel Eyben, "Jugend," in *Reallexikon für Antike und Christentum,* 19.425–26; Nikos Kalogeras, "What Do They Think about Children? Perceptions of Childhood in Early Byzantine Literature," *BMGS* 25 (2001): 2–19.

14. Greenfield, *Byzantine Demonology,* 292–97.

15. Barbara A. Hanawalt, "Historical Descriptions and Prescriptions for Adolescence," *Journal of Family History* 17, no. 4 (1992): 341–51; Emiel Eyben, "The Early Christian View of Youth," in Claudia Klodt, ed., *Satura Lanx: Festschrift für Werner A. Krenkel zum 70. Geburtstag* (Hildesheim: Olms, 1996), 251–52.

16. Peter Brown, *The Body and Society: Men, Women and Sexual Renunciation in Early Christianity* (New York: Columbia University Press, 1988), 224–40.

17. Eyben, "Jugend," 390–94, 407–8, 417–18; Peter Balla, *The Child-Parent Relationship in the New Testament and Its Environment* (Tübingen: Mohr Siebeck, 2003), 58–62.

18. Eyben, "Jugend," 431–33; Balla, *Child-Parent Relationship,* 157–201.

19. Arthur Darby Nock, "Conversion and Adolescence," in *Pisciculi: Studien zur Religion und Kultur des Altertums* (Münster in Westfalen: Aschendorff, 1939), 165–77.

20. Leaving careers or home: *Life of Blasios of Amorion* 660–61; *Life of Peter of Atroa* 73–77; *Life of Methodios* 1245cd; *Life of Niketas* 20; *Life of Antony the Younger* 200–203. Refusing marriage: *Life of Matrona* 808; *Life of David, Symeon, and George* 234–36; *Life of Theophanes 2,* 270. Dreams of monastery: *Life of Gregory of Dekapolis* 214–15. Leaving family, friends, or monastery: *Life of Sabas* 90; *Life of Procopius of Dekapolis* 314–15; *Life of Domnika* 269–70.

21. *Council in Trullo* 14 [949a], 15 [949a], 40 [961c–64a]. Gnilka, *Aetas Spiritalis,* 170–89; Eyben, "Young Priests," 115–16.

22. Theodore of Stoudios, *Letters* 721–22; *Second Council of Nicaea* 13 [753]. Eyben, "Young Priests," 116–20; idem, "Jugend," 397–98, 421–22; Gould, "Early Patristic Thought," 40–52.

23. *Life of Nicholas of Sion* 26–27; *Life of Theodore of Sykeon* 18; *Life of David, Symeon, and George* 219; *Life of Blasios of Amorion* 659–60; *Life of Stephen the Younger* 173.

24. Dorothy Abrahamse, "Women's Monasticism in the Middle Byzantine Period: Problems and Prospects," *Byzantinische Forschungen* 9 (1985): 35–58; Alice-Mary Talbot, "A Comparison of the Monastic Experience of Byzantine Men and Women," *Greek Orthodox Theological Review* 30 (1985): 1–20; Evelyne Patlagean, "L'histoire de la femme déguisée en moine et l'évolution de la sainteté feminine à Byzance," *Studi Medievali* 3rd series, 17 (1976): 598–623.

25. Judith Herrin, "Women and the Faith in Icons in Early Christianity," in Raphael Samuel and Gareth Stedman Jones, eds., *Culture, Ideology and Politics: Essays for Eric Hobsbawm* (London: Routledge and Kegan Paul, 1982), 68–69.

Chapter Ten. The Devotional Life of Laywomen

1. See also Ioli Kalavrezou, ed., *Byzantine Women and Their World* (New Haven: Yale University Press, 2003).

2. These and other saints' lives are available in English translation in Alice-Mary Talbot, ed., *Holy Women of Byzantium* (Washington, D.C.: Dumbarton Oaks, 1996).

3. On this topic, see Alice-Mary Talbot, "Women and Mt. Athos," in Antony Bryer and Mary Cunningham, eds., *Mount Athos and Byzantine Monasticism* (Aldershot: Ashgate, 1996), 67–79, reprinted in Alice-Mary Talbot, *Women and Religious Life in Byzantium* (Aldershot: Ashgate, 2001), part 4. The acts of other monasteries, such as the Lembiotissa near Smyrna and St. John Prodromos on Mount Menoikeion near Serres, await study from this perspective.

4. This can be proved for the *typikon* of Theodora Palaiologina for the convent of Lips (see Alice-Mary Talbot, "Empress Theodora Palaiologina, Wife of Michael VIII," *DOP* 46 [1992]: 299 n. 40), and may be true of other *typika* as well.

5. See, for example, *Life of Stephen the Younger* 3, ed. Marie-France Auzépy, *La Vie d'Étienne le Jeune par Étienne le Diacre* (Aldershot: Ashgate, 1997), 91.

6. Edgar R. A. Sewter, *The Alexiad of Anna Comnena* (Harmondsworth: Penguin, 1969), 178, 374.

7. Michael Psellos, *Chronographia*, book 6, in Edgar R. A. Sewter, trans., *Michael Psellus: Fourteen Byzantine Rulers* (Harmondsworth: Penguin, 1966), 188.

8. See Kalavrezou, *Byzantine Women*, 274–305.

9. Harry J. Magoulias, *Decline and Fall of Byzantium to the Ottoman Turks by Doukas* (Detroit: Wayne State University Press, 1975), 208–9.

10. For more detailed discussion, see the chapter in this volume by Nicholas Constas, "Death and Dying in Byzantium."

11. Michael Psellos, *Funeral Oration for His Daughter Styliane*, in Konstantinos N. Sathas, ed., *Mesaiōnikē Bibliothēkē* (Paris: Maisonneuve, 1876), 5:67; Michael J. Kyriakis, trans., "Medieval European Society as Seen in Two Eleventh-Century Texts of Michael Psellos," *Byzantine Studies/Études byzantines* 3, no. 2 (1976): 86.

12. *Life of Mary the Younger* 5 in Talbot, ed., *Holy Women of Byzantium*, 260.

13. See Sharon E. J. Gerstel, "The Byzantine Village Church: Observations on Its Location and on Agricultural Aspects of Its Program," in Jacques Lefort, Cécile Morrisson, and Jean-Pierre Sodini, eds., *Les villages dans l'Empire byzantin* (IVe–XVe siècle) (Paris: Lethielleux, 2005): 165–78.

14. Sophia Kalopissi-Verti, *Dedicatory Inscriptions and Donor Portraits in Thirteenth-Century Churches of Greece* (Vienna: Österreichische Akademie der Wissenschaften, 1992), 35–37, 67–69, 89–90.

15. Robert F. Taft, "Women at Church in Byzantium: Where, When—and Why?" *DOP* 52 (1998): 27–87.

16. Sharon E. J. Gerstel, "Painted Sources for Female Piety in Medieval Byzantium," *DOP* 52 (1998): 89–103.

17. *Life of Thomaïs of Lesbos* 10; *Holy Women of Byzantium*, 308–9: "She used to go regularly to the most divine church at Blachernai, and would walk the whole way at night sending forth hymns of supplication to God and entreating His all-pure Mother." Chapter 12: "[Thomaïs], who was accustomed to frequent the divine churches and rejoice in the all-night hymnody, went once to the holy church of the Hodegoi."

18. See Angeliki Laiou, "The Festival of 'Agathe': Comments on the Life of

Constantinopolitan Women," in *Byzantion: Aphierōma ston Andrea Strato* (Athens: [N. A. Stratos], 1986), 111–22.

19. John Nesbitt and John Wiita, "A Confraternity of the Comnenian Era," *Byzantinische Zeitschrift* 68 (1975): 360–84.

20. For the egg bread, see Theodore Balsamon's commentary on canon 23 of the Council in Trullo in Georgios A. Rhalles and Michael Potles, eds., *Syntagma tōn theiōn kai hierōn kanonōn* 2 (Athens: G. Chartophylakos, 1852), 355. For the Easter festivities, see Adriana Pignani, *Matteo di Efeso, Racconto di una festa popolare*, 2nd ed. (Naples: M. D'Auria, 1984), 32–35.

21. Gerstel, "Painted Sources," 96–98.

22. Numerous examples can be found in the Dumbarton Oaks Hagiography Database, available online at http://www.doaks.org/hagio.html.

23. See Alice-Mary Talbot, "Female Pilgrimage in Late Antiquity and the Byzantine Era," *Acta byzantina fennica*, n.s. 1 (2002): 73–88.

24. Richard H. Greenfield, *The Life of Lazaros of Mt. Galesion: An Eleventh-Century Pillar Saint* (Washington, D.C.: Dumbarton Oaks, 2000), chap. 95.

25. For more details, see Talbot, "Female Pilgrimage," 80–84.

26. Alice-Mary Talbot, "Epigrams of Manuel Philes on the Theotokos tes Peges and Its Art," *DOP* 48 (1994): 137–65.

27. See Richard Greenfield, "Drawn to the Blazing Beacon: Visitors and Pilgrims to the Living Holy Man and the Case of Lazaros of Mt. Galesion," *DOP* 56 (2002): 213–41.

28. Jan Olof Rosenqvist, *The Hagiographic Dossier of St. Eugenios of Trebizond in codex Athous Dionysiou 154* (Uppsala, Sweden: Uppsala Universitet, 1996), 268–71.

29. See Alice-Mary Talbot, "Byzantine Women, Saints' Lives, and Social Welfare," in Emily A. Hanawalt and Carter Lindberg, eds., *Through the Eye of a Needle: Judeo-Christian Roots of Social Welfare* (Kirksville, Mo.: Thomas Jefferson University Press, 1994), 105–22.

30. See Jane Baun, "The *Apocalypse of Anastasia* in Its Middle Byzantine Context," Ph.D. diss., Princeton University, 1997.

31. Aleksandr N. Veselovskij, "Razyskanija v oblasti russkogo duchovnogo sti-cha," *Sbornik Otdelenija russkogo jazyka i slovesnosti Imperatorskoj Akademii nauk* 46 (1889–90): 10–76.

32. English translation in Kyriakis, "Medieval European Society," 96.

33. Ibid., 96-98.

34. See Alice-Mary Talbot, "Late Byzantine Nuns: By Choice or Necessity?" *Byzantinische Forschungen* 9 (1985): 103–17.

35. Alice-Mary Talbot, "Building Activity in Constantinople under Andronikos II: The Role of Women Patrons in the Construction and Restoration of Monasteries," in Nevra Necipoğlu, ed., *Byzantine Constantinople: Monuments, Topography and Everyday Life* (Leiden: Brill, 2001), 329–43.

36. Franz Miklosich and Joseph Müller, *Acta et diplomata graeca medii aevi sacra et profana*, 4 (Vienna: Gerold, 1871), 393–96.

37. *Actes de Zographou*, ed. Wilhelm Regel et al., in *Vizantiiski Vremennik* 13 (1907) supp. 1, no. 5.9–12 (anno 1142).

38. *Actes de Lavra*, ed. Paul Lemerle et al., III (Paris: Lethielleux, 1979), no. 173.10–11 (anno 1471).

39. For an overall survey of the pious observance of Byzantine men and women, see Sharon E. J. Gerstel and Alice-Mary Talbot, "The Culture of Lay Piety in Medieval Byzantium (1054–1453)," forthcoming in Michael Angold, ed., *The Byzantine Orthodoxy and Society: Lay Piety and Culture* (Cambridge: Cambridge University Press).

40. See Judith Herrin, "Women and the Faith in Icons in Early Christianity," in Raphael Samuel and Gareth Stedman Jones, eds., *Culture, Ideology and Politics: Essays for Eric Hobsbawm* (London: Routledge and Kegan Paul, 1982), 56–83, esp. 68–75.

41. Sharon Gerstel is currently preparing a book on village churches that should provide further evidence on rural lay piety.

INDEX